W9-BVY-325

ABORTION

ABORTION

A Doctor's Perspective
A Woman's Dilemma

Don Sloan, M.D.
with Paula Hartz

DIF

DONALD I. FINE, INC.
New York

Library of Congress Cataloging-in-Publication Data

Sloan, Don M.,
    Abortion : a doctor's perspective/a woman's dilemma / by Don
Sloan, with Paula Hartz.
        p. cm.
    Includes index.
    ISBN 1-55611-341-2
    1. Pro-choice movement—United States—History. 2. Abortion—
United States—Moral and ethical aspects—Case Studies. I. Hartz,
Paula. II. Title.
    [DNLM: 1. Abortion—personal narratives. 2. Physicians—
personal narratives. WQ 225 S634a]
HQ767.5.U5S565 1992
363.4'6'0973—dc20
DNLM/DLC
for Library of Congress   92-54459
                                                                      CIP

Manufactured in the United States of America

10   9   8   7   6   5   4   3   2   1

Designed by Irving Perkins Associates

This book is dedicated to those women, past, present, and future, whose disenfranchisement disavows them their rights to qualified total health care and denies them a means of exercising a choice over their own lives.

For as long as one woman is denied that right, all women are.

Acknowledgments

I thank Gerry Zatuchni who likely doesn't remember that he first suggested I chronicle my abortion experiences; I thank my revered teacher, the late Michael Joe Daly, who taught me that I couldn't be a complete gynecologist until I understood womens' emotions; I thank Irv Saxe who proved to me that you never get too old and should never get too complacent to give each patient your every skill; I thank Allan Chase whose guidance and historical savvy showed me that no issue that concerns people can be grasped in a geopolitical vacuum or divorced from the economics of life.

And I thank my beloved Frankie Sue who is my severest critic, who always demands my very best, and who remains my inspiration.

—Don Sloan, M.D.

I thank my friends, Sheila Crowell and Ellen Kolba, whose commitment to womens' issues has been instrumental in shaping mine, and who provided practical and moral support and helpful comments throughout the writing process. And I thank my mother, Rachel Hartz, who long ago taught me the meaning of choice and the importance of having one, and whose encouragement and enthusiasm never falter.

—Paula Hartz

Authors' Note

The cases in this book center on abortion, an intensely personal, frequently painful decision as well as a controversial and volatile political issue. In preparing the cases for publication, care has been taken to protect the privacy of both patients and medical personnel whose lives and careers might be adversely affected by having their associations with abortion known. All patients' names have been changed, along with identifying details. An asterisk (*) denotes a pseudonym.

Contents

1 *The Making of an Abortionist*

The phone rang in the on-call room sometime in the dark hours of the night. A woman was in trouble from a "wire-hanger job," the ER clerk said, describing yet another botched amateur abortion, and I was the medical resident on duty. Shaking off the heaviness of much-needed sleep, I started down to the emergency room.

I had learned about abortions in med school and seen women in plenty of trouble from very illegal and very crudely performed neighborhood abortions in the emergency room where I did my internship, but up to now, the experience had been somewhat of an academic exercise. Watch and learn, sure. But it wasn't my responsibility, and I didn't get emotionally involved. I saw about it what I wanted to, took from it according to my priorities and closed my eyes to the rest of it. I was there to learn. But this night it was my watch and my responsibility, and it was going to become quite vivid. I was about to mature.

As luck would have it, I had drawn the July fourth holiday for duty. Working that weekend, I saw and cared for my first septic abortion, and it was different from the ones I learned about in class and had only academic appreciation for. It was a rude awakening and an education.

I had just started my residency in gynecology at a big-city hospital in central Philadelphia. Today there are regulations about on-duty hours and unions to enforce them, but then we often worked forty-eight hours straight or more—a hundred or more hours a week was common—grabbing a few minutes of sleep in the on-call room, for two hundred bucks a month and a free midnight snack. And we felt lucky. We were getting an education, seeing and doing things that put us light-years ahead of people getting their experience in quieter places. Even in those days—the sixties—people used the emergency room for primary care as well as accidents and sudden illnesses. There in central Philly, we also got our share of weekend boozers and brawlers. They were our "Saturday-night specials."

Actually, looking back, the times seem pretty tame. Drugs as we know them now were not that big an issue. The JFK trip through Dealey Plaza in Dallas was yesterday's news, and Vietnam was tomorrow's. Occasionally we saw someone on a bad trip from a hallucinogen, sometimes a bad mix of drugs and alcohol, or an attempted suicide. Sometimes we saw couples who had tripped together. We got street stabbings and bumps and bruises from driving under the influence. And we got the victims of back-alley abortions.

"Wire-hanger" abortions were only one way to describe them. Other terms were "poker jobs," "tin cans," "church keys" (when the instrument in question was a beer-can opener) and "barbed wire." I don't think I ever actually saw one that used barbed wire—it just seemed that way. The description fit.

Sometimes the patient came in with a piece of spool wire clutched in her hand. The trick was to take a wire hanger, uncoil it at its neck and then twist the end into a coil that would act like a corkscrew. A little piece of the wire was then wrapped at the portion of the hanger that would go into the uterus to make an easier grip for its eventual removal. Some people created a makeshift handle out of the far portion of the wire, and some were even clever enough to shape it in the form of a perfect handle grip. It took some ingenuity to do such a thing, I guess.

The pliability and strength of a hanger made it ideal. Metal stevedore tools, such as a long corkscrew, were fine in that they were strong, already shaped and even had wooden handles, but they were not pliable. The local abortionists learned that going straight in didn't work because of the direction of the uterus, tipped at its midportion toward the rear or toward the front. They learned to make the proper angles. They had the tools, but of course they didn't have the proper conditions to prevent infection, and they knew it.

At the hospital, we made a distinction between "infected" and "septic" abortions. The line was clear and sharp. Infection, you could often clean them up and send them home. Septic was really bad—coma, urine output low or maybe none, temperature below normal because the body was reacting to the trauma. It was an insult to every major organ—the liver, the kidneys, the adrenals, the thyroid and finally the brain. When that happened, death was close at hand. And not rare.

In a septic abortion, the first thing that hit you was the odor. If it had been more than a day or two, then the odor was one of bacteria, likely from fecal contamination—a coliform odor, we called it, to mark the presence of the coliform bacterium that is a normal inhabitant of the rectal canal. Occasionally there were perforations of the rectum when the patients would jam the wire up into the birth canal and miss—or were stoned on something, and just didn't care. Lots of times they were high on Thunderbird wine, the brand that was the cheapest in the local liquor stores. Or they would have gone out of state, over to Jersey, and gotten something even cheaper, and worse. And then there were the combinations of uppers and downers and alcohol. They made the patients incoherent in the worst way.

If the abortion had taken place within a day or two, maybe the coliform bacteria hadn't yet had a chance to spread and infect the area. Then the odor was just dirt and old blood and stale urine and sweat, unless the patient had added something to the wire hanger—mustard, tar-based salves and astringents that could be bought over the counter for boils and bruises. I had seen and remembered that from my medical school days in Brooklyn. The patients knew they needed something strong to get rid of a pregnancy, and figured if it would burn the skin or eat through grease, it would kill an embryo. They were right. It would do that and more.

As a rule, we would not see too much blood at first. Frequently patients didn't have much left in their bodies to bleed—they had done that already. Then they went into shock or vascular spasm, and the bleeding cut down. And often they had cleaned themselves up. Not knowing what they would meet up with in the ER—empathy if they were lucky, but often hostility and scorn—they wanted to be as polite and presentable as possible.

The first thing to do was to get a history. If we were lucky, there was someone there to provide it—a spouse, a relative, a friend, a lover. The police and ambulance drivers were often not that helpful. They acted resentful that the woman was giving them grief. Their behavior seemed somehow belligerent and even racist to me, since so many of our patients were African-American, and I often got into confrontations with them—even tussles sometimes. On top of that, it could be hard to find nurses who were sympathetic, nonjudgmental. That was a constant problem. All too often they had an attitude, a subtle anger and a subtle resentment simmering just under the surface. I was thinking all these things as I made my way to the ER that July fourth night.

Inside the swinging doors of the ER, odor and blood hit me like a wave.

The patient was in her early twenties—and frail. They usually were frail. She was lying on a litter with her legs drawn up in a fetal position, knees up under her chin, in a spreading pool of maroon-colored blood, moaning and groaning in pain. Pain. I could not describe the pain. I was not even able to touch her without her screaming out in anguish. Pain was everywhere.

My patient that night had done well. She had her little spool wire, the bend in the hanger perfect for her uterine direction. She knew she was pregnant, as the history evolved, by about five to six weeks. Remember, there were no home pregnancy kits in those days. A woman assumed pregnancy if she missed a period and couldn't keep her breakfast down. Although a lot of women were hung over from cheap wine, and morning sickness as a clue to pregnancy was a hazy concept, many others were nondrinkers and knew the feelings of pregnancy. They were usually right.

The young woman had taken the hanger, deftly worked it into the corkscrew shape and sat, cross-legged in a yoga position, in a bathtub with a few inches of warm water. She had inserted the instrument into her vagina and groped around until she found the cervical os—the opening into the uterus. The first pain would have come when she entered the uterus, pushing through into the cervical canal. After that, the pain might not be so bad.

Sometimes a patient would know that all she had to do was get the bleeding started, and then she could come to the ER to have the job completed. I welcomed that kind. More often, the patient got carried away as my patient had, grinding and scraping vigorously, and caused a mess. Sometimes it wasn't the patient but the local practitioners, in the back of an apartment on a kitchen table, who didn't want to leave the job half done. Call it pride in their work.

My patient that night had done her own abortion, although I learned later that she'd had a helper—like a guide. Many of the abortionists were only that—guides. They were paid to talk women through the procedure, to share the guilt and the ugliness. The young woman in front of me had aborted herself at least two to three days before. The odor gave her away. Not the odor of death—that would have been better. You could put on a mask and get away from that, or put the victim in a makeshift body bag and seal it up tight. Coliform odor was penetrating. And it was everywhere.

The patient was cold and clammy. I sized up the situation and called for help—all I could get. Nurses and fellow residents. IV fluids, oxygen, massive antibiotics—penicillin. That was the best then. We never had time to find out if the patient had any drug allergies. Who was there to ask—and who knew? I don't recall any damage we did with the penicillin. At least, I hope there was none.

The standard treatment was to empty the uterus. There wasn't a chance of saving the patient if the source of the bacteria and infection was not removed. Anesthesia was tricky. If the patient was unconscious, then we could get her prepped, cleaned and in position to get a sterile curette up the cervix, take away the rest of the fetal tissue we were sure to find—it only took a pinhead's worth to create and continue a massive infection—and then hope that nature, the penicillin and prayer would pull her through.

If she was awake enough to feel pain, as this woman was, then we needed an anesthetic, which would be given without obtaining much of a history. It was not likely that the patient had eaten for several hours or even days, so food aspiration was not a question. But there was always a risk that she had taken some water to swallow pills, or a slug of whiskey for the pain. You just never knew.

The ER wasn't equipped for general anesthesia. By the time I got my patient to the operating room, fifteen minutes or so later, her blood pressure had fallen through the bottom. Oxygen was all we could use now, and I still had to clean out her uterus. It seemed like a further insult, but it had to be done. If the infectious source stayed, we would never catch up. I did a D & C—a dilation and curettage—dilating, or stretching, the cervix until the opening was large enough to admit a curette, or scraper, and removed the contents of the womb. I found the expected—dirty tissue, blackened and with a stench that filled the room, like a gangrene odor almost. It was bad, but it could have been worse. Sometimes I found parts of a wire, or paint chips that had fallen off the hanger as it was moved in a thrusting motion during the abortion.

The woman's temperature was normal, which was not so good. I would have felt better for her if she had been burning up. Normal was low, meaning shock. Then her urine output slowed. Over the next few hours, three or four, she deteriorated. Then she was dead. Twenty-three years old, and she was gone.

I was angry. I wanted to know who, and where, and why. I wanted to shake the patient and yell, "Didn't you know what you were doing? Didn't you know what could happen, that you might die from this?" I kept going over it in my head. One of the senior residents offered me what passed for reassurance:

"She was sour when they brought her in. You did everything right. Forget it." But I didn't want to forget it. I kept biting on it like a sore tooth. This was a young woman, younger than I was. She had had her whole life ahead of her. I wanted the person responsible. I wanted justice.

Eventually, I realized that my anger was misdirected. Not that I felt any compassion for those who had guided her, but anger was futile. Blame never meant anything, then or now. Who was there to blame? Later on, I even found out the names of the most frequently used "high-wire men"—another sobriquet for the neighborhood practitioners. Some patients told me themselves, after I had earned their trust. But mostly, I learned, it was the patient herself, in desperation, taking up the idea from a cousin or sister or aunt.

Trying to understand, I asked anyone who would listen why women aborted themselves. I got a lot of shrugs and a lot of attitudes. One of the senior nurses, with lots of experience and very wise, old eyes, asked me, "What choice do they have?"

"There must be a better way to deal with it," I protested.

"Unless you've got connections or a lot of money—which they don't—it's the only game in town," she said. "It's do the abortion, any way you can, or have the baby. And they don't want the baby. Besides, you only see the ones that go bad. Some of these people get lucky—more than once."

That wasn't a lot of consolation.

By the middle of my first year, I had seen enough infective and septic abortions to make them closer to routine than I ever dreamed. When the call came from the ER clerk to get there fast, there were some questions I asked to help me decide *how* fast: Was it a tubal pregnancy? Was it a botched abortion? Septic? Infected? Not all the patients died. I had many—from teenage on up—for whom the only lifesaving option was hysterectomy. To get inside and see what a wire hanger and dirt could do to a uterus was an education in itself. The uterine muscle would be black from necrosis—tissue death.

I remember one patient, bleeding heavily from a self-induced abortion attempt, who hadn't even been pregnant. At forty-seven and heading for menopause, she had missed a period and assumed pregnancy—this in spite of having had her tubes tied seven years earlier, right there in the hospital. She was actually infertile.

The nurse reported that the woman had tried to abort herself. No one knew more. The patient was bleeding heavily. The blood was brighter and fresher than usual, so the nurse figured the abortion had been done within the past hour or two. The patient was alert and quite responsive.

When I got there, the sheets were covered with blood. I made sure the patient was IV'd and the standard tests were under way before I made my diagnosis. I was still quite green, and I wanted to have the right information before I called my senior resident. It wasn't appreciated if you woke up your boss when you didn't have the right information or data. That was a no-no.

Through my speculum, I could see fresh scarring of the cervix and bright red blood—lots of it. A church-key job for sure, I thought. Then I checked the patient's history.

The tubal ligation threw me off. By the time I finished reviewing the history, I knew it wasn't an abortion, in spite of what the nurse had said and even what I had seen. I used packing to hold back the hemorrhage. It slowed a little under pressure.

I couldn't do much more without anesthesia and surgery. I told the nurses that this was not an abortion attempt or a miscarriage, and alerted my senior resident because I could not see the source of bleeding. I was a little puzzled by that, but otherwise sure of myself. There was always a mild sort of rivalry between the old-hand nurse and the novice resident, and I was feeling pretty smug for having one-upped the nurse.

The senior got there in a few minutes, listened to my history and smiled knowingly. I didn't understand why. He asked the patient to repeat the story of the tubal ligation. Then he asked her, "Did you do anything to yourself to bring this on?"

She looked down. "Yes," she admitted in a low voice. When he waited, she went on. "With a knitting needle. Did myself years back, too, same way, and it worked fine. This time I must have missed."

I couldn't believe it.

We took her to the OR, found the source of the bleeding and fixed her up. Luckily she had come in right away. She was fine.

My chief resident gave me a lesson in social medicine. He said that the elapsed time since the tubal ligation had told him he was looking at an abortion attempt. Among many cultures, he said, the number seven has powerful significance. In this woman's circle, it manifested itself in the belief that a tubal ligation lasted only seven years, and then the tubes came untied. It was part of the folklore of sevens—seven days of the week, seven seas, seven continents, seven ages of man. There was a belief in the seven phases of womanhood: ages birth through seven, childhood; seven through fourteen, preadolescence, onset of menstruation; fifteen through twenty-one, age of majority; twenty-two through twenty-eight, prime of life; twenty-nine through thirty-five, end of active childbearing; thirty-six through forty-two, premenopause; forty-three through forty-nine, menopause.

That she wasn't pregnant didn't matter. That she thought she was and did something to herself did. She told me, when my fascination with the folklore of sevens led me to ask her about it, that she had been informed by her godmother that yes, her tubes had come untied, and yes, she was indeed pregnant, according to God's will. She described to me her crying and trying to convince her godmother to allow the abortion and even to do it, but the godmother had remained intransigent, saying that it was "God's will" and the woman's duty to have the child and add to the flock. The patient tried living with the idea of another baby at her age, but couldn't stand it, and did the damage. She went home in a few days, a little wiser. So was I.

I didn't stay a novice for long. Soon, when a botched abortion came in, I was the one they called.

On my infrequent nights off, I liked to relax at a little bar and lounge around the corner from the hospital. It drew its customers mostly from the neighborhood people rather than the hospital staff, and I liked that. The food was both budget-priced and good, and there was live music: a better-than-average jazz pianist, sometimes a trio and a singer named Carole. She had a pleasant-enough voice, not really big enough for the kind of songs she wanted to sing, but not bad, either. She was maybe thirty pounds overweight, kind of lumpy, but she had stage presence, sparkle. The patrons liked her, and so did I. She was friendly and easy to listen to.

I was there often enough to become a regular, and Carole used to drift over on her breaks to talk to me and split a beer. She told me her dreams of making it big in show business, and sometimes about her boyfriend, Hurley, a not-always-employed bass player, who, in Carole's words, "wasn't much." I asked her why she stuck with him, and she shrugged. "Better'n nothing, I suppose. But he's mine." She said it with a wide smile, so she must have gotten something from the relationship. Sometimes he joined us, but never for very long. I wondered at first if he didn't like hanging out with a white guy: In those days, interracial friendships were uncommon. But it was just his way. My being white didn't seem to bother Carole, and I was comfortable with her and her friends. Hurley eventually warmed up to me too.

"What've you been up to?" Carole would always ask, and I'd tell her a hospital war story or two. She was a good listener. So she knew what I did, knew that I handled a lot of botched abortions.

One evening when she joined me, she spent more time staring into her half of the beer than drinking it. I finally asked, "Is something wrong?" I assumed it was Hurley again.

She looked me in the eye. "If I asked you something, like a favor, and you didn't want to do it, would you promise not to get mad?" she asked.

"If I don't want to do it, I won't do it. I won't get angry, I promise. What's going on?" I had absolutely no idea where she was heading.

She looked away. "I've got one in the oven, and I don't want it," she said. Her lips barely moved. "Hurley isn't taking it too good. I need to do something, and quick."

I don't remember saying anything, but I must have made a sound, flinched, or put up my hands, because she reached toward me.

"Oh," she said, "I don't mean you should do it. I mean, do you know somebody who'd do a colored girl, safe? A name? The doctors that do it around here for real money don't do colored. I've got some other names, but I don't know how they'd be. There's supposed to be this guy, a doctor, out west of here, in the country. They say he'll help you, no matter what. I figured maybe you'd . . ." she trailed off. "It's OK. I'll use who I've got. You don't have to . . ."

I found my voice. "Promise me," I said, "that you won't do anything or go to anybody until I see what I can do." I had no idea how I was going to do anything, or if I did do it what it was going to be, but I wanted to make sure she didn't go to a back-alley operator and end up on my ER litter—or worse. I didn't think she'd try to do herself, but . . . "Promise," I insisted.

It must have come out more vehemently than I meant it to, because she looked a little scared. She wasn't the only one.

"I promise," she said. I believed her.

"I'll find somebody," I said. "Just be cool."

Why didn't I try to talk her out of it? I don't know, except that I sensed it wouldn't do any good. I could have lectured her about having the baby and putting it up for adoption, but I knew I would come off as pious and patronizing, and it wouldn't have helped. Carole was determined. She didn't need me to tell her what to do—only how to do it.

I had never expected to find myself looking for an abortionist, except possibly to see him (or, more likely, her) put out of business. Now the idea of abortion carries with it a load of unresolved moral and political questions, but then the opinion on abortion was unified and clear-cut—it was dirty, evil and, most important, criminal. Doctors who did abortions risked going to jail, losing their licenses, their careers, everything. Back in the fifties, a doctor in a nearby town had committed suicide— rumor had it that he had been doing abortions and was threatened with exposure. I was bold enough when it came to medicine, but getting involved in an abortion was something else. The idea gave me a sick, clammy feeling. I broke into a sweat.

I had been working in the city long enough to have some contacts there, but like Carole's, mine were not very reliable or very safe, or they were one other "very" that ruled them out— expensive. It was no trick to get contacts in places such as Puerto Rico or Sweden, but jaunts like that were not for the hoi polloi. I had to find someone reliable, safe, accessible and affordable, and I had to do it fast. The clock was ticking.

I was not sure which of my colleagues I could trust. Certainly there were those I could not trust. I didn't know how far or deep I could go with my inquiries, even among my friends. I didn't dare approach any of my superiors, not even the ones I felt close to and liked, and who liked me. I found out later that my instincts were right. If I had approached them about abortion, they would have turned against me, and my career could have been threatened, maybe damaged beyond repair. Abortion was that dirty, that taboo.

I remembered the ER nurse with the wise, old eyes. Hadn't she said something about "connections"? Nurses were supposed to know these things, weren't they? So I asked her.

"What do you think I am?" she snapped. "Clean up your own messes." She stalked away.

I went after her. "It's not my mess," I said. "And a mess is what I'm trying to avoid."

She softened a little, but not much. "I can't help you. I'm sorry." Her tone told me she might not be.

Now what?

I thought about Carole's guy "west of here." I envisioned him in a steel town around Pittsburgh, working in his dirty kitchen in a black apron. Well, if Carole had heard of him, others must have too. I started making phone calls.

My detective work paid off. Over the next couple of days, I began to get names. A doctor from a Washington hospital was said to do abortions on weekends at his Pennsylvania farm, on a well-scrubbed kitchen table. There was a woman, a nurse, on the Jersey shore, but that recommendation came with reservations—she wasn't always neat and clean. And yes, there was a doctor west of Philly, near mining country. His name popped up more frequently than the rest. It even showed up on a little piece of paper in my uniform jacket pocket one night after I'd been in the ER. The nurse with the wise, old eyes? I never found out.

The name was Spencer. He sounded too good to be true— like a fictional character. Maybe I had my man. All I had to do was find him.

I grabbed the medical directory and matched the name with a town in a place where it should be—Ashland, Pennsylvania. I called the number in the directory and got his office receptionist, I guessed. Her local drawl didn't sound too professional. But it was as simple as that. I made an appointment.

My next day off, I drove out to Ashland to meet this doctor, if indeed that's what he was. He might be all he was supposed to be, and then again, he might not. I wasn't quite ready to let him work on Carole without checking him out first.

Ashland reminded me of every sleepy little coal town I'd ever seen. About a hundred miles northwest of Philadelphia, it was near nothing except a lot of other sleepy little coal towns. The whole place consisted of only a few square blocks. It's not much bigger now, if you don't count the shopping malls. The wide, elm-shaded main drag, Center Street, held all the shops and offices—a little grocery, the bus depot, the local barbershop, a drugstore with a soda fountain, a luncheonette, the town hall. The hospital, a squat, sprawling gray brick building tinged with coal smoke, stood on the outskirts. The town was right out of Norman Rockwell—still is, although the elms are gone, fast-food joints have replaced the luncheonette and the building on

Center Street where Spencer had his office has a new stucco facade and is painted an ugly brown and beige.

In 1966 it was white clapboard, a big, rambling place with a wide front porch. I had no trouble finding it.

It was an afternoon in early winter. I parked in one of the slots in front of the building and went up to the door where Spencer's shingle hung. I entered an ordinary, small-town doctor's office, unremarkable in every way. There was a pregnant woman, a man with a bad cough and an older woman nursing a bandaged hand. I sat down to wait my turn.

I felt nervous and guilty. In Ashland, anyway, I needn't have worried. Everyone in the town, all six thousand people, knew everybody's business, Doc Spencer's included. But he was the one who delivered their babies and sat up with their sick and dying, and they treasured him. I found out later that if no one was in Spencer's office to answer a call, the local telephone operator—the town didn't have dial phones yet—would cut in and make the appointment for him.

Dr. R. Douglas Spencer (the "R," for Robert, rarely used) was Dr. Spencer to the townspeople of Ashland, Doug or Douglas to his close friends and "Dr. S" to thousands of women up and down the East Coast and as far west as Ohio. He was a stockily built man of medium height with slightly bowed legs and a mane of silky white hair that framed and softened a squarish face. I guessed him to be in his late sixties. He was wearing a white shirt open at the neck (characteristically, I learned; on the rare occasions when he wore a tie, it was a bow), baggy tweed pants, heavy for winter, and square-toed black shoes. Perched on his nose were horn-rimmed bifocals. He had even, white teeth. He bragged that they were his own, but that one boast I doubted.

When my turn came, he took me into his office. It was clean and neat—a little old-fashioned, but somehow that fit his image. He waved me into a chair and studied me through his horn-rims, sizing me up, trying to decide whether I was a legitimate patient or trouble or what. "Now, just what is it that I can do for you?" he asked.

Instead of playing it cagey and cool as I had planned, I found myself blurting out the truth and the point of my errand. I gave him a bio in twenty-five words or less: "I'm a doctor, an OB-GYN resident in Philly. One of my clinic patients needs a therapeutic. I want to find her a safe one." "Therapeutic" was polite doctor-to-doctor talk for abortion in those days.

Without making a comment, he consulted his calendar. "She can come on Saturday at one o'clock," he said.

"She doesn't have much money."

"Tell her money won't be a problem."

"She's a black woman," I told him. "I wouldn't want to send her all this way if you—"

"Why should that make a difference?" he asked mildly, and smiled when I shook my head—I never had been able to figure out why it should make a difference either.

The transaction was apparently complete; he made a little notation on his calendar. "Well, then, Dr. Sloan, have you had lunch?" he asked.

I had not.

"Would you care to join me? We'll go to Ashland's finest—and only."

I would.

He called ahead and booked a table at the local luncheon-ette—it could get crowded at lunch hour—and because it was for Dr. Spencer, we got the best seats in the house. When we walked in, he gestured vaguely at the waitress, who brought us coffee and two BLTs on white toast smothered in mayo, without being asked. It was his standard lunch, and the first of many things we found out we had in common. We spent our time there with him talking as he ate.

Over the next hour or so, I learned a great deal about R. Douglas Spencer. Born in Missouri, he had done his medical training at the University of Pennsylvania in Philadelphia, and had practiced in Ashland most of his life, except for the time he had spent as an army doctor during World War II. He had two grown children from an early, failed marriage, and a new, younger wife, twenty years his junior—Eleanor, whom he clearly cared for deeply. They were the best of friends.

For a country doctor, he was surprisingly up-to-date on some of the newer procedures like gastroscopy and esophagoscopy—techniques he had more or less taught himself with the help of fast-take training courses and medical journals. His army training helped too. The thing he told me that shocked me the most, I think, was not that he did abortions in his office, but that he had done lots of office procedures that were considered somewhat courageous—even risky. But by then, I had the feeling that Spencer was a risk-taker. A careful one.

As the lunch progressed, I realized how much I liked the man. He was taking a chance, reaching out to me, hoping I was the right person to tell about his work. The more he talked, the more I felt I was. As we got up to leave, he looked me in the eye.

"Ever done a therapeutic?" he asked.

"No."

"Seen one done?"

"No. Just cleaned up a lot of bad ones."

"If you're interested in seeing one done right," he said, "you might want to come back some Saturday. You'd be welcome. It's a simple operation, really, but I could show you a few things. And I could use the help. Call ahead, and I'll let you know if anyone's coming in. That way, you won't waste the trip."

Carole went up to Ashland and had her abortion a few days later. I wish I could say Hurley went with her, but he'd made himself scarce. She came back to me at the hospital clinic for a checkup afterward, and she was fine. She told me Spencer had asked her how much she could afford to pay, and when she told him, he asked her for a little less. As far as she was concerned, he was a candidate for sainthood. I would have seconded the nomination.

The following week, I went back to Ashland. I felt relaxed about going, but at the same time I was aware enough of what I was doing that all the way up I kept checking in my rear-view mirror to see if anybody was following. I thought that every state trooper in Pennsylvania was onto me. When I got to the office and rang the bell, Spencer himself let me in and showed me where to hang my coat and where to wash up. By the end of that morning, we were on a first-name basis, and Douglas had showed me the ropes of an abortion—a real one.

He was a good teacher. As a doctor he may have been a renegade and a risk-taker, but in surgery he was steady and sure. It seems hard to believe now, but at that time, most doctors weren't very skillful at determining the duration of a pregnancy from a physical examination. There weren't any sonograms or sophisticated tests. You just took the woman's word for it and trusted your hands. Douglas was an expert. He would not do an abortion beyond a safe and early first trimester, and he was good at making sure the patient was telling the truth. He was daring enough to work outside the law, but he wasn't foolhardy.

R. Douglas Spencer and I soon became a habit. I looked forward to the days I would spend in Ashland.

We had to work by hand. I was a well-trained senior resident in GYN by that time, so I knew my way around an operating room, but in Doug's office, he was boss. I think back on it—I was trained in gynecology, and he wasn't, but experience wins every time. He knew what he was doing. Suction, the standard technique for most abortions today, was still some years in the future. I can't imagine now doing what we did without the technique of suction. But we did it.

We scraped. We used a kind of handmade suction to collect some of the blood, the uterine lining and embryonic tissue, but it was nothing like the present-day aspiration technique now in routine use. We didn't have the special tips and cannulas (a thick Bakelite or polystyrene pipe the size of a drinking straw) or the proper vacuums that are in common use today. The procedure took time, up to an hour a patient. Scrape and look at the materials, scrape and look again. The cases I did were almost always early, no more than several weeks. Very few patients made the mistake of waiting too long—fewer than you would think. Of course, some did, and then Douglas would stretch a little bit or just wouldn't do the procedure. He knew when to say no. His record for safe, successful abortions was phenomenal.

We were very, very careful about technique. Sterile instruments—always. The table was always covered with a clean sheet, and there was a pillow with a fresh pillowcase at the patient's head. We had a kind of panty-hose thing with no crotch that the patients wore—when we had one available. We did our own laundry, and sometimes we ran out.

For anesthesia, we used mostly hand-holding and talk. A local, a little Novocain, to get past the cervix, and that was about it. The dilators and the rest of the equipment were antiquated but adequate—just. Today it would all qualify for the Smithsonian.

Afterward, the patient lay on a cot in Doug's little back room for an hour or so with a blanket over her and a cold cloth on her head. He'd give her something for cramps and instruct her about calling him if anything out of the ordinary happened, and send her on her way. Occasionally, as a precaution, he'd prescribe prophylactic antibiotics.

It scares me, in the atmosphere of medical litigation we have now, to think of what we were doing. But I don't remember ever being scared then. As long as I was with Doug, in the office or in his company, I never worried. I knew that if I ever got into trouble with a patient—which fortunately never happened—he would be there to help me out. But on the drive up and back, I never stopped looking over my shoulder for the cops.

In between patients, Douglas would chat about so many things—his hobbies, his habits, his travels. He was a rock hound, an amateur geologist; he and Ellie traveled all over the country collecting fossils and rocks. He also had a custom-built car that he could drive into water, and the two of them, and sometimes a friend, would go car-boating, or whatever it was called. I think he liked the look on people's faces when he drove right out into the middle of a lake. Though he invited me a few times, I never made it.

But our relationship was mostly a working one. He kidded me sometimes about my newfangled ideas and my residency—such formal training had been unheard of in his day. For my part, I found it difficult to remember that his school was mostly on-the-job stuff—he was that good. He shared his medical knowledge with me sparingly, as though I might judge him by it and find him wanting. It seems almost silly to think of it. I was in awe of him.

I never found out just how he got started doing abortions. Later, I learned that to many young women of that generation, he was an almost legendary figure, "the Angel of Ashland," the hero who would rescue a woman in distress. They had stories about him. One was that he had lost a family member—a daughter, a sister—to an abortionist, and had then devoted himself to helping women in trouble. But it was nothing so dramatic or romantic as that. Ellie told me later that it was a natural progression of things: "Douglas just never could say no to anyone in need of his skills. Anyone."

He did have some early experiences cleaning up local women who had gone to Philly or Cincinnati or Pittsburgh and been hurt by back-alley guys there. He hated that—he really cared. I could picture him saying, "Don't go to someone else if this happens again. Come to me." And because he was the person he was, they came to him, and he helped them.

Danger? Did that enter into it? Did he think of it that way? And did I? It just never came up. I wasn't the only helper he had. There were one or two others, over a longer period of time, local men. Like me, they had absorbed his philosophy. If someone was in trouble and Douglas could do something about it, he did. His attitude was all the more remarkable for the times. Deadly abortions were commonplace. And those were the ones we saw. There were plenty of deaths that never became public: poor or black women who never got to a hospital. Some of them never even got to be statistics. They were buried in someone's backyard or basement and never missed, at least not by the world at large.

I think we all had a good feeling when we did a neat and

clean procedure, and the woman was safe. I know I did. Doug's office was a safety valve for me after the pressure of a week in a big teaching hospital in the city. The scenes there were so bizarre. Sometimes a woman came in handcuffed to a cop, and the cop wouldn't take off the cuffs while we worked on her. We'd throw sheets over the pair of them, like Siamese twins. I would bring back these horror stories, and Doug would say, "Too bad we didn't get her up here before she found her bum." "Bum" was a bad word to Doug. In that way, he reminded me a little of my father.

Somehow he found time to read. When the occasion called for it, he could quote Samuel Clemens or Karl Marx, and, although he wasn't obviously religious, the Bible. His favorite Bible quotation was Matthew 19:24: "It is easier for a camel to pass through the eye of a needle than for a rich man to enter the kingdom of heaven."

He lived by it, too. Money just never seemed to be important to Doug Spencer. He seemed to borrow a page from Willie Sutton's book. Doug did abortions because that's where the need was. Although he was not above charging an obviously well-to-do matron in a fur coat a hundred bucks or more, we did many abortions for five dollars or less, some for barter—a dozen eggs or a bag of fresh vegetables—and quite a few for nothing at all.

Patients came to Douglas Spencer from all over. All sizes, all shapes, all colors, all economic strata. College women and coal miners' daughters, society women and housekeepers, we saw them all. They came with husbands, lovers, girlfriends, mothers or alone. If Douglas felt the abortion could be safely done, he did it. No one was ever turned away.

In Ashland, Spencer's sideline was an open secret—the local telephone operator who made appointments when he was out made abortion appointments for him as well. But because he was the person he was and had the respect of the community, it wasn't a problem. At least, that's the way it seemed to me. There were people against abortion—in those days some would have said every decent, straight-thinking person—but the antiabortion movement wasn't organized, at least not the way it is now. Douglas must have figured that Ashland was in the middle of nowhere, and no one was likely to bother him. He was generally right about that, but it wasn't always true.

I remember at least one time when a man called and threatened Doug with exposure if he did not pay up—I think the amount was a thousand dollars, an awful lot of money in those days. I don't know whether the man was a disgruntled family member or friend of a patient or just an outsider with an ax to grind, but he had blackmail on his mind. Douglas called the police in Ashland and told them he had gotten a call from an extortionist.

The police wanted Doug to go ahead with the meeting so they could nab the guy. Typically, Doug said no—he didn't want to get anyone in trouble! He was actually planning to pay the money. The police pointed out that extortionists rarely quit, and this could happen again and again, but Douglas said once in a while was OK, because he felt sorry for anyone who was so emotional about his beliefs on abortion. Doug could be like that.

On this occasion, though, the police prevailed. They arrested the blackmailer, although Douglas convinced the authorities to keep a low profile because he didn't want the exposure. I'm not sure how many other times it happened—when he paid without mentioning it to anyone. He never wanted trouble, and that was his way of doing things.

In my almost two years with Douglas Spencer, I acquired his philosophy as well as his technique. His example carried over into my work at the hospital, as I tried to emulate his compassion, his gentleness and his serenity. He was a man with many, many friends.

We were colleagues and more. He hoped, I knew, that I would find a way to stay with him in his work, and I was tempted. But I wasn't ready to define my career so narrowly or settle for life in rural America. As my residency drew to a close, he said to me one day, "You'll be leaving soon." It was a statement, not a question.

"Yes," I told him.

He nodded. "I thought you would," he said. He didn't press me to stay. He knew I was homesick.

A few months later, when I finished my training, Douglas and I parted company, and I headed for New York and home. We corresponded once or twice, his letters typed on the same 1910 Remington that he always used for prescriptions. Then the correspondence trailed off, and I let it go. I never saw him again.

Douglas rarely complained about his own aches and pains, so it came as a surprise to me when I learned that he was seriously ill. A scant two years after I left Ashland, he died, with Ellie nearby. She told me he had worked up to the week of his death. Knowing him as I did, I wasn't surprised.

2 *The Bad Old Days*

". . . still so little. I just don't see how I can manage another one right now. It's just too soon!"

Coming into the hall, I could hear my youngest sister, deep in a confab with our parents in the next room. We were close in age—she was only a couple of years older—but she was already married with a newborn, a "family woman," while I was still in school, the kid brother. Her concerns these days seemed light-years away from mine.

". . . have an abortion." Her voice, sharp and clear, drifted into the hall. I hadn't planned to listen, but now I was transfixed. I could hear my parents demurring.

"You always said it should be up to the woman," my sister said, and I knew she was addressing our father. She continued, "You can't mean it for someone else and not for me. You must know of someone! Just get me a name. I'll do the rest."

Another rumble from my father, and the softer murmur of my mother's voice, soothing. I'd heard enough. I backed away to think.

My father would do anything for his children, but I half hoped he wouldn't honor my sister's request. Abortion was illegal and far from safe. Just the word ruined reputations—about the worst thing you could say about a girl in high school was that she'd had an abortion. I didn't know much, but I knew that women who'd had abortions died or were hurt so badly they couldn't have babies. I kept thinking, Not my sister, not my beloved sister.

Herman, as our father was called by just about everyone,

certainly believed that women should be the ones to decide
whether to bear a child. He and his friends weren't nonsexist in
the sense we understand it today, but the rights of women were
on his political agenda. Steeped in the traditions of European
socialism, he had a powerful sense of social justice.

He found her a "name"—that was the way people in shady
businesses were described back then—and reluctantly passed it
on. Over the next couple of days, I could feel the tension in the
house in little whispered conversations and silences and see it
in my parents' grim expressions. They were worried sick, but
still, on principle, they supported my sister's right to make the
decision. When she decided not to go through with it, their
relief was palpable.

When she said, "You must know of someone!" my sister
knew what she was talking about. Herman had his finger in a
lot of pies. I don't remember a time in my life when my father
wasn't immersed in some form of social or political activity. He
was an involved citizen.

During World War II, when the other kids on the block were
playing touch football, my father, who was over the age for
military service, had me out on Saturday afternoons airplane-
spotting for the local civilian air patrol—my contribution to the
war effort, along with saving tinfoil. By the time I reached
college, I was using my weekends to support a picket line or to
ladle out soup for strikers on a work action. I spent many a
Sunday morning in migrant-worker camps in central New
Jersey and upstate New York, handing out food vouchers or
doing my darnedest to get the workers to read union literature.
Did I mind? Not one bit. It was all a marvelous part of growing
up in my father's image.

Politics was my first love. A few years after college, when I
decided I wanted a profession, I first considered political science
or law. But medical school gave me a lot of options. Medicine
could make me a solid citizen, and there was plenty of politics
to play with in the medical community. It was a natural for me,
but not so clear to Herman.

He was disappointed when I chose doctoring. He had pictured

me as a farmer—in overalls, a hayfork in one hand, sitting in
the cab of a John Deere tractor. He had always longed for a
farm of his own. If I had chosen that route, I would have had a
partner for life. To his way of thinking, medicine was too elitist,
too establishment. He was concerned that I would turn out to
be "just another rich doctor," a traditional practitioner. I guess
I should have been insulted, but my father's concerns always
grew out of love, and his criticisms never hurt. Before he died, I
was able to show him he need not have worried.

I did my internship at Kings County Hospital—KCHC, as we
knew it—in the heart of the Brooklyn ghetto. I hadn't had a
privileged life, and, thanks to my father's tutelage, I thought I
knew what poverty and privation looked like. But the things I
saw there are etched into my memory forever. Who could ever
forget?

There was not even Medicaid in those days. Public hospitals
were the health-care system for poor women. Not that it made
much difference—poor and down is poor and down. Many of
those we saw were immigrants and illegals and domestics. They
depended on KCHC and places like it for their lifeline, which
means they depended on medical students, interns and residents. They were teaching cases, and, for the most part, not
much more.

As I watched women die in their own blood and pus, I
wondered about abortion—how could anyone be desperate
enough to do this to herself? But they were and they did. They
still do.

Daily, they streamed into the emergency room, half aborted—
and half dead. What I saw a few years later in my residency in
Philly was just another page from the same book. It was rarer,
to be sure, but not impossible, to see an upper-middle-class
housewife or working woman, well enough off and well enough
educated to know better, who had gone to one of these neighborhood butchers and ended up on the same litter or morgue

slab. The color of their skin and the cost of their funerals were different—that's all.

The thing that got to me most was their faces. You have never seen such fear. Fear on their lips and in their eyes. God, what looks they gave us.

We usually saw them late. It was lucky for us when we got women who had been aborted recently and had only an early infection. Usually, they'd had the infection for days, and it was draining the life out of them. Sometimes they would have gone back to the one who did the damage and asked for help. Why not? These women trusted their local abortionists, not us. The person was often a neighbor, a friend or a relative—a mother-in-law or sister or uncle.

Sometimes when women went back for help, they were further brutalized, because the abortionist realized that there was a part of the pregnancy left behind. Digging around in the infection only spread it. In many cases, I guess, they likely hoped the patient would die, so as not to expose what had happened. Sometimes, with their competency called into question, they would beat up a patient with a baseball bat or something. We saw it all.

Worse—if that's possible—were the abortions that were not done with instruments, but with various solutions. The abortionist would convince the woman to allow a liquid to be introduced into the vagina, strong enough to penetrate the cervix and get into the uterus. It was senseless. The cervical os, the opening into the womb, is closed. Nothing passes through it without force.

Sometimes a woman who had had children would have a loosening of the os, allowing some of the stuff to seep up and through into the uterus. But mostly all it ever did was sear the tissues. The solutions ranged from washing detergents to Lysol, Flit, insect sprays and even household lye or Drano. Lye was the most horrible. It burned right into the lining of the vagina. We saw vaginas that were black—pitch black—from burns. It was hard to imagine the tissue destruction—and the pain. Or that look of fear.

One of the first "liquid jobs" I saw was on a Sunday night when I was assigned as a resident assistant. Inexperienced as I was, I could see that the patient was in great distress. Her breath was coming in short gasps, and she was doubled up, clutching her belly in pain.

I felt a little shock. I knew her. She was an eighteen-year-old girl I had met a few weeks before, when she came to the hospital outpatient clinic with an older sister for routine care. That day she had been saucy and flirtatious. She had been wearing hand-painted stockings that she proudly told me were her trademark.

That night in the emergency room, she was still wearing them, but they were covered in blood. Hers.

My resident knew what he was looking for. He bent over her, half shouting to break through the pain into her consciousness. "If we're going to fix you up, you have to help us. You have to cooperate. Do you hear me?" She gave a little nod, too deep in the grip of fear and pain to resist. He yelled to me back over his shoulder, "Grab her legs. Get her in the stirrups."

I had to hold her bloodstained, torn-stockinged feet in the foot braces while he got the speculum in place. He motioned me to look. The mottled black and brown color of the normally rosy red vaginal wall told the story. The odor completed the diagnosis—undiluted Lysol.

"Let's go!" he said.

We rushed her to our down-the-hall mini OR and gently flooded the area with copious amounts of water, mild soap and absorbent oils—anything to stop the chemical burning of the phenols in the Lysol compound. If we got there early enough, and there were no systemic effects from absorption, such as vomiting and shock, time and soothing support would leave only a light scar in the vagina—and a deep one in the memory.

She was still pregnant.

We cleaned her up, sedated her well and prepared for the completion of the abortion. Finally, when we had done all that we could do, we left her, still whimpering in pain, to the ER nurses.

She was one of the lucky ones. For her, it all ended up OK.

There were other women who had done it to themselves. They'd heard of the locals doing it, and they figured they would save a few bucks. They couldn't do worse. The mess and the burns and the pain were no different. The odor of the human body burned by Flit or detergents would make your eyes water and your stomach churn.

The ingenuity of these people was amazing. Channeled in the right direction, it would have made them brilliant physicians. Detergent tablets, for example—there weren't many on the market, but they found them and used them. One favorite item was the blue commercial-strength disinfectant tablets that hung in the public toilets in train and bus stations. They were snitched for the express purpose of doing in an unwanted pregnancy in some desperate woman.

The numbers of abortion deaths during that period were all just guesstimates. Too many were never known about. How could anyone know? A vast number were not reported—either to avoid legal retribution or because nobody cared. The quoted statistics for illegal abortion at that time were one in forty dead. The real numbers were probably a lot higher, and even more shocking compared to the current rate of maybe one in 400,000. After *Roe v. Wade,* Planned Parenthood did its first 200,000 abortions with no deaths. None at all. And their record was not unique.

Of course, I was seeing only one side of the coin. My father had earlier pointed out to me, and I later confirmed it with my own experiences, that there was a decided double standard at work in the abortion business. For the affluent, there was no problem, or at least less of one.

If you had enough money, you could fly off to Havana for the Cuba Libre weekend. When I went to Cuba in the seventies as part of a medical exchange teaching program, doctors there who remembered "the good old days" told me about these jaunts made by those who could afford them in the days before the Revolution of 1959.

Special travel agents in New York, Miami and Los Angeles—"names" that people had if they were "in the know"—offered a package deal that included first-class airplane and hotel accommodations and a first-class pregnancy termination. A woman would plan to arrive on a Friday afternoon, and later that evening, a limousine would pick her up and take her to the American Hospital—now the Ramon Gonzalez Coro Maternity Center, renamed for a hero of the revolution.

The abortion done, the patient had the remainder of the weekend to relax—onto the beach for sunning and an afternoon or evening of shopping or visiting the gaming tables in the hotel, followed by a gourmet dinner. Then beach and cabana-clubbing on Sunday, and back to the States for Monday morning. Sometimes they brought along their husbands or lovers and extended the weekend, sort of a vacation-abortion combo. All very convenient—and very expensive.

"Sure, I did them," one of the old-timers told me. "Many of us did." We were sitting around the Floridita Bar, an old Hemingway hangout, over daiquiris, and he had become expansive.

"The cost? I think it was $1,200 or more for the weekend— hospital, hotel, everything—plus the air fare."

In the early sixties, I commented, that was real money to a lot of people. He raised his eyebrows. In present-day Cuba, it is still a lot of money.

"I guess to those people, it was a bargain," he shrugged.

He remembered names, some of which I only vaguely recognized from the society and business pages, but others from the entertainment world that I had to know—top names in show business. "Naturally," he said, "they got star treatment—incognito, but with all the trimmings. Champagne, flowers."

I jokingly reminded my companions that Hollywood and Broadway gossip columnists would pay nice finders' fees for such information. Today's supermarket tabloids would be having a field day, and for a change, they'd be right.

But it wasn't absolutely necessary to go to Cuba. New York had its own form of "Saturday-night specials" for wealthy women who didn't want to go to the trouble of flying off to the Caribbean. For them a few doctors—you could count them on one hand—had the Park Avenue business sewed up.

A call would come in to the hospital switchboard to page certain residents that Dr. So-and-So was sending in a patient he had seen in his office that day with bleeding. No one bothered to mention that the blood usually came from a needle stick in the cervix. Those few drops of blood were enough to get the patient past the ER crew and put the wheels of a D & C into motion.

The patient was diagnosed as a miscarriage, and she went directly to the operating room for her procedure. Within a few hours it was all over, and the various people involved were splitting the patient's fee. The patient could easily afford the tariff, and everyone involved was rewarded.

Needle sticks weren't the only trick. I knew of cases where red vegetable dye was used to simulate blood, thus saving the patient an uncomfortable encounter with a needle. Watered-down catsup was another possibility. The patient ran the risk of smelling like a hamburger and having the admitting doctor be unable to keep a straight face, but it worked more than once.

I once did a Saturday-night special as a favor for a colleague whose fiancée had turned up with an untimely pregnancy. Legal abortions were still about a year away. He knew of my experience with Doug Spencer, and fast came the needle scratch in the cervix. It was all over in about an hour. After all, they were VIPs. I remember feeling powerful that night, knowing that I was being called on for my special expertise, and that I was able to do something that scared others off because of its clandestine nature. I was especially pleased that it all turned out so well. It would have been most embarrassing if it hadn't, but the possibility of failure was an afterthought. It never occurred to me at the time.

A year or two into medical school, I was still looking around for a specialty that would combine medicine and social responsibility—I was going to be a doctor, not a farmer, but I was still my father's son. About that time, my chairman at Downstate Medical Center arranged for me to meet Dr. C. Lee Buxton, a friend of his and chairman of the department of obstetrics and gynecology at Yale University Medical School, when Buxton came to lecture at our staff meeting.

Dr. Buxton was a fascinating guy. In 1961, shortly before I met him, he, in his position as medical director of the Planned Parenthood League of Connecticut, and Estelle Griswold, its executive director, had opened a birth-control clinic that dispensed materials and devices. They were openly defying a Connecticut state law that made it illegal to use "any drug, medicinal article or instrument for the purpose of preventing conception." Their premise was that it was stupid, poor social medicine and probably unconstitutional for married Connecticut couples to have to smuggle condoms across the state line and risk fines or jail to use them. They examined married women in the clinic and prescribed contraception.

As Griswold and Buxton had expected—maybe even hoped— the cops shut down the clinic and arrested them under another section of the law providing that "Any person who assists, abets, counsels . . . another to commit any offense may be prosecuted and punished as if he were the principal offender."

The Connecticut court found them guilty. Two appeals courts concurred. The case eventually went to the United States Supreme Court.

Griswold v. Connecticut became a landmark. It established that married couples have the right to privacy and the right to use whatever they like for their bedroom activities. The decision invalidated Connecticut's law and all other state laws (Massachusetts, for one, had similar legislation) against the prescription, sale or use of contraceptive devices.

The highest court found that there was a right to privacy, maybe not spelled out in the Constitution, but implied nevertheless. Delivering the majority opinion, Justice William O. Douglas wrote, "Would we allow the police to search . . . marital bedrooms for telltale signs of the use of contraceptives? The very idea is repulsive to the notions of privacy surrounding the marriage relationship." The origins of the right to privacy could be traced back to seventeenth-century England—the "property in one's person" dictum that inspired the Puritans and many of the settlers in colonial America.

The Griswold case eventually paved the way for subsequent cases involving privacy. It was to be crucial eight years later in a case called *Roe v. Wade*.

The court decision on *Griswold* was still years in the future when I decided that gynecology was the perfect choice for someone who—like Buxton—wanted a medical specialty that involved both social and psychologic aspects. I approached my chairman to say that I wanted to do postgraduate work in that area, and he arranged for me to go to Philadelphia. He knew people there who, he promised, would see to my training—and they did. He couldn't know, nor could I, that Doug Spencer and Ashland would be part of that training.

By the end of my residency, I was itching to get home. Philadelphia was a city, but it wasn't *my* city, as my Philly colleagues knew—they called me the "Cosmopolitan Kid." It was great to get back to New York—the smell, the grit, the noise, the concrete, all of it.

I was up to my eyeballs in debt—like practically everybody I knew, sure, but that was no comfort. I was already older than a lot of others starting out, and I felt that I was going to be playing catch-up forever, especially since I was starting another training program, in the field of psychosomatics and human sexuality, my special interests. I found hospital work as a staff GYN to help pay the freight, but that meant that I was working around the clock and grinding away, studying and taking exams in my "spare" time. Politics got shoved onto a back burner.

In those days, the mainstream medical societies, such as the prestigious American College of Obstetricians and Gynecologists (ACOG), were officially mum on the subject of abortion. It was too hot a potato for them then. Today they have a clearly stated pro-choice policy, but then—nothing. There was abortion reform politicking going on, though, and I guess with my background I was bound to find it—or it me. I was ripe for the politics of abortion. It was just a natural arena.

I did some moonlighting in the Bronx for Planned Parenthood—not abortion; this was before the law changed. It was there that I met people who were working with NARAL, the National Association for Repeal of Abortion Laws (now the National Abortion Rights Action League).

NARAL had its beginnings in New York's medical community. One of its cofounders was Dr. Bernard Nathanson, a respected OB-GYN who was known for his outspoken opposition to antiabortion laws. NARAL volunteers started letter-writing campaigns and kept track of cases and data they could use to help sway legislation votes. A lot of nurses and doctors belonged. It was something you could do, something you could turn to when you started to feel burnout from treating so many "wire-hanger jobs."

And medical people weren't the only ones speaking out against the abortion carnage. Down at the Judson Memorial Church in New York's Greenwich Village, the Reverend Howard Moody had an active abortion-referral service in full operation. Moody's Clergy Consultation Service on Abortion eventually grew to include as many as fifteen hundred ministers, rabbis and even a few priests who formed a network that funneled women to doctors who would help them.

The CCSA, or "the Moody network," was using practitioners in this country—including Douglas Spencer—who were frankly flaunting the law, so their activities were legally sensitive. But in most cases sympathetic authorities looked the other way. As time went on, that referral source became public knowledge. Many women benefited from the work of the Reverend Mr. Moody.

By the late sixties, the whole atmosphere surrounding abortion was changing. For one thing, it was much more public. From being something that was mentioned only in whispers, it was becoming more and more accepted and "decent"—almost. You could look in certain newspapers and find a classified ad labeled "women referrals." All kinds of people imbued with the entrepreneurial spirit were getting into the act.

I remember hearing about one guy who worked for a publishing house in midtown. I don't know where his contacts came from, but he had a network of doctors on tap. He placed ads in newspapers across the country and, from his publishing desk, matched women up with practitioners in London or wherever. He set up the appointment, the trip and the hotel reservations, and took his vigorish. Everybody felt he deserved a cut, I guess. *The New York Times* got hold of the story, and that ended his publishing career—at least with that house. But there wasn't any law against what he was doing, and he wasn't particularly secretive about it.

At the time, I was working in the New York City hospital system. From a NARAL mailing, I'd received notification of an abortion reform strategy meeting coming up in Chicago, including Planned Parenthood, NARAL, NOW and a lot of others—I don't remember all of the sponsors. The idea got my political juices flowing, but I'd tossed the literature out. Between my schedule and my finances, I didn't have a prayer of going.

At the hospital, we'd been hearing rumors of gang activity in our catchment area—Harlem and Spanish Harlem—and we already knew our image needed work. As part of a PR plan, the hospital powers-that-be decided to hold a meeting and invited some leading neighborhood representatives to a public hall at the medical school. Since there were women's health issues involved, I was asked to sit in for my department.

We had our meeting, a lot of exchange, and we all felt we had taken a giant step forward. My chief was pleased with our start in a community outreach program. Talking to him later, I figured out what I wanted for a quid pro quo. When he said,

"We owe you one," I suggested a round-trip air-shuttle ticket to Chicago, a room at the Ambassador and a meal allowance.

"I think I can swing that," he said. "Try to share a room."

Minutes later, I was on the phone, looking for somebody to take my shift.

The air in Chicago was thick with excitement. You could feel it. At one question-and-answer session, I got carried away enough to grab the mike and speak out publicly. I don't remember what I said, but I do remember the glare of the lights, the noise, the sound of my voice reverberating in the room. I had wanted to be part of what was happening, and I was.

Those of us from New York, though, got a clear message from the other delegates: New York might not be a state on which to spend too much time or effort. The Archdiocese of New York, with its strong conservative tradition, first under Cardinal Spellman and then Cardinal Cooke, was considered a powerful force against abortion reform. With some noted exceptions, New York had a history of electing Catholic governors and lawmakers and was also thought to be resistant to abortion change. In fact, we were considered to be one of the last states likely to get reform.

Even so, everyone paid attention to the people from New York. We came from what was then the most populous state, with a great deal of clout in national politics—we had the most electoral votes. We were a flagship state. And we were the state with the abortion reform leaders—Planned Parenthood, NARAL. New York was looked on by the other states as I had been looked on in Philadelphia—as the Cosmopolitan Kid.

The conference was wonderful, exhilarating—and exhausting. I was proud of my part in it. I left Chicago with a sense of accomplishment and belonging and empowerment. More of us were working for reform than I had realized. And more important than numbers, we had determination, passion, going for us. For the first time, the goal seemed reachable.

The meeting spurred us all to go back to our home states and redouble our efforts. We New Yorkers had taken our share of lumps. We felt protective and vowed that we wouldn't let our state be left behind. Leaving the hotel, I ran into a delegate from California who made a joking remark about New York having to wait a while yet.

"We'll be there when the time is right," I told her. "We might even beat you. Just wait and see."

If you were into abortion rights, people assumed that you wanted to get into the business in a big way and make some fast money, because it was there to be made. Sometime early that spring, I was approached by an enterprising doctor, then semiretired, who was recruiting for a clinic outside San Juan. Puerto Rico was another option for women seeking abortions— not as ritzy as Cuba, but they had a thriving business there. It was quite illegal, but buyouts and payoffs were easy to come by.

"It's a good setup," he told me. "They need you about three days a week. You fly down, run through the cases, collect your dough and fly home. That's all there is to it."

"Illegal?"

"Yes, but city hall understands that they'll be taken care of. Someone else handles the money. You won't be involved. It's safe and sound. And the place itself is clean. Just trust me."

"You've worked with them?"

"Well—let's say I know what I'm talking about. All they need is the doctor. You won't be the first."

I told him I'd think about it. And I did, but not seriously.

Victoria was a long-time patient. I had delivered her two children, and I did her mother's hysterectomy. I knew that an abortion was part of her history, but I hadn't heard the details until years later.

* * *

"I was single, less than a year out of school, working my first job—an "entry-level position," you know? I was making almost nothing, just living from paycheck to paycheck. I didn't have anywhere to turn. The guy was a total loss—but by the time I realized that, it was already too late. My parents had really sacrificed to send me to school, so I could make something of myself, have a chance to do better than they did, and now I was pregnant. I was afraid they'd disown me—they were that uptight about sex. God, what a month. I was frantic. My phone bill was out of sight . . ."

"Your phone bill?" I asked. I didn't make the connection.

"Over two hundred dollars. I called all over the world. London. Sweden. Even Tokyo. I couldn't sleep, couldn't eat, I was throwing up—part morning sickness and part just nerves, probably. I was scared to death. What was going to become of me? All I could think was that my life was going to be over if I went on with this pregnancy. I would lose my job, my family, any chance I had at a career or marriage to someone who loved me. I had a little savings account, a few hundred dollars, but not enough to live on for more than a few weeks. How could I take months off to hide a pregnancy and have a baby? What would I live on? Illegitimacy—it's an ugly word, isn't it? There was still quite a stigma in those days. The whispering, people talking behind your back. People still talked when a couple's baby was 'born early'! I was sharing an apartment with a couple of other girls from school—I couldn't stay there pregnant. Where would I go? How could I take care of a baby alone? I'd have to go on welfare. It was the end of the world.

"One of the calls I made just over in New Jersey—Fort Lee, Hackensack, someplace over there. I know it was just over the George Washington Bridge. I got a call back from that one, in the middle of the night. It was a man with a deep-sounding voice. He told me to drive across the G-W, make a right, pass two lights, turn into an alley and wait. He would meet me. I followed the instructions. Would you believe it? I actually did such a crazy thing. Me. I can't watch scary movies in my own living room! I found the place, or what I thought was the place, and sat in the alley and waited. I jumped at every noise. It was awful. There was trash all around, and I'm sure there were rats—I could hear them skittering around the garbage cans. Somebody threw an empty bottle out of a window, and it smashed right in front of me.

"I sat there for ages. Then, somebody rapped on the car window. It was the guy I'd spoken to; I recognized his voice. He was a giant of a man—six feet four, two hundred fifty pounds, at least. The alley was so dark that I couldn't make out his features, except that when he spoke I saw he had very white teeth—I remember because they were really all I could see. He was neatly dressed and polite enough, spoke like he was educated. But I was spooked by the whole thing. I hadn't expected it to be so—it made me feel like a criminal. I stammered something about having changed my mind and got out of there as fast as I could."

Years later, in the safety of my office, Victoria could smile about it. But she hadn't been smiling back then, when it happened.

"I tried the Moody network, but I didn't get a call back. I didn't know what to think. It had worked for other people I knew, but not for me. I just could never make that connection.

"Finally, I got a call back—collect—from someone in Puerto Rico. I had called so many places I couldn't remember what was what anymore, but Puerto Rico was closer than Sweden, at least. Or Tokyo. The man on the phone told me to come down and stay in a particular hotel. He gave me a telephone number, said it was a dentist's office. When I got there, I was supposed to call, and they would see me right away. I had to bring three hundred dollars—in cash. I withdrew all my savings from the bank and caught the first flight out of JFK. It was still called Idlewild then.

"When I got there, I called the number. I gave my name, and the voice said, 'Not today, not today. Call tomorrow.' I called the next day, and the next, and always the same thing—'Not today. Call tomorrow.'

"I was desperate. I had to have the abortion—had to. I was

tormenting myself with what I had done, who I had done it with. How could I have been so dumb? Have his child? I couldn't, just couldn't. There was no way to have the baby. By this time, I had already spent I don't know how much of my savings and used up most of my vacation time. It was this or nothing, so it had to be this. There was no going back.

"On the fifth day, I think it was, they finally gave me an address and said to come in. I took a cab; I couldn't have found it otherwise. It was a two-story wooden building, unusual for Puerto Rico. The office was on the second floor. There was a guy at the bottom of the stairs, a big, burly guy, like a bouncer. He looked like he could really hurt you. I said who I was, and he took me upstairs. There was a woman in the reception room—a nurse, maybe? She looked at me like I was dirt and told me the price was nine hundred dollars.

"I didn't have it. I had spent everything getting there, staying at the hotel, waiting.

"I just broke down completely. I sobbed and pleaded. I was hysterical to the point of insanity. I don't know what I said, but I must have said something right. Maybe they were afraid to let me go out again, the condition I was in. Afraid I'd blow the whistle on them. They took me for the three hundred.

"There was no anesthesia, nothing at all for pain. The abortionist just motioned me to get up on the table, and he went to work. Boy, did he ever. I guess it didn't take very long, but it seemed like an eternity. I could feel everything. The pain was terrible. They're scraping around in your insides with something sharp, and you don't know—maybe they're doing permanent damage, maybe you'll die. You're so helpless. I was terrified.

"But I got through it somehow. I survived it. The big, burly bouncer guy took me downstairs and put me in a cab. It was too late to make my plane, so I spend the night in the hotel and I got back to Idlewild the next day. What a relief!

"Later, much later, I found out that what happened to me was not that unusual. Lots of girls and women thought they were going to legitimate clinics in Puerto Rico—I mean, it was all illegal, but we heard it was open, permissive—and then they were put off and told to come up with more money. These guys were abortionists-extortionists. And a lot of girls who had the contacts at home and could do it got money from their parents or husbands or boyfriends and paid it. Why they took me, I'll never know."

There were real doctors and clinics in Puerto Rico, but it was not a network I wanted to be part of.

In the spring of 1970, I took a day off to drive up to the state capital in Albany for what we called "the Albany watch"— waiting around in the halls of the senate office building for the results of the vote on abortion reform. Along the Thruway, trees were haloed in yellow-green, the grass was greening up—it was country even a cosmopolitan kid could appreciate. Working two jobs and trying to get a practice started, I really didn't have time to take off and go lobbying, but I couldn't let my friends or myself down. So there I was.

I was part of a relatively small group of regulars from the predictable organizations—Planned Parenthood, NARAL, the women's groups. Few as we were, we were the only ones lobbying this issue either way. The chance that any state, much less the Supreme Court, would tamper with the existing laws against abortion seemed so remote that protesting for abortion reform was deemed unnecessary. Especially in conservative New York.

I knew the drill. We'd go up and down the halls, visiting the offices of assembly members and signing their guest books, adding a note about our purpose. Sometimes a representative would happen out of his office (it was always *his*; there were no *hers* in those days). We'd corner him on the spot and deliver our pitch. I was a practiced lobbyist, with my pitch down pat.

Then we'd wait for the vote, to see which reps we'd have to buttonhole the next year, or who was "softening up" or which ones we might be able to work on for "next time." At that point, we hadn't yet thought that there might not be a next time.

That day, we thought we knew how everyone would vote. But when the vote was tallied, the impossible had happened. The New York State Assembly had approved legislation to decriminalize abortion, to make it the province of the medical code, a matter between doctor and patient. We were astounded.

One of the other lobbyists had a look of total bewilderment on her face. "Is that it?" she asked. "We've won? Just like that? What happened?"

We began to piece it together. We had needed only a single precious vote to go our way, and one conservative upstate lawmaker had switched his vote at the last minute, teaming up with downstate and city liberals to tip the balance. Going over the roll call, we could see the mechanics, but not the reasons. Not yet. On the strength of our victory, we decided to go out and celebrate.

Later, we quietly tried to analyze the events of that day.

"You know why he did it, don't you?" a colleague asked. "It wasn't altruism. Far from it. He's gambling that abortion will keep the welfare rolls down, that there won't be so many poor babies. It was part people who want to put abortion into the medical code where it belongs and part racism. Well, maybe racism's strong. Call it 'political pragmatism.' "

Actually, it was political suicide, and the assemblyman was well aware of it. The next day, *The New York Times* recounted his anguished statement from the assembly floor as he changed his vote, predicting that it would mean the end of his career— which it did.

But I could understand my colleague's skepticism. I hated to think that abortion reform had come out of such a philosophy, but I knew plenty of people saw abortion as a way to control the poor. Well, Doug Spencer had a Bible quotation for that: "Ye have the poor always with you." Ending poverty would never be so simple as getting rid of poor babies. But if indeed that had been the reason behind the vote, it wouldn't have been new in history.

For openers, there's Margaret Sanger, America's birth-control pioneer. Popular thinking has her down as a great champion of women's rights, and indeed, her work brought reproductive freedom to untold numbers of women. But freedom for women was not the main goal of her crusade. Far from it.

Sanger was a Malthusian, a believer in the theory that population increases faster than its food supply, and that, unless it is checked, it will result in poverty and the ultimate collapse of the culture. In the late eighteenth century, Thomas Robert Malthus wrote that the checks on population growth were famine, war and natural disasters, but later he added "moral restraint," the notion that people could control population growth voluntarily. Eugenics, the study of human improvement through genetic control, became a science—scientific racism.

As a follower of Malthus, Sanger joined the company of a number of noted American intellectuals of her day, including H. L. Mencken and later Nobel Prize winner William Shockley in espousing eugenics and racist thinking: If the poor couldn't restrain themselves, it was the duty of those who knew better to help them do so, through birth control.

In 1926, Sanger delivered the graduation speech at Vassar College. Her topic was the function of sterilization. She said that while "we have taken steps to control the property of our own population through drastic immigration laws . . . we must make an attempt to cut down the rapid multiplication of the unfit at home."

Like other Malthusians, Sanger saw birth control primarily as a means of controlling the poor—not of liberating women, necessarily. The ultimate elitist, she would probably be leading the fight for abortion today for the same reasons. Politics makes strange bedfellows.

I had to concede that my colleague had a point. Many of the voters that day probably weren't thinking about upholding the rights of women; maybe the only one voting his conscience in that regard was the guy who changed his vote. The irony was that that assemblyman was genuinely trying to do the right thing, and his constituents, whom he had served well for years, turned against him for it—that one vote, that one issue.

Anyone who thought that a vote for legal abortion was a vote against welfare was wrong. It was a vote to end a hemorrhage— a flood of dead and dying women—whether it was meant to be or not.

Driving back to New York after the Albany session, I got to musing on the role of abortion in my life. One thing just seemed to lead to another—my father's attitudes, my hospital experiences, Douglas Spencer.

And then, I recalled my own mother's story. I don't know where it had been in my memory all that time.

It was early in my medical-school years when I got an urgent message from my sister. My mother was in the hospital with complications from the diabetes she had suffered with for some time. She was listed as critical.

"They're saying she probably won't make it," my sister said. "You'd better come."

When I got to the hospital a few hours later, my sister had gathered the whole family. Herman was there, of course, and all three of my sisters and their husbands. They were involved in a family powwow.

It seemed that my youngest sister was pregnant again, this time with a wanted child. She hadn't planned on telling anyone yet, but my other sisters knew, and they were urging her to share the news. They said, "Momma should know. You know how she is about grandchildren." We all knew. Her world revolved around her status as a loving grandmother. If she seemed crotchety or down, just reminding her of her grandchildren was enough to pick up her spirits. My sister looked at me, and I nodded. It was unanimous. She shrugged and agreed.

We all gathered at the bedside and my sister made her announcement in a rather matter-of-fact way.

Momma was cheered by the news considerably. She sat up, cleared her throat and, uncharacteristically for her, started to speak about her own childbearing years, her own pregnancies. We all listened attentively.

My mother had her first two children, both girls, early in her marriage. There was the usual traditional importance attached to having a boy, a male offspring, but finances being what they were, she and my father agreed, at least tacitly, to stop at two. Then after ten years, in her late thirties, she became pregnant again.

"We decided to go ahead with it," Momma said. "Of course, I felt too old. And the kidding. Everyone teased that we were trying for a boy—and at our age." She looked at my youngest sister. "But you were another girl." It brought a blush to both of them.

Then, two years later, she found herself to be pregnant yet again. Now in her forties, she wanted none of it. "Herman, he said he was sorry, that enough was enough, but he thought I should go through with it. He didn't have to be pregnant, dragging around for nine months with a backache and swollen ankles, as big as a house. I made him find a good name for me—he knew what and where." Again, a "name." She went on with her story. "I pestered him until he gave in. Finally he gave me the money—a hundred dollars. I think it was a hundred-dollar bill—an awful lot of money. He didn't like any of it, but he agreed with me—he wasn't the pregnant one."

Momma had never been one for confidences. My sisters and I exchanged looks; we didn't know what to think. Even my oldest sister, who had been a teenager at the time, had had no inkling of this. But our mother wasn't given to fantasy. We had to accept it as truth.

The appointment was made. She was to take a train from Penn Station to Newark, over in New Jersey, have the abortion and return home late that night. Where, exactly, and by whom had gotten lost in her memory. Quite out of character, my father had let her make the journey alone, as a showing of mild protest.

She was packing for the trip when a telegram arrived. My father's mother, the mother-in-law she had never met, was arriving for a surprise visit. And what a surprise it was!

The grandmother we had never seen but had heard so much about had sent her children to America from czarist Russia early in the century, but she herself had remained behind. Immigration quotas and then age had proved barriers that no one expected her to surmount. A determined woman, she had made her way to Canada, and now she was on her way to her son's home, bent on meeting the daughter-in-law and grand-children she had never known.

"I was stunned," said my mother. "She was arriving at Grand Central the same day and the same hour that I was supposed to be across town taking the tubes to Newark."

Momma smiled. "I thought, the house is a mess, I have to wash the curtains, what will I serve for dinner?" Her smile became a chuckle, as she turned up her palms as if to say, "What was I supposed to do? Tell her I couldn't see her because I was getting rid of her grandchild? And me with no sons." She jerked a thumb toward my father. "I canceled the appointment. He got his boy."

Herman remained silent. He seemed to be embarrassed, but recalling the time fondly, in a way. I saw it in his eyes. He was as surprised as anyone that Momma was speaking up like this. I knew he was glad to have a son, but like my mother, he wasn't one to share his private feelings. What had he thought when she wanted an abortion? Whatever it was, principle had won out. He had given her her choice. He had to practice what he preached.

I thought about my mother's decision. She had died—not that night, but a short time after—from complications of her diabetes. Could it have been the demands of a later-than-usual pregnancy that brought it on and led to her early death? The onset of diabetes is well documented as being stressed by pregnancy. Might her reluctance to subject her body to that pregnancy have arisen from some intuition that she had had enough? Would my mother have been wrong to have gone through with it? She was already the mother of three, with a great responsibility to remain alive and well for them. I was glad she had chosen to continue the pregnancy—not that I would have known if she hadn't. But mostly I felt satisfied that she had had an option.

On my way home to New York that night, I realized that my life was about to change profoundly. I would no longer have to hide my expertise, or deny it, or practice it in an atmosphere of fear and guilt. I thought about twists of fate and chance, and wondered what was coming next. It wasn't long before I found out.

3 Abortion on Demand—the Women's Center

The honey-smooth voice on the telephone told me I was dealing with a southerner—a gentleman, unless I missed my guess—but it didn't tell me much else.

"Dr. Sloan? This is Roy Parker*, here from Tampa and Miami." He pronounced it "MY-yam-i." "You don't know me, but we have a number of mutual friends. I understand that you've been—how shall I put this?—interested in the abortion question. That you can handle what I have in mind. Your name has come up in quite a few conversations I've had with my people, and they tell me you know your way around an OR. I have a proposition that I believe might be of some interest. I'd like for us to get together, if that would be possible." With that kind of flattery from that kind of voice, who could resist?

It couldn't have been much more than another sunset after the flash had come from the Albany assembly that New York had voted in abortion reform. I was just back from Albany, and I was riding high, feeling victorious. "Sure," I told him. "About what, exactly?"

"Well, since abortion is about to become legal in the state of New York—is, to all intents and purposes, legal right now— I'm looking to set up a center to do safe, legal abortions. As I see it, the people who set up clinics now will be in an admirable position, from a business point of view. I mean to have mine be

*Asterisk indicates pseudonym.

the first. I need the right people with me. I'd like to talk to you about it in detail. Are you interested?"

My practice hadn't really taken off yet. I was working at the hospital and planning to complete my training as a sex therapist, but I wasn't exactly burning up with a patient load. I figured I could juggle one more thing. Especially abortion. I was still in debt.

"If you can make it, we're having a press conference tomorrow at noon," he told me. He gave me an address in midtown, across from the Empire State Building. "I look forward to seeing you there," he finished. It was settled.

The next day was fine May weather, a weekday. I walked down Fifth Avenue to the address he'd given me. People were out on the avenue and the library steps, enjoying the sunshine. I found the address and the room easily and went in. A decent-sized crowd, mostly reporters, had gathered and were milling around, chatting and joking. Some of them I recognized from having seen them in Chicago and Albany. One or two gave me a casual, "Hello, how are you?" or a nod. I felt a part of the crowd.

A young woman tapped me on the arm. "Dr. Sloan? Dr. Parker said to ask you to go right up and introduce yourself to him when you got here. That's him, right over there."

She pointed toward a pleasant-looking man dressed in a gray suit, a shirt so white it fairly gleamed, collar and cuffs starched stiff and a slim black tie. He was about medium height, but looked taller, with a slight, wiry build, a receding hairline and a round face accented by rimless glasses. I guessed him to be about forty.

When he saw me approaching, he broke away from the group he was with and came forward, reaching out to grasp my arm and shake my hand. "Dr. Sloan, how do you do?" he said. "I'm Roy Parker. Thank you for coming. I'm so happy you could be here. We're getting under way in a few minutes. I hope you'll have the time to stay afterward so we can talk? Good, good." I still wasn't sure how he or anyone else had recognized me. I took a place in the front row.

The press conference went well, I thought. Parker began by saying how proud he was that New York had done what it had, that there was now a place where women with unwanted pregnancies could have them terminated safely, by professionals in a medical setting, ending the scourge of back-alley abortions. He was vague about his plans, but he did imply that he had come to New York City to set up a unit in which women could exercise their legal rights to "specialized health care." Everybody in the room understood that he was talking about abortion. It was funny how the word still had an uneasy ring to it.

Most of the rest of his comments had to do with how happy he was to be coming to New York. He made it sound like his second home. The reporters were taking it all down, and I figured city government—from the mayor right down to the cop on the beat—was being sent a message. I had to admire his style. He was a diplomat of the first order, as smooth as silk, and quite a salesman. He could have sold me a used car.

The crowd dispersed, leaving Roy and me and a few others, mostly women, his inner circle, those he referred to as "my people." One of the women, I later learned, was his steady companion, another served as an administrative assistant, some were his counselors. He took me and one woman by the arm and led us, with the others following along, into a little room just down the hall from where the press conference had been held.

We all settled ourselves around the table, and Roy began to explain his plans in detail. He had, he said, made arrangements to take over the lease on a professional suite and was seeing to it that the offices were outfitted with the very latest in medical equipment. The speed with which he worked was impressive, to say the least. Astonishing was more like it. From the press conference, I'd understood that he was talking about having a clinic up and running sometime soon—I was thinking maybe by the end of the summer—and I was wondering how he could have put everything together so fast. It was almost as if he had had inside information.

It was all the more amazing when I learned that he was ready to put things in motion within a few days! He convinced me that although the law said July first, he had the moxie to get a running start.

Well, I was ready to start too, without his persuading. It was all go for me. I sat and listened to his quiet, rather musical southern drawl and tried to take his measure. He was a marvel of efficiency, organization and deftness at handling people. The reporters had practically been eating out of his hand, and his "people," those gathered around the table that day, were obviously loyal and devoted to him. Like Parker himself, they were mostly out-of-towners, and like him they had picked up and come to relocate in New York on what couldn't have been more than a couple of days' notice. He was not someone I felt drawn to—in the time we worked together, we never became warm friends—but I had to admire his skills. He was truly effective. I liked him in a distant sort of way.

Strangely, I thought, he didn't ask me much about myself. I wondered if he was preinformed that I was "qualified" and that all my medical credentials were in order—at the time, I had no idea how important that was to him—or whether all that mattered to him was that I was obviously happy with the change in the abortion statutes and ready to go to work for real. He did ask me if I had any more information about what had taken place in Albany a few days before. In view of how much of a jump he had on everybody, I figured he knew as much as I did, and probably more.

No, I told him, I was as surprised as anyone by the change in the law, the swing vote from the upstate assemblyman.

"The power of the good Lord at work is a surprising thing," he said. "They may not understand it themselves, as yet." I was struck then by Roy's imputing abortion reform to the power of the Lord, but when I got to know him better, I found that he saw the Lord's hand in everything. The thought crossed my mind that he would have made a magnetic evangelist preacher. It was well before the days of TV evangelists, but Roy was out of that mold. He could have been a real rainmaker.

We shook hands and agreed to meet in a few days.

On the weekend, I met him in his apartment—which was, by coincidence, in the same block as mine—and he took me around the corner to the center. Its full name would be the New York Center for Reproductive and Sexual Health. I suppose it was about that time that he began to talk about my involvement as a "partnership"—mostly in terms of needing someone from New York, "so we won't look so much like carpetbaggers," he said affably. He was right about my knowing the local scene. It sounded all right to me.

I had been impressed by hearing Roy talk, but I was even more impressed when I saw what he and his people had put together. He had taken a whole floor in a medical office building. In a matter of a few days, he had outfitted the ORs with updated equipment, and that equipment was excellent—autoclaves for sterilizing instruments, good suction units, adequate laundry service. We would be working as a doctors' office, not a clinic, but there was no problem with that; in-office procedures were OK. We would not offer general anesthesia, only local injection, with the doctors doubling as anesthesiologists.

I met a few of the people who would be my colleagues—the nurses Roy had either brought with him or who had been hired through his New York contacts and the counselors. I later learned that Roy recruited many of his counselors from women who had turned to him for abortions themselves. The law at that time was sketchy. It didn't mandate counseling. All it said was that abortion, like any other medical procedure, fell under the medical code of New York State, rather than under the legal or judicial code. It was a matter to be decided between a doctor and his or her patient—and that was that. Regulations and guidelines came later. It would be several months before the state worked out regs about counseling and safety equipment and such. Roy was way ahead of them. We were truly a prototype.

Some of the other doctors who would be working at the center were there that day too. I knew one or two by sight and some by reputation—the Doug Spencers of New York, in the sense that they did good, safe abortions, although not always with his altruism. There would eventually be eight or ten of us.

Roy wanted only experienced doctors with good track records for safety and skill—the best. And he had scored a coup. One of our number was to be the outspoken proponent of legalized abortion and cofounder of NARAL, Dr. Bernard Nathanson.

The new law was scheduled to go into effect on July first. We actually started up two weeks earlier, on June 15; Roy kept assuring us that the law was loose enough that no one would stand in our way, and no one did. He had done his homework well.

We were mobbed.

Overnight, we had become the abortion capital of the world. Literally. Roy had asked me and a few of the others to get the unit started; we did, and we became its mainstays. Roy pretty much limited himself to administration and kept regular hours. He was gone at 5:00 P.M. after an eight-hour day. The rest of us worked around the clock. We just all seemed to know what to do and when.

When patients came in, they met with a counselor in a group for an overview, and then each patient was assigned to one of the nurse-practitioners—all trained nurses—who would stay with her through the whole procedure. That nurse would be the woman's personal counselor, meet with her one-on-one and give her a chance to express any fears or concerns she might have—how long would it take, would it hurt, what about afterward?—and then get her ready for the procedure. These nurses were good, very good. I found out later on that every one of them had had an abortion with Roy Parker. Putting aside an occasional and minor personality clash, the medical staff quickly came to respect them as qualified and able counselors and technicians. They had earned that respect. They had mine.

Once in a while the nurse would want to say a few words to the doctor alone about something—an anxious patient or a tense situation because of a low pain threshold or maybe even a special friend of someone in the office.

* * *

"The patient is twenty-three, married two years, two kids, fifteen months and four months. Seems collected."

"Did you talk to her about birth control?"

"She was pregnant before she got back to the clinic to get something. Didn't know it could happen when she wasn't getting her period. Husband didn't know either. I gave her the address of Planned Parenthood."

What a summer that was! It was hazy, hot and humid as only New York can be, heat radiating up from the sidewalks and being trapped at ground level by all the steel and concrete. The day started a little after dawn, and we worked into the wee hours of the night. Sure, there were supposed to be appointments, but friends brought friends and some just showed up, having heard of us by word of mouth. We squeezed them in. Many came from far away, often spending their last few dollars getting the plane or bus fare or their vans filled with gas and camping out until we saw them. Imagine camping out in a van in midtown Manhattan in the silk-stocking district! But they did it, until we could do their abortions and send them home.

I would leave my apartment and walk to work, just a few blocks away, wondering what I was going to see, what the street in front of the building would look like. It was early morning, and the city hadn't really come awake yet. People had spread sleeping bags or blankets in doorways or in their vans and cars and were sacked out everywhere. It felt like walking through some gigantic sleep-in, a city Woodstock. I don't know if any neighbors realized what they were in the middle of. After all, the area was known for medical doctors of all kinds, and patients often spilled into the street.

Every night by 10:00 or 11:00 P.M. or later, as I was leaving, the crowds were building up. Many were the friends and consorts of the patients, waiting for their people to be discharged. They sat on the curbs, playing guitars and eating sandwiches and pizza, drinking beer and soda. They were always very quiet—I don't remember a rowdy moment. If there were drugs, we didn't know about it—maybe a little pot, but that's all. It was a rare case when a hard-drug user would show up so much in trouble that we would have to cancel or postpone her procedure. Our campers rarely consumed anything stronger than pot or beer.

The married women, young executives, the MBAs and the career women mostly came during the day. The night crowd was of a special order. We came to know them well.

The staff was a heterogeneous crew, a mix of Park Avenue and the boroughs, old-timers and latecomers, New Yorkers and Roy's out-of-town contingent. Somehow it worked. We respected one another's skills and professionalism and quickly pulled together as a unit.

"The patient is twenty-seven, apparently in good health. Nothing unusual, except that this is her second abortion. The first one was a butcher job, and she had a bad infection. She's a little worried about whether she'll be able to have children later, if she wants them."

"I'll talk to her."

"Thanks, Doctor S."

The nurse had no idea what memories she had just jogged.

I guess there is an esprit de corps in every profession—people working together get close and fall in love and things like that. But when you think of it, medicine, hospital life, is special in that regard. In the center, we worked together day and night. We were plunged into living with each other. As interns and nurses we had learned to live our patients' lives and histories. Anybody who couldn't take that kind of familiarity with the body and bodily functions was very unhappy in medical life and didn't hang around long—especially in GYN. Most of us at the center were medical professionals, RNs and MDs, all coming from that kind of background, so modesty quickly went by the boards. No one had time to be dignified or polite—or even to close the door to the john. We just became family very, very fast. And with abortion being the only thing we did, sexual organs and sex, sex, sex became all we ever talked about. Makes you very tight. Very.

"Marjory is forty-six, unmarried, a secretary in a big law firm. Just got back from a vacation to Greece. Thought she was going into menopause, but got suspicious when she started throwing up in the mornings."

"Hello, Marjory. I'm Doctor Sloan. Any questions?"

There was a friend of Roy's from Tennessee, a general practitioner from cotton country who entertained us between cases with Civil War stories. He would fly up on Friday, arriving close to midnight, and go to work immediately. Saturday he'd grab some sleep and show up for work in the afternoon, work late into the night, repeat the whole thing on Sunday, and then fly back to his practice in Nashville, or wherever. We kidded him about leading a double life, and he kidded right back, enjoying the idea for its romance and intrigue, but cheerfully denying that he had any time on the weekends to do anything but work—he was right.

Even with the air fare, the buck was worth it to him. We worked cheap, but there was volume, and since we were paid by the case, an old regular like him was able to churn out a bunch of them over a weekend—well over a hundred—and it certainly paid him to come up. "It pays the rent," he used to say.

Then there was the doctor I'll call Ben*. He was a big, heavy, disheveled-looking guy—downright sloppy, really—with a thick Eastern European accent. You'd never take him for an associate of the fastidious Roy Parker, but there he was, right in the middle of things. He had a booming voice and a Falstaffian lust for life; he did everything in a big way. Poker, the track, gambling at Vegas and Reno, the Caribbean, France. I don't think he ever carried a wallet—he just stuffed his pockets with cash.

The rumor was that Ben was "connected," that he had ties to the Mob or some such shady outfit and that he had done "therapeutics" on well-connected women. In return, supposedly, they gave him tips on the fight fixes and the races, and he got his payoffs. He was good at what he did, no question, which, I guess, was why Roy took him on. One thing counted with Roy, and that was skill at doing abortions. Business was business.

Ben was a decent guy. We became friendly, and a couple of years after I left the center, he called and asked me to take on a new obstetric patient. He was no longer doing deliveries, although he had done many in his day. The patient owed him for past consultations, so he told her that his fee would be included in whatever I charged and told me I should bill her and send him a check for his portion—all fair and square. I readily agreed.

I was happy with the arrangement. Like him, Ben's patients were nice people. It was a good fee, and if the patient was satisfied, she would send me her friends. When I collected the money, I sent Ben a check for his share, over a thousand dollars.

The check was never cashed. My bookkeeper told me about it three or four months later, and I called and asked his secretary to please either cash it or let me know if they wanted me to send him another. I never heard from him.

A couple more months passed. Then, tragically, Ben showed up on the eleven o'clock news. He was on his way home from a late night on the town, and as he entered his apartment building, apparently two gunmen rushed in and shot him several times, gangland style. The papers the next day described the event as a "mob-style hit on a doctor," so I guess the rumors were true. But it wasn't abortion that got him into trouble. Indeed, it kept him out of it for a while. He was an unforgettable character— one of so many I met in the abortion business that I sometimes felt I could fill a whole Reader's Digest by myself.

* * *

"This lady is twenty-eight, five living children, two miscarriages, a stillbirth. Youngest child is a year old, oldest is eight. She says she uses birth control, but it just doesn't work." The nurse shrugs as if to say, "Who knows?"

I think, Eight pregnancies in eight years—she's been pregnant almost a whole decade. This one never menstruates. "This her first abortion?"

"She says yes. Her husband just left her—two weeks ago—and it doesn't look as if he's coming back. She doesn't see how she can manage what she's got, let alone another baby."

By bus, by plane, train or van, you name it, they got there. All ages, all stations of life, all races, colors, denominations, nationalities. Women came from Ohio, Pennsylvania, Massachusetts, California, Florida, Missouri—I wouldn't be surprised if we had all fifty states represented. I don't remember anyone from Hawaii and Alaska, but I did have patients from Manila—more than once. And Europe.

"The patient is thirty-one, two children, husband out of work for almost a year now. He's with her. They wish they didn't have to do this, but—"

"They've agreed it's the best thing."

"Right."

"She's OK with it?"

"She's more OK than he is, I think. He feels responsible."

"That's better than not feeling responsible."

"You got that right."

The bubble lasted on and on. Summer became fall, and then winter. The cold weather made the street camp-outs a little more difficult, and sometimes we had to provide—under duress, because we were cramped anyway—some more protected areas for the friends. Our hallways and anterooms became mob scenes with people waiting.

It was a cash business. The price was as right as the services provided. That, along with our being legal and safe, was a big part of the reason so many women came to us. No one was turned away. We were a bargain.

But we had volume. The receptionists at the desk collected the fees, and when the cash boxes overflowed, as they did nearly every day, they filled the drawers. We often got paid in small money—singles, even coins—and counting it was time-consuming; sometimes it didn't get done right away. When the banks weren't open, we just closed off a room and put the none-too-neat piles of money in it. By the end of a weekend, you'd open a door and walk into a sea of money. At the time, we thought nothing of it. We had all kinds of people in our halls, just hanging out, and we were ripe for robbery, but somehow it never happened. Maybe we were lucky. Maybe we were just always respected by a grateful clientele.

"My patient is twenty-eight, one child. She's got intractable morning sickness, and she's decided to pack it in."

"You told her her doctor could help her?"

"Sure, but apparently she had the same thing all the way through her first pregnancy, and nothing worked. She's just unable to function. Last week while she was stretched out on the bathroom floor the four-year-old got hold of a book of matches. He burned himself before he burned the house down, nothing too serious, but her husband is working two jobs, and he's furious that she can't even watch the kid. She's not kidding—we had to give her a basin to get her through counseling. She says she just can't stand the thought of spending the next four months with her head in the toilet bowl."

"Can't argue much with that."

"Not really."

*   *   *

Over the next thousand days, our unit performed over one hundred thousand abortive procedures. The demand was positively staggering.

When you think about it, all doctoring is work on demand, either stated or implied: Cure the itch, stop my pain, stitch this cut, set this ankle, take out this tumor. There are a few jobs in medicine that are considered purely elective, such as cosmetic surgery, but even that can be emotionally a cure: People are happier and healthier when they feel good about the way they look.

In gynecology, there are only three procedures that we consider purely elective: sterilization and its opposite, tubal reconstruction, *in vitro* fertilization and the like—although you could make the argument that infertility is a pathology—and abortion.

Abortions are elective. There are very few conditions—now maybe none—that require the termination of a pregnancy. When I was in training, there was one: a rare condition of the inner ear, exacerbated by pregnancy, that causes extreme and permanent deafness. I never heard of a case or saw one, but it was in the medical books as an indication for termination. Maybe it still is.

But with everything else, if a woman with a serious illness—heart disease, say, or diabetes—gets pregnant, the abortion procedure may be as dangerous for her as going through with the pregnancy, although statistically, full-term pregnancy and delivery carry a higher risk for all women than early abortion.

Take the case of a cardiac patient, for example. There are actually studies to prove that women who have heart disease and become pregnant live longer than those who don't. Why? Because their cardiac condition is discovered in routine prenatal care, and heart disease is often not found until it is too late to give the patient real help, particularly among the poor, who aren't getting regular medical care otherwise. With diseases like lupus, multiple sclerosis, even breast cancer, the chance that pregnancy will make the disease worse is no greater than the chance that the disease will either stay the same or improve. And medical technology has advanced to a point where even women with diabetes and kidney disease can be seen through a pregnancy safely by a doctor who knows what he or she is doing. We've come a long way since my mother's time.

For someone that sick to get pregnant may not be wise, but that's another question. Pregnancy may shorten her life; her child may be an orphan at a too-early age. But a belief in reproductive freedom dictates that a woman has the right to bear a child if she wants to. It works both ways.

In the days before *Roe v. Wade,* before abortion was considered a purely medical procedure rather than a judicial one, one of the ways to go was to have two doctors certify that a woman was "suicidal." This stemmed from the old-time statute that required professional certifications from two licensed psychiatrists in order to arrange a legal commitment to a mental institution. That "two P-C" rule was loosely applied to abortion, although it was never spelled out in law. That was one way the rich and famous did it. They simply made two psychiatrists an offer that couldn't be refused, and they were on their way. In the vast majority of cases, no one believed that the woman would actually do herself in, or that the doctor thought she would, but the certification of her "suicidal" state became the means to a safe, clean hospital procedure. It was just part of the game. The main reason this seemingly simple ploy wasn't used too often—apart from expense—was that patients were always afraid of the blight of "suicidal" on their medical records. Their fears were justified. False medical records, especially of this nature, could come back to haunt them later in life.

The idea of abortion to save the mother's life is something that people cling to because it sounds noble and pure—but medically speaking, it probably doesn't exist. It's a real stretch of our thinking.

Abortions, then, can be seen as always purely elective—not necessary from a medical standpoint.

Why, then, perform them?

It was clear, from the steady stream of clients who came to the unit, that there was an enormous demand for abortion services. Women in vast numbers were pregnant when they did not want to be. We weren't soliciting their patronage—they were seeking us out. It was as though no matter how many we did, there were more women waiting in the wings.

The alternative? I had seen the alternative in hospital emergency rooms in Philadelphia and Brooklyn, and I didn't want to see it ever again.

"This patient is pretty upset. She started out in a convent school and wanted to wait until marriage, all that stuff. She'd been going with this guy, and he talked her into letting him go a little farther than she wanted to, but she thought she could trust him, and the next thing she knew, she couldn't stop him. First and only time. So now she's pregnant, and he's unavailable."

"Didn't respect her in the morning, huh?"

"Didn't respect her at all, it looks like. She's a wreck."

Roy Parker made the point—as had Doug Spencer earlier—that a pregnant woman is in a bind. She's already in a tough spot because she's a woman in a society that is going to pay her less, value her less and generally make things harder for her than for a man. She's probably young and immature, and now she has to turn to the medical establishment, which is overwhelmingly male and full of itself.

She is often embarrassed and ashamed of what she has done— as if she got pregnant all by herself. She's "made a mistake," "got into trouble," "messed up," "got caught" or any of those other clichés that young women use to describe their plight.

What is the result? She will seek out whatever help she can get, and often that help is not safe. Even in New York, where Medicaid abortions still exist, we get people going to unlicensed or unsafe facilities, even—rarely, to be sure, and only in the ghetto—wire-hanger guys. This kind of thing happens especially in the industrial states that have urban centers and all of the inner-city problems that follow, but have no Medicaid abortions. New York, with public funds allocated for Medicaid abortions, is one of the few exceptions.

It seems that women will accept a low standard for abortion—shame and embarrassment get in the way of their good sense. Women all too often look on an unwanted pregnancy as "dumb," "stupid" or "How could I have let this happen?" I've had patients who would come to me for Pap smears and deliveries and yeast infections, and then run out of town for an abortion, so they won't have to face me, an "authority figure" who they'll have to deal with the rest of their lives—as if telling me about it later is better. It happens all the time. Likewise, I have aborted many women who came to me rather than their longtime and trusted gynecologists in order to avoid what they considered the risk of a negative judgment from someone they held in great esteem.

Thus women will tolerate and accept lesser standards of care for abortion, as if they didn't deserve better. They look for ways to blame themselves. And there's this—until it happens, most women think it won't happen to them. Nobody says, "I'd better safeguard abortion rights because I—or my sister, mother, daughter, best friend—will probably need an abortion." But statistically, they're wrong. It will touch them.

An atmosphere in which respectable practitioners are being scared out of abortion practice only opens the door for goof-balls and quacks and amateurs to get into the business and do real harm—even if their intentions are good. If abortion becomes disreputable, it is more likely to attract people who shouldn't be doing it, like the New York practitioner—licensed, but does it matter?—who tried to perform an illegal late abortion and only succeeded in tearing off the baby's arm.

By early 1992, with the Supreme Court chipping away at *Roe v. Wade* and the prospect of its being overturned looming ever greater, various sorts of people are conjuring up all kinds of methods that they bill as ways of assuring a source of safe and clean terminations. For example, so-called "women's self-help groups" have been springing up around the country. Their stated goal is to learn more about their own bodies through such means as palpating one another's uteruses and ovaries and using a speculum to examine the vagina and cervix. But they're also learning to perform a type of "menstrual extraction," which uses a Rube Goldberg–type apparatus involving tubing, a suction-creating pump and a collecting receptacle. Its proponents say the procedure is "not necessarily" for abortion, but if a woman "happens" to be newly pregnant, the device will, of course, extract the pregnancy too. In practical terms, it's "self-abortion" in a group setting.

Such groups are addressing the very real possibility that women may find themselves without access to abortion, and trying to give them a safer alternative to wire hangers. Their hearts are in the right place. But encouraging homegrown surgical procedures flies in the face of good sense.

The implications are enormous.

First—despite good intentions—such proposals open up the business of abortion to a new brand of back-alley weirdos. Anyone can go into business with stuff they can buy in a pharmacy, a hardware store or a supermarket, and probably will. Even the best of us, trained and experienced, can get a woman into trouble: Infection, hemorrhage, perforation and all of the sequelae of incomplete jobs are possibilities. It happens. To say that is a "minimal risk" is folly. A woman who dies or suffers permanent damage at the hands of her friends in a group is just as dead or damaged as one who goes to an old-time, back-alley butcher.

Suggestions like these also serve to divide the pro-choice movement. You don't have to be an old conservative fuddy-duddy to understand that restraints and regulations on abortion aren't necessarily all bad. Some of them are intelligent and welcome. There is a difference between those aimed at protecting the woman's health and safety and those restricting her right to a clean, medically safe procedure. "Do-it-yourself" quackery only plays into the hands of the antichoice groups, who will use the complications of such procedures as ammunition in the battle against safe abortions done by well-trained physicians in certified abortion clinics.

The polarization of the two sides in the abortion battle has everyone over a barrel. The pro-choice people find themselves fighting good, healthy, correct state regulations because many of those regulations are emanating from antiabortion pressure groups as a political ploy. On the other side, antichoicers find themselves unable to compromise on any point, even when common sense dictates it, as in the case of a severely malformed fetus that cannot survive or the impregnation of a twelve-year-old through incest or rape.

A case in point is the Supreme Court's decision in *Webster v. Reproductive Health Services* (1989), which took a bite out of *Roe v. Wade* by affirming the states' right to limit access to abortion and may have merit when it stands alone. It's what it is meant to do—establish legally that a conceptus is a person and begin the breakdown of reproductive freedom—that is dangerous.

An abortion performed by a doctor is still usually safer than childbirth. In 1970, when we started them in New York State, the death rate from legal abortion was 6.2 out of 100,000. In 1978, that was reduced to 0.6 out of 100,000. And it's still falling. Risk goes up as pregnancy progresses, but eighty-five percent of the procedures are done in the first seven weeks.

The medical literature is dotted with many reliable and well-controlled studies and reports that demonstrate the safety of the abortion procedure performed under proper conditions by qualified physicians. In its annual report, the U.S. Department of Health and Human Services' Centers for Disease Control (CDC) confirms this safety with its study of almost 1.4 million yearly procedures up to 1990. This report represented a cross section of all ages, all states, all weeks of gestation and all types of services. The extremely low rates of maternal death, sepsis, hemorrhage or any other complication serious enough to require hospital evaluation clearly showed that such negative outcomes were not a factor in deciding on the merits of abortion.

*   *   *

"This gal is sixteen, here with her mother. Get this—she didn't have intercourse. She and this guy were fooling around, petting, and he ejaculated between her legs . . ."

"Why not, huh?"

Roy was always there for us. We were good at what we did. Particularly after the first few months, complications were rare. But every case was special, every patient different. And every patient needed that special attention. Nobody ever just missed a period, killed the rabbit, snapped her fingers, hopped up on the table and spread her legs without some feelings about what she was doing. It was never easy. Pregnancy is a major event in a woman's life, with important ramifications and consequences.

The patient before me was a woman in her early thirties, the mother of young children, in the middle of a divorce and in a bind. She was early in her pregnancy, maybe six or seven weeks.

I had a good nurse with me, one of the best. I trusted her insights—you eventually got to know who were the more capable nurses. When the patient bounced around on the table, sighed and wouldn't hold still, I looked at the nurse. She shrugged her shoulders.

Then she moved around to the side of the table and took the patient's hands into her own. "Are you OK with this?" she asked. "We're not going ahead unless you're sure."

The patient's eyes immediately filled with tears and she turned her face away. The nurse looked to me. "She's not sure if we should go on," she said. "Let's give it a minute."

The patient was crying in earnest now, almost sobbing. We helped her sit up. "Look," I said. "We don't want to rush you into anything you don't want. Can I make a suggestion here? Why don't you go back and talk things over with the counselor some more?"

I glanced at the nurse, and she nodded. As she opened the door to summon the counselor, Roy was heading down the hallway. Coincidence. "Anything I can do?" he asked mildly.

I told him that the patient was returning to the counseling room.

He came in, rolled up his sleeves, took off his spectacles and polished them, taking his time and letting things settle down a little. Then he pulled up a stool to the head of the table, so he was eye level with the patient, and started to draw her out. The master was at work. I watched and listened.

Under his gentle probing, she unfolded her history—from the Midwest, involved in a messy divorce, pregnant by a lover and now feeling all sorts of guilt and anguish over having an abortion. He listened with his whole attention, occasionally repeating something she'd said as if to underscore it. That was all. It took about five minutes.

"This is no time for a baby," the patient said. "The divorce, my kids—they need me now, and a baby would take me away from them. Or I could lose them. The court mess, everything." Roy was nodding. It was decided.

The patient lay back, took a deep breath and said to proceed at once. Roy bent over her and called her by name. "You," he said with a stern conviction in his voice, "*you* are making the right decision." With that, he nodded to me to go ahead without delay. I did so, and that was that. Everything went well at my end of the table.

Later on, Roy and I met for a few minutes at the coffee urn. He liked an occasional smoke, and as he lit up, we talked about that type of case. He explained his role, what he had just done in my room, and what he thought mine should be.

"We are the authority," he said. "It is our job to give the patient help. Every woman deserves an abortion if she wants one, and every woman deserves an abortionist she trusts." A pearl if ever I heard one.

He went on to say that the thought he wanted to leave her with, the words he wanted her to hear, were that what she was doing was right and correct. Then he surprised me. "If she had gotten up off the table and gone home," he said, "I would have said the same thing—'*You* are making the right decision.' The patient has to hear it from us."

There were times later when he—and then I—did just that. One of us told an ambivalent patient she was right in not having the abortion, and she would get up and leave. No hard feelings, fee cheerfully refunded. Sometimes she came back in a few hours or a few days, and then we told her she was right to have it. When you did it right and with the right philosophy, it all sounded so healthy.

"Ah, the patient says she's eighteen and has a birth certificate to prove it, but she's very nervous, and she doesn't look more than fourteen or fifteen."

"Problem?"

"Not on that. We've got the BC. But—you ought to know—she says the father is her uncle. No way to check on any of it, but I tend to believe her on the uncle thing."

"Okay. Thanks. Let's go to work."

"Thank you, Doctor. If you're ready, I am."

Teenagers were a dicey deal. The law was flaky then as to the age of consent, but those of us who were MDs cautioned the administration that we should try to be circumspect.

The law was vague on age for many reasons. There is a special legal designation—emancipated minor—that has nothing to do with chronology. If a ten-year-old can prove emancipation, she (or he—the law applies equally) is entitled to medical care without parental consent. Pregnancy itself presents a technical problem. Once she becomes a mother, a female—whatever her age—is considered emancipated. But she is legally not a mother until her first birth and at the very moment of birth.

A pregnant teen living at home is a minor, and parental consent is required. But if she goes into labor and delivers a baby, she's emancipated. If a pregnant minor comes to you in need of care, it may not be so urgent that you can claim life or death, but who knows? There are no pat answers.

Runaway kids, throwaway kids—we never knew much about them except that they were streetwise and would probably get themselves wire-hanger jobs if we didn't help them. So we did—all the time. I had done it with Doug Spencer, but then he was responsible. This was different: Now and here, I had a career and a license to lose. We were supposed to be like bartenders and not serve anyone under eighteen. Only we weren't bartenders, we were doctors. So much of the time we went ahead. We never got into trouble over it, though we were walking a very fine line. But, as in Ashland, those kinds of doubts just never prevented any of us from doing what our hearts and guts told us was right.

"Her name is Laurie. She's nice—a student at a women's college. She was at a fraternity weekend, had a little too much to drink, and the next thing she knew, her date—I guess it was a fix-up, not someone she knew—had invited a bunch of his fraternity brothers in to have a go at her. They just took turns. She's pretty upset, blames herself for the whole thing. She's got no idea who the father is. But she's sure of when, because other than that weekend, she hadn't had a date all semester. Now she never wants to have another one."

"Hope she gets past it."

"Hard to predict."

The holidays came and went. We were closed on Thanksgiving, Christmas Day and New Year's, and that was all—no time for partying. At Christmastime, Roy went out and bought turkeys and hams and gave everybody in the office a choice. The next year, a repeat. I forget what I took—one of each, maybe. It was typical Roy.

*   *   *

"My patient is thirty-three, a loan officer in a bank. She'd been going with this guy for four years, and he took her out to dinner last week and told her he was getting engaged to somebody else. This week, she finds out she's pregnant."

"Bad timing, huh?"

"The worst."

By early 1972, we were overworked, overcrowded and overused. *Roe v. Wade* was not on the horizon yet—we figured we were going to work like this forever. We were outgrowing everything. The place really wasn't set up for the kind of use it was getting. We managed to keep a semblance of order and cleanliness, but we were bulging at the seams.

"Doctor? I need a minute before we start." Louise, the nurse-practitioner on the case, drew me into one of the examining rooms. "We're going to be doing two patients, one right after the other."

This was nothing unusual. "OK, so what?"

"They're mother and daughter. Thirty-five and sixteen. And they're both nine weeks pregnant."

I raised my eyebrows. "That must have been quite a weekend at their house."

"That's not the half of it. They got pregnant on the same day. By the same guy. Apparently he's in the habit of going from room to room. Not the girl's father. But that's about all that's missing. They actually think it's a gas—both getting caught the same time."

My first of many ménage-à-trois abortions. I shrugged my shoulders and went to work. By then, I figured that if I hadn't heard it all, I soon would. I did the mother first, then the daughter, both totally uneventful procedures. But they were the talk around the coffeepot later that day. Apparently this was not an isolated event in their lives; we might see them again, although perhaps not together.

It was a little unusual to see a mother and a daughter on the same day, but it happened. And more than once a patient came in one day and then came back a few weeks or months later with a daughter or a mother or even a grandmother or two.

The antichoice forces were growing more vocal. New York State was under fire for its position on abortion. A lot of people didn't like being the abortion capital of America, and let their politicians know it. I always think of how that upstate assemblyman who switched his vote to make abortion legal lost his assembly seat in the next election. Those of us who followed abortion politics knew about *Roe v. Wade*, then making its way through the courts, but we didn't figure it would make its impact until maybe 1974 or even 1975. In 1972, we were still thinking it was at least a few years away. The actual date of *Roe v. Wade* was January 22, 1973. It changed our lives forever.

"It's birth-control failure—the patient says the condom broke."

After a year or so, Roy Parker was around less and less. Rumors were flying about his status, his management and mostly about the fact that he was getting rich out of the business. In truth, we were all doing pretty well, but on the volume, not because we were ripping anybody off. When you work sixteen hours a day, seven days a week, it just tends to happen. Most of the stuff we were hearing was empty rumor. As far as I knew, Roy was never dishonest about money or greedy—it just wouldn't have meshed with his personality or his beliefs. But he did have a problem.

Roy Parker wasn't a medical doctor. I don't know that he had ever actually said he was, but his homegrown contingent always called him "Doctor," and he never corrected them. He understood medical procedures and techniques, was up on the latest equipment and acted like a professional, but he had neither a license nor a medical degree. There were hints that he had attended medical school and was a doctor in all but license, but even that was apparently not true. It seemed he had no formal medical training at all. That was one reason he had been so scrupulous about getting MDs on his team, so generous about sharing the titles, taking me on as an associate when he scarcely knew me. That had been true with all of us.

When the news broke, we were all a little surprised and bemused. Nobody was angry or steamed. The unit had become an experienced, well-oiled machine, no longer dependent on Roy Parker for its inspiration or operation. Roy was a simple kind of man, a true believer, kindly and gentle but never vicious, so he never evoked a bitter or vicious reaction.

The MDs on the staff put their heads together. The center had a terrific record, and on the whole, things were settling down. The "New York experiment" hadn't brought disaster to the state—far from it. Little by little, abortion was being accepted as a legitimate choice for women who, for whatever reason, did not want to bear a child, and we wanted to keep it that way. The antichoice movement was getting organized, and we didn't want to give them ammunition. As a unit, we had always bent over backward to keep everything on the up and up. We didn't want to make waves. And we didn't.

But Roy had to go. He knew it. I think he may have wanted to move on as well. We arranged for the board of directors to sit down and work out a buyout. It was only fair: All the upfront money and equipment had been his. There were rumors that he was demanding millions of dollars, but greed, as I said, was never Roy Parker's motivation. A settlement was reached and the buyout was made. The break was clean.

He took the check. He put it in his breast pocket without looking at it, wished us well and left. Later I heard he was somewhere in Europe. I had an address, but when I tried to contact him, I didn't get a response. That was the last I knew of Roy Parker.

* * *

"The patient didn't know she could get pregnant during her period."

We managed to entice a legal and licensed physician to act as director, and the unit kept rolling. Eventually we hired a chief operating officer from outside, a highly respected former chairman of the OB-GYN department of a large medical school. He came on—a nice guy, capable and good to work with, although maybe not all that comfortable in the world of abortion.

The move to bigger and more modern quarters came sometime in early 1972. We found a new place and moved to quarters designed and engineered for our work—a million-dollar renovation, with all the amenities. We could afford it. Quite a change. We settled in, and we got our act together—bookkeepers and cash drawers, men's and ladies' rooms, a record room and a place to stretch out. It all seemed too elegant!

Now we had the best of equipment and service quarters and workrooms—real junior ORs that met the myriad state regulations that were the result of both proper medical scrutiny and antichoice lobbying. If some of the new regs struck the oldtimers as being too restrictive, at least they erred on the side of the patient's welfare. So they were OK by us. Complaints and grumbles were minimal.

"The patient—are you ready for this?—is a practicing MD. Says she just didn't see how she could be pregnant, so when she missed her period, she thought it must be something else. She's almost twelve weeks—pretty late—"

"No bigger, I hope."

"I'm just reporting, Doctor, not explaining."

"How did she get through her medical boards?"

"Well, her specialty isn't GYN."

"I could tell."

*   *   *

As we moved through 1973, I was growing tired and jaded—
not with the procedures or the patients, but with the volume. It
was hundreds and hundreds a week for those three years. The
numbers added up fast. Although abortion was now legal in all
fifty states, many women still came to New York, and to the
center. We had the experience and the reputation, and our
safety record was well documented, both by the public network
of referral services and in the medical literature.

Now there were others well organized into smaller units, and
I allied myself with another doctor who had started up his own
network after the New York law changed. There was still much
to learn, as always, and I found myself a new teacher.

But Roy Parker and his legacy stayed with me. Through him
I came to understand that abortion's just being legal wasn't
enough—it also had to be practical, within financial reach and
safe, both medically and emotionally. Our unit proved that such
a thing was possible on a grand scale—and one-to-one.

Looking back, I remember it all as a remarkable few years:
meeting Roy, the group, the nurses, all types—tough, easy, soft,
clever, stupid, mean, kind, gay, straight. We had them all. But
we were a family. I meet once in a while with one or two of
them, at the hospital or at my office, and we talk over the old
times—and fondly. The memories were and are great, and I
have no regrets. I had a leg up with my Ashland experience, and
since then, I've carried on on my own, with more experience
than anyone can imagine. But it was an era.

4 Conflicts of Interest: My Dual Career

"Mister—ah, Mister Sloan. What's the safest way to deliver a baby?"

I was a third-year medical student on teaching rounds when the professor threw that one at me. By the third year, you're feeling pretty secure—you've made it. There are very few flunkees at that stage of your schooling. "Only getting hit by a truck in Times Square will do you in" was the way we put it. You're thinking the wheat has been separated from the chaff—and you're the wheat.

The question-answer aspect of grand rounds was part of the game. I was supposed to field the question and snap back the answer. The safest way? All eyes were on me. Everybody was waiting. My brain whirred and clicked and came up blank.

The prof was clearly enjoying my discomfiture. "In a taxicab, Mr. Sloan, in a taxicab," he said dryly, and received the anticipated laugh at my expense. In time I came to learn that he was only using one of his many teaching techniques to give a valuable lesson to his students.

It was his way of pointing out that most babies are born naturally; they don't just pop out, but nature does do most of the work, most of the time. The obstetrician is there mainly to guard against trouble—predict it when possible and act to prevent or minimize it.

Whenever medical students get together for rap sessions or just to pass the time of day in a rare moment of relaxation, the choice of residency training and specialty is a favorite topic of conversation. It's a juicy area for speculation—and not just among the students. I remember a time when one of the profs went around the room and asked about our plans for residency training, if any. One of my classmates said, "Pediatric allergy, sir."

The prof peered at him. "Son," he said, "you'll be the richest and busiest man in the world. Every parent will pay a fortune to get rid of allergies in his kid."

But that didn't create a stampede to pediatric allergy. On the contrary. Maybe the choice of a specialty is predestined. Students who prefer the esoteric world of science to personal contact often go toward radiology or pathology or medical research. Those who like the personal involvement but shy away from the blood and guts stuff lean toward medical specialties— cardiology, oncology, internal medicine or even the quieter specialty of dermatology. Then there are the rest of us, who seek out careers in areas of high trauma, such as general surgery, orthopedics and gynecology and obstetrics.

One of the duties of a chief resident is to play host to departmental guests, and I remember a time when my chief asked me to take a guest speaker, a medically trained anthropologist, to lunch in the cafeteria. His double interests made a fascinating combination. As we sat and sipped coffee, he asked me if I knew the other people coming off the cafeteria line, and when I nodded, he offered to guess their specialties in a game of skill.

He was eerily accurate. He explained that he used height, weight, dress and eye-hand coordination among other parameters of anthropologic training. Orthopedists, he said, taking one example, were usually tall, lean, male, mature-looking, dark clothed, with lots of starch in their hospital uniforms. Cardiologists? Shorter, with receding hairlines. A lot of generalization, but, all in all, good fun and I loved it. I didn't ask him about OB-GYNs, though—and he was tactful enough not to tell me.

We obviously must prefer to work with women. *Why* is always a topic of lively debate. Do gynecologists love women?

Hate them? Or is it a love-hate relationship? It's one of those imponderables that the Dr. Kildare wannabes never get tired of arguing and, of course, never settle. The answer would be far too revealing.

Obstetrics usually attracts a certain segment of any medical school class. It's called "the happy specialty," because it offers the doctor a chance to share the euphoria of childbirth over and over again. And most cases, maybe nine out of ten, are happy from beginning to end.

It's with that other one or so that the doctor gets tested. And then it's a real test. An obstetrician is the only medical specialist who deals with two patients—the mother and the fetus—and two sets of anatomy and physiology simultaneously. It's quite a challenge.

Every pregnancy represents enormous change, creating what the disciples of Sigmund Freud called "physiologic anxiety"— the kind every pregnant woman has. They said that anxiety arose from a conflict between two essential parts of the Freudian psyche, the id and the ego. The id, the part of us that contains our subconscious drives and irrational dreams and wishes, is always subjectively pro-pregnancy. People want to have sex, they want romance, they want to procreate and pass a bit of themselves on to posterity. The desire to become pregnant has been labeled a basic drive of women.

Why is the ego in conflict with this? In our physical lives, all objective aspects of pregnancy are negative. There are the morning nausea and ill feelings, weight gain, ungainliness and swollen ankles, any one or more of which are universally associated with early gestation. There's the expense. If a woman has a career, she may have to put it on hold and may never get it back on track. Then there's potential health damage and even maternal mortality—you can die! A lot of women feel anxious in pregnancy. The anxiety of ambivalence occurs as the id and the ego wrestle with each other in every pregnant woman's mind. That's not just common—it's resoundingly normal.

But generally, in the woman who chooses pregnancy, the up side outweighs the down—the id outweighs the ego. For a normal woman with a healthy ego, the goal of a chosen pregnancy is the knowledge that there is something good coming at the end of it—the reward of a healthy baby.

It's the same for the obstetrician. Some doctors who want to work with women gravitate toward other areas—gynecological cancers, endocrinology, sexuality—not obstetrics. The "happy specialty" means sleepless nights and always being on call—babies arrive at all hours of the day and night. But for those who choose the field, it's well worth it.

The idea in all wanted pregnancies, really, but especially in a high-risk case, is to do everything possible for both maternal and fetal well-being, to keep the fetus in utero for as long as possible, to get it to a stage where it can survive in the extrauterine world. It takes time and effort—and lots of money. There's a great sense of accomplishment when we work with the mother through her complications and problems with bed rest, diet, medication of all kinds, monitoring, sonograms, and see the baby come to full bloom. The obstetrician's reward is identical to the patient's—a healthy mother and a healthy offspring.

We get the baby to the point of survival, and then we turn it over to a pediatrician and watch it grow. I have to admit that it's satisfying to see a baby go home and live a full life and give the intended joy to its parents. It is a grand feeling.

In creating the womb, nature has provided the quintessential place for a fetus to develop. A perfectly healthy fetus born too early can be a very sick and troubled newborn. Technology has pushed the age of survival down a little, but there's always a floor it can't go below. As yet, there's no hospital equipment that can substitute for the healthy uterus where the immature fetus is concerned.

At a recent international obstetrics meeting, I took part in a round-table discussion on high-risk pregnancies. We were reviewing the organic and ethical problems and issues surrounding the resuscitation of babies born in great breathing difficulty, learning the ins and outs of infant nasal suctioning, the techniques of inserting breathing tubes and trying to understand the biochemistry of the newborn and its pulmonary system, and the bioethics of it all. Even a full-term newborn is different in both obvious and subtle ways from an adult or an older child. Its broncho-vascular tree, its linkages from lung to heart, are unique in order to allow for the use of the mother's blood rather than its own source of atmospheric oxygen.

I looked about the room. Not all of my colleagues there, as far as I knew, did abortions, or "therapeutics." But some did. And now, with recertification and qualifying exams being a constant in our medical lives, every one of us was being exposed to all of it.

I was rapping this through with a friend of mine, a perinatologist, whose specialty deals with high-risk pregnancy. His career was devoted to saving the littlest, sickest babies and to working with that five to ten percent of women whose pathology needed the skills of the highest order. But as the head of a hospital OB-GYN department, he had to step in and do whatever was necessary whenever his staff needed him. One of his interests, and something he got called on to do, was abortion. "Not often, but often enough," he explained with a complaining tone to his voice.

"On some mornings," he said, "I leave my office, and if I turn right, I go down the hallway to the TOP clinic and terminate. I am a destroyer of pregnancies. If I turn left down the same hallway, I go toward the nursery and the labor and delivery unit and take care of the myriad complications in women who are in the throes of problem pregnancies—and I do things to help them hold on. It's all so schizophrenic. I have a kind of split personality."

A dilemma? Sure. OB-GYNs face dilemmas every day. A doctor trained in the management of high-risk pregnancies can get a woman with almost any condition through almost any pregnancy. Almost. Does that mean it's wise? Pregnancy bombards a woman's system with powerful hormones and other stresses. If she's taking medication to control a preexisting condition—lupus, say, or manic depression—the drug can easily do damage to the developing embryo. But is it safe for her to go off the drug for the duration of a pregnancy? Indeed, by the time she discovers she's pregnant, there may already be damage to the embryo. Now what?

If she's had a prior pregnancy complicated with diabetes or kidney failure, the chances are pretty good that the condition will recur and perhaps become chronic. Many do. She may not die, but her health may be permanently impaired and certainly compromised—I still remember my mother and the course her life took. Some conditions, like multiple sclerosis, can worsen dramatically in pregnancy, soon leaving the woman wheelchair-bound or hospitalized for the rest of her life. Even in a mild case, is it worth the risk?

And there are hosts of other complications, not life-threatening, perhaps, but troubling just the same.

Ginny was thirty-eight when she came to me in her third pregnancy. She and her husband, Joe, had always talked of four kids, but with the costs of raising the first two, the demands of their careers and Joe's chronically ill mother needing their help, they had scaled back their plans to three. Now they had a problem with this one.

Ginny's first pregnancy had ended up as a cesarean section, the second as well, and for the same reason: recurrent herpes. She had had a lesion before pregnancy, and they figured that one or the other of them must have contracted the disease before their marriage. They were very together and secure, and it had no effect on their relationship. But in her first pregnancy, another lesion broke out just before her due date. Lab work confirmed the presence of the virus. A c-section was required.

It went well. Ginny got her reward—a healthy baby.

With her second pregnancy, Ginny and Joe were eager for a trial of labor, and so was I. But a series of herpes ulcerations popped out during her final month, and with a diagnosis reaffirmed, we planned the second section. It went well, and Ginny delivered her second boy. Joe, Jr. was here.

They had high hopes for number three. It might be a longed-for daughter, although they said they would cheerfully accept whatever came along. And there was still a chance for a vaginal delivery. So when they brought up abortion at the second prenatal visit, I was somewhat surprised.

At first, I thought it was their home situation—Joe's business was going through serious growing pains, and his mother required increasing care. They couldn't predict where that might lead. Then they brought up the problem of a third cesarean.

"It's not certain that you'll have to have one," I said. "I've had really good luck with vaginal deliveries after two cesareans. And you haven't had a breakout in years. All your cultures have been negative."

"But it could happen again, couldn't it? Suppose it popped up just at the time of delivery?"

They had me there. It's one of those things that can't be predicted. No matter how I tried to sell them on the idea of lightning not striking three times, I could see they weren't convinced. Maybe I wasn't so confident either. And there was more.

"Even if she doesn't have a breakout, would it be really safe to try labor after two cesareans? Isn't it risky?" Joe asked me.

"Some risk, yes, but . . ."

"Three cesareans? Is that really safe?" He was pressing me.

"It's surgery; there's risk with any surgery. But the cesarean's one of the safest . . ."

Ginny cut in. "I'm just not sure I want to spend the next few months worrying, will I, won't I—have a breakout, have a cesarean. I was a lot younger with the last one, and I had more help, and believe me, recovery was no fun."

I asked them to think about it, but I felt I knew which way they were going, and I couldn't find it in me to convince them otherwise. I just wasn't that sure myself. If they were right, the newborn child would be at a terrible risk—one that could be tragic. Herpes infection can cause retardation, blindness, brain infection, coma. We had to talk cesarean.

Over the next few days, they both called me frequently with questions. Abortion was becoming more and more of an option. The thought of facing a third major operation, the drawbacks of their home situation and their economic problems were all hefted and given consideration.

They came back to the office to talk again in person. This time, I sensed that they were definitely leaning toward abortion—and that is what happened. I saw them both breathe a sigh of relief when the decision-making process was over. In follow-up, they remained firm in their resolve and satisfied that they had done the right thing for their marriage and their family.

These are difficult, even painful questions. When the mother's life is not immediately at stake, but "only" her health, her quality of life, her general well-being, her responsibility to her existing family and her life span, what is the "right" choice? Ginny and Joe chose one way; my mother chose the other. Both ways have consequences.

Historically, even when there were laws against elective abortion, a woman with a serious medical condition could get one. Special hospital boards would hear the case and make the decision. The "two P-C" rule reigned. But rules were applied unevenly. A sick woman might have to go shopping to find a sympathetic hospital board or be able to afford the two psychiatrists.

Women carrying severely damaged fetuses were often out of luck. The rubella, or German measles, epidemic in 1965 left thousands of babies with serious defects from blindness and deafness to heart problems and degenerative brain disease. Rubella is so damaging to the embryo that medical authorities now recommend informing any woman who contracts it in the early stages of pregnancy that abortion must be given serious consideration.

Judy caught German measles from a friend's child. "I didn't know yet that I was pregnant. My friend's kid was sick, and she had to go out, so she called me to babysit. Kimmy was fussy, so

I held her. A couple of weeks later, I came down with a fever and a telltale rash. I felt achy and rotten for a day or two, but it didn't last long. I found out I was pregnant right after that. I told my doctor, and he said it was probably OK. But as I went along, I started to worry more and more. I did some reading and found out about what could happen. And I checked with my friend and found out that Kimmy had definitely had German measles.

"I went to another doctor. He really laid it out for me. It was horrible. I was starting to show—I was wearing maternity clothes already. I had told everybody at work, all my friends. But I decided to have the abortion. I felt so stupid.

"I had to have a salting-out and go through labor. When I went back to work a few days later, I was still out of shape, wearing tents, and people assumed I was still pregnant and would ask me about the baby. It was awful. The only consolation for us was that the baby would not have been normal, and I couldn't stand that—deliberately bringing a child into the world to suffer like that."

It isn't impossible—I've had it happen to me—to have a woman come in for an abortion, and then a couple of years later come back and ask for help in managing a difficult pregnancy to term. That points up the highly individual nature of every pregnancy—each one is a special situation composed of the time, the place, the people involved, their finances, their health, the state of their relationship. For the woman who wants a pregnancy, often no cost is too great, sometimes even at the risk of her own life. The same thing is true for a woman who looks at her situation and decides on abortion.

Abortion is not new in America's history. Until "quickening," when women begin to feel life, it was allowed—and done— from the time of the earliest settlers right down through the nineteenth century. Any woman who wanted an abortion could have one for any reason, if she acted early enough. Seventeenth-century Salem had its witch hunts—but it also had abortion. The stockades in the village square or burning at the stake were for heretics but not for abortionists.

Most of women's health concerns were seen to by midwives, not doctors. The "grannies" had their methods—herbal brews and potions that were supposed to bring on menstruation and who knew what else. Some of them probably worked through the limbic system or coincidence. I don't think they bothered with any well-controlled studies.

Was it legal? Perhaps not in the sense of being written into the law. But then, not much was. In 1850, as we were feeling and exerting our manifest destiny, there were no legal statutes anywhere in America against abortion. Patent medicines adver-tised openly in women's magazines stated that they could be used as abortifacients. Billboards and classified ads offered similar services. Everybody knew what they meant. Some were quite explicit. Nobody objected. Even abortion after quickening was a misdemeanor at worst. Not more.

While a lot of people felt vaguely that abortion was wrong, there were few religious prohibitions against it. The Catholic church had taken a mild stand against abortion as early as the thirteenth century, but the ban would not be absolute and enforced until 1869, when Pope Pius IX set forth the Catholic dogma: no abortion, ever, for any reason. It was seen princi-pally as religious doctrine, something Catholics had to abide by, but others didn't.

Sometimes an irate family member or spouse would bring suit, but juries tended to believe a woman who said she hadn't felt movement and rule that the abortion had been performed early enough. Everyone looked the other way. There were lots of "names" then. By and large, people were happy if the woman didn't die. Many did, of course. But childbirth was also danger-ous. It was a real crap shoot.

Crude as their practices were, it's likely that the midwives in those days had a better record than many latter-day abortion-ists. Abortion has been called "the first medical specialty," and they were the specialists. They operated openly, their success—or failure—rate well known by their clients.

Up until the 1840s, anyone could claim to be a healer and use the title "doctor." Quacks abounded. Not only midwives and doctors, but also barber-dentists and horse doctors and all manner of lay healers practiced abortion. They say the wild West's Doc Holiday did more than a few in his day.

When the American Medical Association, the AMA, was formed in 1847, it began a campaign to control licensure, granting the right to practice medicine only to those who had specifically trained for it.

Only trained physicians, the argument went, should be permitted to perform abortions. Such laws would protect women from quacks and butchers. Moreover, medical science had progressed to a point where doctors knew that the fetus moved before women felt it as quickening. The child had to be protected as well. Indeed, only a doctor was trained enough and astute enough to know when it was safe to do an abortion. Of course, the established medical community had its fair share of deviates and quacks, but nobody mentioned those.

The Victorian Age of Mother England spread to America and the New World. The era saw the beginnings of laws to regulate sexuality and its fruits; the repressive tenor of the times made restricting abortion attractive. "Bad" girls should pay for their flagrant behavior. There was no such thing as a "bad boy."

Sexual probity became a cause. A reformer named Sylvester Graham traveled up and down the East Coast, lecturing on the evils of concupiscence. The prisons of America, he said, were full of people who hadn't been able to control their sexual urges. To keep young people away from a life of crime, he recommended cold showers, hard beds and bread made of unsifted flour. His feel for the times was dead-on. He managed to get a government grant to develop the flour product and peddle it to jails and schools and lobbied Congress for over $100,000—a small fortune in those days—before they wised up to his game. He did leave us a legacy, though—the graham cracker.

Legislators went for the notion that restricting abortion would both save maternal and infant lives and uphold morals. Abortion passed into the hands of the judicial establishment. Doctors were allowed to do the abortions that judges and lawyers approved. Everybody thought they were "saved." Pius IX's edict from Rome was not coincidental.

In those days, of course, women were routinely excluded from medical and law schools, and therefore from abortion decisions. Such arcane knowledge as when and how to terminate a pregnancy was thus left to men. Or rather, to doctors and judges—who were men.

By 1880, abortion was illegal throughout America.

The next generations grew up knowing that abortion was against the law—and therefore wrong. Yet abortion was done. In a time when birth control consisted mostly of "Not tonight, I've got a headache," or "Smoke your pipe and blow the smoke out the window"—your great-grandmother's euphemism for coitus interruptus—there were a goodly number of unwanted pregnancies. From those early days on, just as my father always said, well-off women found ways to get what they wanted. Poor women resorted to coat hangers—or their equivalent—even then.

Betty, now in her eighties, vividly remembers her 1930s abortion.

"It was the Depression. We were Catholic, and I already had two babies. It seemed like every time Bill hung his pants on the bedpost, I got pregnant. I'd had a lot of trouble with the second one, and my doctor had said we should wait for at least a year, but there I was again. I went to the doctor, and he just shook his head. I asked him about an abortion.

"He didn't do them. Oh, no. But when I pressed him, he gave me a couple of names. Said he couldn't guarantee them, but other patients had used them. One of them was a doctor in town. Well, I couldn't use him. If I went to someone in town and people found out, it could hurt Bill's business, and we couldn't afford that. The other name was a woman, in a town about forty miles away.

"So we went there. We had to go at night. It was an isolated place, out in the country. Bill waited in the car—I had to go in alone. The woman wanted the money first, and I gave it to her and watched her count it. The house looked filthy, but I thought if the doctor sent me there, it must be all right. I just kept telling myself that while she worked on me. It hurt, but it wasn't any worse than having a baby.

"By the next morning, I knew I was in trouble. Chills and a fever—I was really sick. I called the doctor, and he came right over. He was furious. He removed the gauze packing and when he did, I remember he said, 'Why can't that damned woman at least be *clean?*'

"He fixed me up and told me to come in in a week. Bill was fit to be tied, he was so mad at the doctor. Why did he send me to her if he knew she wasn't clean? We really didn't have a choice. But in the end, I was fine. And I wasn't sorry—it gave me a little breather between kids. We had three more after that."

Betty was one of the lucky ones. Not all women survived with their lives and their reproductive functions intact.

It was an interesting twist of fate when, following the heat and battle for abortion reform in the 1960s, the AMA worked to overturn the laws it had sought and to liberalize the law, once again in the name of saving maternal lives.

An OB-GYN practice is about more than just keeping part of a woman's body healthy. It implies sex and sexuality. I figured out early on that if I was going to be a good women's doctor, I was going to have to know more about women than just how their plumbing worked.

Part of my postgraduate training in human sexuality and sex therapy was with the master—Dr. William Masters, of Masters and Johnson. At one of our first workshop sessions, Bill—as he liked to be called by everyone but his patients—insisted that sex and marital therapy properly belonged in the bailiwick of the gynecologist rather than in that of the psychiatrist. The psychiatric community may have been first in time and initiated sex therapy, but "they blew it when they had their chance," Bill said, because from Freud on down, they never got the total picture on women. "They didn't do their homework," he claimed.

Does anyone doubt the link between mind and body? Nervousness makes the palms sweat. Fear raises gooseflesh and makes chills run up and down the spine. Sorrow and sometimes joy bring tears. Love makes the heart beat faster and does a few other things.

Psychiatrists accept that the so-called limbic system—the link between the organic body systems and the emotions—exists, but they don't bother to dissect it, although the neural pathways are there to be studied. They focus their attention on the brain. Neurologists study the limbic system to discover its anatomical functions, in order to treat organic nerve disease. Urologists do it to learn only about urinary functioning in both sexes—which is something else Dr. Masters decried. They don't give enough attention to the anatomy and physiology of sexual behavior.

That leaves the gynecologists, the doctors for women only. GYNs are the ones who focus on female anatomy and physiology; we are the ones who can tie women's sexual functioning in with their organic side. Bill kept reminding us that it was therefore our responsibility. More, he insisted that when women are troubled by all things sexual, they seek out not their ministers, beauticians or parents, but their gynecologists.

Male anatomy has always been considered the standard; women's is secondary. I guess that's a pretty hard bias to shake. Or maybe all those early male medical students just felt more at ease with male anatomy. Those physicians who were trained in European medical schools, considered the prototypes, relied on cadavers that were male. It was a special occasion when they trotted out a female cadaver for dissection. And it was not that there were too few female cadavers to go around. They were just uptight about it, or so it seemed—funny for Freudians.

In sex and marital therapy, one of the most significant issues for discussion is family aspirations. What are the couple's hopes and dreams? Children? How many? When? A first baby is a milestone: It makes a couple a family in many people's thinking. A relationship may suffer for many reasons—religion, peers, morals, money—and pregnancy ups the ante. It can be the final blow that forces a couple to stay unhappily within a troubled marriage "for the sake of the kids" or that forces them to *get* married when the relationship is shaky at best. With pregnancy, cultural pressures go up many-fold, and people know it. The bedroom becomes a battleground. In our country, with almost one half of all marriages ending in divorce, marital therapy dictates that couples need all the edge they can get.

Bill Masters used to remind us that in this latter half of the twentieth century any couple who blamed an inability to find an adequate form of birth control for the breakdown of the sexual side of their marriage were fooling themselves. "Don't let them get away with it," he said. "It isn't the reason. It's their ticket of admission to your office." But usually the last thing a couple with marital problems wants is a baby, and the possibility of pregnancy is another stress on an already stressed-out situation. Fragile relationships often break under the strain and never get the chance to do some healing.

It can be mighty comforting to a couple to know that along with adequate birth control, there's a chance for a safe abortion if they want it, or need it.

Nan and Alan Benson came to me by referral from their family doctor. When they showed up in my office for that first consultation, sex had become first unrewarding and then almost nonexistent, to the point of distress. "We want a family," Nan said, "but we don't make love often enough for me to get pregnant—and as far as being able to do it specifically at times when I'm fertile, forget it."

Alan seconded Nan's complaint. Neither was happy with the situation. We worked together in intensive therapy for about a month, and things improved dramatically. The Bensons talked more and more about the family they hoped to have.

Then Nan showed up in my office alone and in tears. "I'm pregnant," she wept. "I just can't have a baby now. Things were just getting a little better. I don't want this—don't want it at all. Can you help me? Can you do an abortion?"

When I pressed her for an explanation, she blurted, "I never really wanted a baby. It's Alan. I thought if he thought he could make me pregnant, it would be easier for him. I didn't think it would happen!"

Another therapy session was clearly called for. The three of us sat down for a little honesty check.

"You thought what? A baby was your idea, not mine," was Alan's response. "I'm more than happy with the way things are. I don't need kids running around, believe me. Not now, anyway." Their communication skills needed more help.

Neither of them, as it turned out, had actually wanted a pregnancy; each was using it as a lure to entice the other into a sexual interlude. They had fooled me as well as each other. "What do we do now?" asked Alan.

They chose abortion, and their marriage improved in an atmosphere of honesty. They are childless by choice.

Even under the bleakest marital circumstances, there are couples who don't want a termination. It's usually both of them, by the way. Every time a couple comes together, for whatever reason, even though they may be in deep trouble and considering a split, a spark of something draws them together. The therapist is hoping to find that spark and use it as a basis for success. That's part of our job.

Couples will tussle over money, in-laws, where to live, how many children to have or even whether to have any. But usually not over abortion. I guess it's safe to say that a courting couple who battle over something as basic as abortion probably won't make it through the premarital relationship. It's too basic a rift.

*   *   *

Carrie and Greg were in their late twenties, married five years. They were in their sexual prime, but their sex life had dwindled to nil when they came to see me.

"I won't be bullied into having a baby," Carrie said. "Greg's brothers and sisters—younger than he is—all have kids, and I know his brothers particularly are giving him a hard time about not scoring, but really, it isn't the Super Bowl, no matter what he thinks. We come home from one of those family things, and he's mad at *me*. Why doesn't he get mad at them? They're the ones snickering and making snide remarks."

"As far as I'm concerned," Greg said, "my brothers are right. It makes me look like I'm no good. And I do get mad at her. She's cut me off."

We talked about the areas of contention within the relationship, and they spoke of love, sex, careers and, mainly, children—why and when to have them. As it turned out, neither Carrie nor Greg felt good about having a baby until their marriage was sound.

I told them we'd have to deal with the question of children, because Carrie was holding sex over Greg's head. "No way," she said, "am I going to spread my legs without either being sure that the marriage is going to last or absolutely foolproof birth control."

She was asking for the impossible. To break the impasse, I pointed out the availability of abortion.

They turned on me in unison. No, they said, that was not an option. They were vehement. And united. It was a lucky break for me—I became the heavy. We finally had something to build on.

It doesn't usually work like that. As a rule, couples in therapy who are resuming sexual relations and don't want a baby feel better knowing that abortion is there as a safeguard, like a security blanket. But either way, the couple find themselves in agreement—most of the time.

People usually know—or think they do—which side of the abortion question they're going to come down on. Most women who choose termination feel that it's the only thing to do, the only route for their own survival.

Experiencing regret and sadness, a well-recognized postabortal syndrome, may follow. The woman has come to a crossroads in her life and chosen one way—what if she had chosen the other? The sting is there. A woman who chooses to end her pregnancy has to accept that. But few, if any, major life decisions are totally regret-free, have no consequences. Why must abortion be? How could it be?

Adoption is touted as an option for the woman who's caught in an unwanted pregnancy. But adoption isn't free of consequences either. Twenty years ago, when she was young and alone, Sarah gave up her newborn son for adoption.

"I'd get over it, they told me. I'd get on with my life and forget it. It wasn't true. Nobody told me that I would grieve for my baby all my life, always wonder what happened to him. I believed them when they said I was doing the best thing. But now I don't know. Since adoption has become so much more open, you hear so much about adopted children—even when they go to loving homes—feeling rejected and second-best because they were given away. And you think, 'Does he blame me? Does he hate me? Does he feel abandoned and unwanted because I gave him up?' "

The emotional pain described by women who give up their babies for adoption is intense and ongoing. "I cried every night for three years," one said. Feelings may lie in ambush, surfacing after a woman marries and has a second child. She may go on to have a career, a happy marriage and a family, but the sense of loss endures. A living child is out there, somewhere—is that child happy? Well? Cared for?

What about women who abort? How do they feel about what they have done?

A U.S. Department of Health and Human Services study on pregnant teenagers, done at the Johns Hopkins School of Hygiene and Public Health, found that two years after an abortion, more than ninety percent of the girls had completed high school, and some had gone on to college. Only ten percent said that they regretted their decision so much that they would not make the same choice again.

Conversely, in the control group—girls who carried their pregnancies to term—forty percent dropped out of school, and their level of regret was high. Apparently, by taking charge of their lives, the young women who ended their pregnancies had increased their feelings of self-worth and independence, positive feelings that drove them to higher achievement.

Other studies, including one commissioned by then Surgeon General C. Everett Koop, an avowed abortion opponent, found substantially the same thing. After abortion, there was some remorse, some guilt, some regret. But for the most part, the regret could be attributed to having gotten into a mess in the first place—simply to having been there. Given his stated bias, Koop probably hoped the study would show otherwise, but to his credit, though it showed no significant psychological damage, he released the findings.

A survey, one of many, out of the Department of Psychiatry of Mt. Sinai Hospital in Toronto reported in the American Journal of Psychiatry on the psychological effects of abortion decisions. The author found anger—not in women who had abortions, but in those who were denied them.

That might be expected. Of course, as the antichoice lobby points out, there is more at stake than just the future of the pregnant girl or woman. There's a potential baby. What about it?

It appears that most women who were denied abortions kept their babies—not surprisingly, since society reserves special opprobrium for the woman who gives up a child. And many had persistent feelings of resentment toward their unwanted children.

Children born to mothers who didn't want them were more likely to be emotionally unstable, unhappy and sick, to fail to make friends and to do poorly academically. More unwanted children dropped out of school, turned to drugs or alcohol and got into trouble with the law. The difference in level of education was marked: Wanted children went to college at twice the rate of unwanted children, even after adjustments for family income and other factors.

Maternal love can't be legislated. The state may be able to compel a woman to carry a pregnancy to term, but should it? With what consequences for the child? And for all of us?

But it would be foolish to say that there aren't ever *some* consequences in abortion. Like any other major life decision, it can come back to haunt a woman years later.

Linda was someone I had seen for routine gynecological exams for five or six years, an established patient in good health. Then on one visit, she confided that she and her husband, Ted, no longer had sexual contact of any kind although their relationship was loving and supportive in many ways. They were only in their midtwenties. Something was clearly very wrong, and Linda was afraid it would eventually break up a marriage that was otherwise good and fulfilling.

I took Linda and Ted on as a couple for sex and marital therapy. And in a few weeks, we had success—enough for them to feel more secure about their marriage and their future together.

About another year later, Linda came in again for her routine gynecological evaluation. Once again, she seemed vaguely worried about something. I got her talking.

"Do you think I'm sterile?" she asked.

"I don't have any reason to think so. Do you?"

"Well, Ted and I are together pretty regularly—not every

night or anything, but often enough. I haven't been trying to get pregnant, but then, I haven't really been trying not to, you know? I just wonder."

"There are lots of variables involved. If you want to go to work on it, we can."

"No—I'm—we're not really ready for a baby yet. But"—Linda twisted her hands into a knot in her lap—"I wonder if"—she took a deep breath and switched gears—"I had an abortion, you know, when I was just a kid—seventeen. And now I wonder, all the time, if I'm ever going to be able to have a baby, because of what I did. If I'm infertile. If it's God's punishment for killing my baby."

Once she started, the words just tumbled out. "The worst thing is, in the same circumstances, I'd do it again. I was just in high school. It would have been the end of everything—my plans for college, my future, my everything. It was the only thing to do. But now I see people on television saying it's murder, and I think—is that what I did? Murder?"

"Do you think so?"

"No. I don't. I really don't. But—how can I be sure? Some people see it that way. How does God see it? And if I'm right, if my not being able to conceive again is God's punishment for what I did, can you fix it? Can anybody?"

Linda was expressing, quite poignantly, one of the dilemmas of abortion. She was going to have to come to grips with her own feelings about it—what it was, what she did and why—and finally see that there is no biologic connection between "God's will" and fertility. Intellectually, she could understand that. But emotionally? That's a longer, tougher process.

There could hardly be two more diametrically opposite problems than abortion and infertility, and the OB-GYN gets to deal with both, sometimes—as with Linda—in the same patient. It's another example of how every pregnancy grows out of a special, individual set of circumstances. No two are ever alike.

More women are delaying motherhood—sometimes by

means of abortion—into their thirties or even forties, when fertility is known to decline. But they wonder. Could the abortion have made them infertile?

I sometimes see one of the nurse-counselors from my days at the women's center. Like many other counselors there, she had had firsthand abortion experience with Roy Parker. After the center closed, she went back to school, got an advanced degree, set herself up in a career and got married to a great guy. They have two adopted children—she was never able to get pregnant again.

"I put myself in his hands," she says, "and as far as I know, he did a good job. I trusted him; I went with him to the center. I wonder, of course. But in another way, it doesn't matter: I had to do what I did, and I'd do it again, even if I knew I'd never have other children. Actually, I'm not unhappy with the way things turned out. I've got a great life, one I wouldn't have had as a single mother trying to support myself and a kid on a nurse's salary."

Infertility is a complex problem, and one that is more properly classified as a couple's issue than a woman's. Whatever's keeping a pregnancy from happening can be peculiar to one partner or both or—in the current state of medical art—neither.

Elise came to me as a fertility patient in her very late thirties. Her petite figure and blond good looks belied a sharp legal mind; she was the youngest partner in a high-powered Wall Street firm. She had all the perks—a secretary of her own and a car with a driver—and she had earned them. She carried her briefcase everywhere and snapped it open as soon as she sat down. She was never idle a minute.

Her husband, Peter, was maybe forty-five. Like Elise, he was fair-haired, slender and fit, good-looking and expensively turned out. President of his own small but rapidly growing industrial design firm, he too exuded confidence and energy and a zest for "having it all." What they didn't have was a family.

They were easy and confident together as they spoke about wanting a child. "Now that I'm a partner, we don't have to worry about the 'mommy track,' " Elise said. "And Peter's business is doing well enough that we can afford reliable child care if we both have to travel. We've got it all worked out, but nature isn't cooperating. What have you got for us?"

We got a fertility evaluation and set a workup into motion. It wasn't long before Elise walked into my office all smiles. "I missed my period," she said. "And the rabbit died."

I started her prenatal care. That was that, I thought. She was an "older mother," so we scheduled an amniocentesis. It showed a normal, healthy boy. Everything was progressing as it should. So I was a little surprised when she showed up a week early for her next regularly scheduled visit.

"What can I do?" she asked. "This baby may or may not be Peter's."

Was I hearing right? "May *not* be?" I repeated.

Her story unraveled. She and Peter were restoring a big old Victorian house in Connecticut, right on Long Island Sound. The senior partner in Elise's firm had a place nearby and had introduced them around. The house was livable, and they'd been spending their weekends there. It seemed ideal.

"Back when I was taking the fertility stuff, we were planning to go out to the house for a long weekend," Elise explained. "We'd both been working so hard that we'd scarcely seen each other for weeks, and—well, it seemed like our best chance to get something going. We had it all scheduled. I'd arranged a couple of days off, everything."

I could see that she was struggling for composure. She went on. "At the very last minute, something came up and Peter had to go to San Francisco. He said he'd try to get back on Sunday, so we could salvage something of the weekend, so I decided to take the time and go out to Connecticut anyway. My hormones were raging and I'd arranged for the time—why not take it?

"Well, on Friday, Peter called to say he'd have to stay over until Monday. I was pretty disappointed, but I figured we'd still have time. But I was at loose ends, in the house alone. And then I ran into someone we'd met recently, and she said they were having a party that night and why not come over.

"I was thinking maybe a dozen people, but there must have been a hundred," Elise said. "They had a band, and waiters circulating with drinks, and I guess I was feeling sorry for myself, because I had a lot more to drink than I usually do. I got to talking to this man, who was somebody's houseguest. He was from South America somewhere and very Latin—very dark and handsome, very courtly. He insisted on seeing me home.

"Then it all gets pretty fuzzy. I keep trying to put it all together in my mind. I know how crazy this must sound to you. I think we sat out on the lawn for a while, and then I know I went to bed. The point is, I don't remember him leaving. What I sort of remember is, he'd gotten into bed with me. I think."

"What do you mean, you think, Elise? Did he?"

"I'm not sure. I really can't remember. I convinced myself the next morning it was a dream. I'm not like that. But I was so out of it. If he did anything to me, I never knew it. I just don't know anymore."

I tried not to let my incredulity show on my face. The story brought to mind a famous teaching vignette from my psychiatry training about the old, old woman who hobbles off to bed and falls into a deep sleep. Suddenly, she is startled awake by a thunderous knocking at her garden door. She is amazed to see a dashing horseman on a white steed. He swoops down, lifts her from her bed and carries her off on horseback to a mountaintop, where he throws her down on a carpet of green moss. He lunges at her nightdress, rips it from her in a lustful grab and looms over her naked body.

"What are you going to do to me?" she quavers.

"I don't know," he replies. "It's your dream."

What was my patient describing? An indiscretion? A seduction? A rape? The way she told it, it could have been some Greek god down from Mount Olympus, spreading his favors. It was her dream.

"Hadn't you been having sexual relations with Peter up to that time?" I asked.

"Well—no," she said. "We'd been so busy before—that's why we scheduled the weekend. And then Peter didn't get back all that week."

We started looking at charts and records. Her time of peak fertility and the weekend in Connecticut coincided perfectly. If the encounter had happened, it was likely the source of the pregnancy. I told her as much.

"Isn't there some kind of test you can do? To find out for sure who the father is?" she wanted to know.

There wasn't—not without blood or fluid samples from both men. No way to get those. There was also a limit to what I would do for a patient, and it stopped well short of outright lying. To anyone. What, I asked her, were the consequences of telling Peter?

She wasn't sure.

We tabled the discussion to give her time to think it over. In two days she was back with a decision: She had to abort. She was now convinced that the baby was not her husband's, and there would be no way to fool him. The father had been of such different complexion. What would she say if the baby looked like him? More, how would she feel? The dishonesty bothered her as well.

I didn't answer. I had no answer. I told her this was not something for a doctor to decide. It was her decision alone.

She crossed her arms across her body and rocked back and forth like someone in pain. Maybe she was.

"We wanted a baby," she said. "Our baby. What have I done? Was I trying to get even with Peter for not being there? Did I want to get pregnant just to prove it wasn't my fault? Is that why this happened? I can't do this to Peter—I can't. It's not that he wouldn't forgive me. It's that I could never forgive myself."

She chose abortion.

I am not sure how she explained it to her husband. I wondered if she used the amnio somehow, said something was wrong with the fetus, but I didn't ask. She said she wanted to wrestle with it on her own. I accepted her need for privacy, letting her know I was there if she needed me. This was a wanted pregnancy; they had both gone through fertility evaluations. She said she told him everything. I hope she did.

Elise and Peter are still together; she has never again become pregnant. Their focus seemed to change in the wake of the abortion. Fertility lost its priority; Elise's biological imperative loosened its grip. How much of a role that weekend played, we'll never know. For them as a couple there will be no children. But Elise can live with that. Painful as it all was, she had a choice.

Obstetrics. Perinatology. Gynecology. Sex and marital therapy. Fertility. Some doctors limit their practices to one or two, but I've always wanted to be able to treat the whole woman, get the whole picture. And part of that picture is abortion. The ability to choose the conditions under which she'll have a child is central to a woman's reproductive life.

The anguish that accompanies the decision to abort generally dissipates once the procedure is over. As with any major decision, it helps a woman to feel she's not alone. That was what Roy Parker understood when he told patients they were doing the right thing. And that is why, to this day, at the last minute, just before I nod to the anesthesiologist to start the pentothal, I ask a fast question. Not "Are you sure?" It's the wrong time for that; that I did in the counseling session. But "Are you OK? Are you comfortable?" and then, when the patient nods, I say, "You are doing fine. You will be just great. I am here."

Every patient has the right to an abortion and a person she trusts to do it. A pearl if I ever heard one.

5 *My Niece, My Judge*

"Uncle Don, could I talk to you?"

My niece Jessica cornered me at a Thanksgiving Day family affair. My three sisters and I were all born within two weeks of that last Thursday in November, so it was a special celebration in the Sloan household. I always tried to make sure I was there. From the look in Jessica's eyes, it appeared that I was about to be called on to perform some avuncular duties. I hoped I was up to the task.

"Sure, Jess. What's up?"

"Did Mom say anything to you about the frog thing?"

"No. What 'frog thing'?"

"I have to, you know, dissect a frog? For biology lab. And—well, the frog's alive. I mean, can't I learn the same stuff from a book? It's *alive*. Why do I have to kill it? It's all so gross."

I had never known Jessica that well, but we weren't strangers, either. I thought if there were anything startling about her, I would have known it. Her devotion to the preservation of life had never come up before—yet it had apparently been there all along.

"What happens if you don't dissect the frog?" I asked her.

"I guess I flunk. Maybe not *flunk*, but even if I ace the written final, a third of my grade is lab, and I'll get a big fat zero in that." Jessica sighed. "For sure, it's going to mess up my average. If I really flunk, I won't have enough credits to graduate. It's a required course. Mom and Dad will go bananas. They're already partway there. Especially Dad. You know him." She shrugged. "But it's *my* frog, isn't it?"

* * *

I was just beginning to think about the dilemmas of the abortive patient, forming concerns that I hadn't had when I was working with Doug Spencer. I thought more in those days of the women we were helping—not of the fetuses. The life or death of embryos never came into the picture. We never gave it a thought.

What I had engaged in early on was a fight to save women's lives from the horrors of the ugly abortions I saw in Brooklyn and in Philadelphia. That was the simple attraction of my work with Doug Spencer. Even women's rights didn't enter into it—not until we had time to think of what we were doing. It never came up and for one good reason: We never doubted it. We just assumed that a woman had the right to do what she wished with her body. It was a cliché, perhaps, but clichés are true sometimes.

"You do abortions on pregnant women, don't you?" Jessica asked, as if there were some other kind.

The question took me by surprise. I also hadn't known Jessica was aware of what I did. High school is a whole other place from when I went there. The sexual revolution, explicit language, advertising, rated movies, MTV—all the media push kids into growing up fast now, even faster than they want to, maybe. Jessica obviously knew about abortion, knew it was controversial. And she had made a connection. It brought me up short. I hadn't tied the two together myself. Was abortion the same as "killing frogs"?

"Yes, Jessica, I do abortions. It's an important part of my work."

"How can you do that? I don't even want to kill a frog. Isn't that like killing babies?"

"No. It's not." I answered her abruptly. I wanted her to make her point.

There are some pundits who argue that if we are allowed to kill fetuses, we should be able to kill newborns too. After all, there's not much difference between a newborn and a fetus, and if you can destroy one, why not the other?

But to me, it's a specious argument. Jessica's problem got me thinking.

I was offered the chance to kill a baby once; I guess "kill" is the right word.

It was early in the days of legal abortion in New York. I was spending most of my time at the women's center, but I had a budding private practice. I'd set myself up in an office and bought myself a small suction unit, and I was in business. I was the second coming of Doug Spencer.

The appointment came through the regular channels. The patient, a sixteen-year-old girl scared like a jackrabbit, arrived in a gray stretch limousine with smoked windows, accompanied by her father, an uncle and her not-so-elder brother, all nattily dressed in dark suits, white shirts and skinny ties. I remember a big bow in her hair, something only a mother could have put there—although her mother was missing from the party. But even when the brother asked to be seen with her, I was more puzzled than suspicious. My mind started playing tricks on me. They all moved so deliberately, I didn't have time to form any scenarios about what might be going down.

I made sure, as I always do, that the patient didn't object to having someone else there. Even with a legal requirement to notify the parents of someone under seventeen, I wasn't sure a brother was appropriate. None of this had ever happened before. When I found out she was pregnant, I could have dismissed everyone. The law is loose as to when a doctor can consider a pregnant female emancipated—major enough to be seen alone. I sensed the situation called for a family conference.

The history I got was vague. She was hiding something—likely that she was too far along. The exam—and my eyeballs—confirmed it. She was well past the second trimester—over thirty weeks.

There was no way I could go on. First of all, the girl was just not very responsive. I felt stymied with every question. She mumbled her answers and wouldn't look me in the eye. And then there was the not-so-elder brother, who acted older and older as he took charge. The situation got stranger and stranger. I wasn't scared, although I felt a little trapped. We got down to the case at hand. They wanted the pregnancy ended, and now.

I explained that a termination was not possible—not here, not anywhere. This early in the legal abortion era, late cases were just not considered. And, I explained, if anyone agreed to do it, it would not be safe for mother or baby. I had to say it over many times and in many ways to make my point. The young man finally got up, motioned for his sister to follow and they both exited the office onto the street and into the smoky-glassed limo.

About an hour later, my nurse buzzed me. The father of the girl had returned and was asking for a few more minutes of my time. I welcomed him in.

I almost preempted his request, but instead I decided to hear him out. People in trouble need to talk. And talk he did. "She got into a mess with a bad kid in the neighborhood," he said. "You know how these things are. Her mother knows nothing. It would destroy her."

Sure. In my experience, mothers know, and they roll with the punches. But in his, the mother was supposed to cry, I guess. The patient was peripheral. I hinted strongly that maybe this was a wanted pregnancy—the girl having kept it secret all these months.

"No, no, no," he said. "She was just innocent and scared. Didn't know what was happening to her until it was too late."

Sure, sure, I nodded. Somehow, I half believed him. But it was too late. Other arrangements would have to be made.

He stood up, reached into his breast pocket and brought out a leather-bound checkbook. He flipped it open and wrote in my name and the date. Then he wrote the number five in the amount section and tore the check from the book. He slid it to me across the desk, face up. "Doctor," he said, "take my check and put down as many zeros as you want. No matter. Whatever you think it's worth. The check is as good as gold. Take the baby. Just get rid of it."

It was all so preposterous, I didn't know what to say. I felt all-powerful. The whole scene was unreal, like the set of a B movie. I wouldn't have been surprised to hear some sinister music in the background. The check lay between us. I didn't make a move toward it.

He tried to chat me up, man-to-man. He seemed, in many ways, like a nice guy. He talked about his love for his daughter—I wondered what he meant by "love"—and about the disgrace for the whole family, in the church, among their peers, in the community. "Is it more than money?" he wanted to know. "Is there something else you want done? Anything." He was trying to make me an offer I couldn't refuse.

I finally found my voice. I first-named him. "No, Lou, I've got a fee schedule, and I work for that. Period. It's just that there's simply no way to do what you want," I said. "She's too close to term." I tried to suggest alternatives—adoption came to mind. There was a great demand for healthy Caucasian babies.

He shook his head. It was intolerable—unthinkable. But then suddenly he pushed the check toward me. "OK," he said. "If we do it now. Take the baby and give it away. Whatever. Just do it now. We need a quick fix."

"Look, Lou. Listen to me. I cannot deliberately take out what would be a very small and sick baby, when in a few more weeks, it will be mature and healthy. That would be the same as deliberately killing it. No. We have to wait. That's it," I said. I explained the obvious. There would be nurses and other doctors who would work to keep the baby alive and would likely succeed, but the baby might be blind, spastic, brain damaged—unadoptable.

Without a word, he swept the check off my desk and walked out the door. It wasn't rudeness. More like exasperation. He wasn't accustomed to not getting his way.

There are some who argue that if we can justify destroying embryos because they're not "like us"—like human adults—

then we might as well kill newborns, because they're more like fetuses than they are like grown people. But rationally most people know there's a difference. When does a fetus become a person? There's no clear dividing line. When does a stream become a river? When does a child become an adult? We may not be able to put an exact date on it, but we can tell the difference. And it's better to err on the side of caution. I'll do abortions, but I did draw a legal, medical and ethical line that I could live with.

"How does a woman make up her mind?" Jessica asked earnestly. "If the woman doesn't want a baby, and it's going to mess up her life, I know, but still, it's a *baby*. Not right then— later on, it'll be a baby, right?"

"Yes, it'll be a baby. What kind and how healthy, I don't know. But that's irrelevant. That's just what the woman doesn't want. Jessica, at the time when we do most abortions, it's not a baby. It's an embryo or a tiny fetus that has an existence only inside the woman's body."

"But the baby—the embryo—it dies, right?"

"It can't live outside the uterus. It gets everything from the mother's body. It's living tissue of sorts. So, yes, in one sense, it dies. But it was never viable—able to live on its own." I kept wondering how much of this Jessica was understanding.

"You say it's not a baby—it's an embryo or something. But if it'll be a baby someday, what's the difference?"

"Think about acorns and oak trees. The acorn is the fertilized egg of the oak. That doesn't make it an oak tree, right? And even after it starts to grow, you don't call it a tree. You call it an acorn that's sprouted or a seedling. It's a potential tree, but it's not a tree yet. Something very special is going to happen to that growth to make it into what we know is a tree because it's able to do what a tree does. There's no clear moment when it becomes a tree, but that doesn't mean you can't tell when it's a tree and when it's not. It's the same with fetal growth."

"That sounds too simple—and weird. People aren't oak trees. You make it sound like fetuses aren't human life."

To Jessica, "weird" was an all-encompassing term. You had to interpret what she intended it to mean.

"I wouldn't deny that they're human tissue. Of course they are, as I said. And while they're attached to the woman, that tissue is alive. But they're not independent life, and they're not people as we know them. They don't have brain waves and sensitivity to pain yet."

"Don't they jump if you poke them?"

"Yes, but that doesn't mean they're feeling pain. Anything jumps if it's poked—an amoeba, an earthworm. Or your frog."

"Oh, gosh, yes. My frog. I almost forgot about that."

"What is it, exactly, about killing the frog? Do you want to keep it for a pet? Is it a special frog? Would you be thinking differently about someone else's frog?"

I was thinking of the 4-H kids who raise calves, shower them with love and care. The payoff is that the best calf fetches the highest price and goes off to be beeved—turned into steak. I've known some Texas ranchers who cried when a favorite steer or calf was led off to slaughter. But it wasn't that.

"No. It doesn't know me from Adam. It's just a frog. But it's hopping around. It breathes. It eats flies and stuff. It's enjoying itself." She grinned. "I mean, I guess it's enjoying itself. Who knows? But it's not hurting anybody. Why should I hurt it? Doesn't it have a right to be alive?"

"Generally speaking, no. Only people have rights—or can have them taken away."

The phrase "right to life" sounds good, but courts have traditionally found that the right to life is not absolute—especially where the rights of others are concerned. Not long ago, the father of a twelve-year-old boy with leukemia sued the mother of his three-year-old twins, the product of a liaison, to allow them to be tested as possible bone-marrow donors. The older boy's only hope was a bone-marrow transplant, and his half siblings represented his best chance for life.

The mother refused on the grounds that testing the twins was intrusive and a violation of their bodily integrity. She argued that it might be frightening or even harmful to them.

The court found for the mother. She could not be compelled to allow her children to be tested. Their half brother did not get the bone-marrow transplant, and he died.

The rights of the two sides collided. You might argue that children have become bone-marrow donors for their siblings on any number of occasions and no harm came of it; you might argue that the twins' mother was morally obligated to try to save the life of their half brother; you might argue that a twelve-year-old boy deserves a chance at life even if somebody else's rights have to be violated just a little. But the fact is that one person cannot be forced to use his or her body to save another, no matter what.

At least not so far.

Jessica sighed. "The thing is, I don't want to kill the frog, but I don't really want to give up graduation and stuff for a frog, either. I'm stuck. I've got two choices, and they're both bad. Either I murder my frog, or I flunk my course." There was no gray area for Jessica at this point.

"Even if you kill the frog, Jess, it wouldn't be murder."

"Murder, kill. What's the difference? Isn't it wrong, all the same?"

" 'Wrong' is a value judgment. Lots of things that are wrong to some are not to others, and they're not against the law. It would be wrong, I think, to torture the frog, but it's not a crime. *Murder* is a loaded word. It makes things sound a lot worse than they are. You're putting a value judgment on your actions when you use such terms."

"A lot of people call abortion murder, don't they?"

*   *   *

Is abortion murder? All killing isn't murder. A cop shoots a teenager who "appeared to be going for a gun," and we call it "justifiable homicide"—a tragedy for all concerned, but not murder if the gun was there and the cop was acting in the line of duty. And then there's war. In theory, soldiers shoot only at each other. But in practice, lots and lots of other folks get killed. We drop bombs where there are noncombatants—women and children and old people—and when they die, we call it not murder but "collateral damage." Our soldiers get killed by "friendly fire"—often by people who aimed directly at them. Is that murder? All killing like that, to me, is morally wrong. But murder?

Calling abortion "murder" doesn't make it murder. We are hearing someone's value judgment placed on what others do.

"Take it one step further, Jess. You said you just read *Les Misérables* in school. Was Jean Valjean a thief when he stole bread to feed his starving children?"

"Well, he stole it, but he had to, didn't he?"

"When a hungry man kills in the act of taking food from someone who denies him, is that murder? Or self-defense?"

"I don't know. The guy wasn't coming at him with a knife or anything, but if he hadn't done it, he'd be dead just the same, you mean? I never thought about that. Self-defense, I guess, wasn't it?" I wondered if Jessica was now thinking about the novel in a new light.

Self-defense, then, isn't considered murder; in our culture, there is a right to kill in self-defense. There are people who try to make the case that abortion is a kind of self-defense: The woman is defending her health, her peace of mind, her way of life against an unwanted intruder. If a stranger tried to take these things away from her against her will, might she not be justified in exercising her right to self-defense? Legal tradition upholds that idea—the notion of abortion to save the life of the mother.

Of course, if the fetus has an absolute "right to life," as some would say, then even if the mother's life is at stake, the abortion should not be performed. Not ever. No exceptions. If that were true for me, I would never have done the first one.

But there are always exceptions. What about ectopic pregnancies? We destroy such pregnancies because they're not viable. An embryo that attaches itself outside the uterus can cause internal damage, bleeding, even the woman's death. Nowadays, with microsurgery, we can remove an embryo from a fallopian tube, saving the tube and possibly the woman's reproductive function. The alternative is waiting for rupture—a certainty in medicine. There are cases on record where hospitals, bound by religious convictions and not permitting abortion, also do not permit a gynecologist to remove an eccyesis until it has been ruptured—and is therefore no longer "alive."

In an era in which fertilized ova in a petri dish can be called "children" in a court of law, will ectopic pregnancies, too, have a "right to life"?

One fascinating dilemma in the abortion debate is the right to abortion in cases of rape or incest. If an embryo is a person and abortion is murder and no one has the constitutional right to kill another person, how can it be OK to kill only at certain times—as in rape or incest? Isn't killing always wrong? If, indeed, it is a killing? Is it murder sometimes and not murder at others?

It seems that people who say they're against abortion except in cases of rape or incest are basing their judgment on something other than whether or not abortion is killing. Clearly, their feelings about abortion have to do not with the "innocent life" of the embryo or fetus, but with the mother. The idea of forcing a woman or girl to carry the product of rape to term is repugnant to most people. Not to all, just most. When pressed, they'll say that they're against abortion for "birth control," but not in cases of rape or incest, because then the woman didn't "intend" to get pregnant—she was an "innocent victim." Rationalization to fit an accepted scheme? You tell me.

Presumably, then, at other times the woman isn't "innocent." It's a case, if you'll pardon the expression, of "She made her bed, now let her lie in it"—she "chose" to get pregnant, or at least to put herself at risk for pregnancy by having sex, playing what in the pre-pill days used to be called "Vatican roulette." The logical conclusion to that thought is ". . . which she *shouldn't have done* if she didn't want to get pregnant." She's been irresponsible. Now let's see that she pays for it. A lot of the arguments about abortion are really about controlling women's sexuality or just controlling women, period.

And as far as "using abortion for birth control" goes, it's a red herring. American women don't, and in our almost quarter-century of legalized abortion there are no signs that it is a factor. In some of the Eastern Bloc countries after World War II, where birth control was hard to come by, women had a dozen or more abortions. That's using abortion for birth control, and it hasn't happened here. We see women who are mostly responsible, who have maybe a thirty-minute lapse. Are we supposed to say to them, "The punishment for that is the next eighteen years of your life"? We see teenagers getting pregnant because they're naive, or because they can't get birth control at all. Why not? Because they "should" be abstinent.

Former Surgeon General C. Everett Koop summed it up: "We are at a very strange place in history where the people most opposed to abortions are also most opposed to the one thing that would stop them, which is contraceptive information."

"The fact is, Uncle Don," Jessica sighed, "I don't want to kill *anything*. OK. So the frog doesn't have rights. What about *my* rights? Don't I have any?"

Jessica was getting to the crux of the matter, just where I wanted her to go. What are rights? And who has them? Are the rights of an embryo the same as those of a mature woman? And if the unborn have rights, do they not also have the right not to be born if they will not be wanted and loved and healthy?

The idea that we might abort any fetus that doesn't meet some standard of "perfection" smacks distastefully of eugenics—who's going to set the standard? But Mary Calderone, a founder and long the head of SIECUS—the Sex Information and Education Council of the United States—has written that the unborn child has a right to be born free of disease or serious defect. Never mind the rights of parents not to bring a deformed or defective child into the world—Calderone says it is a violation of the rights of the child. The dilemmas seem endless.

Ron, an intense, athletic-looking young man, sat gripping his wife's hand. "I'm one of three children, and I'm the only survivor. Cystic fibrosis. My sister died when she was six. My brother lived to be twenty. I know that medical science is pushing the boundaries for CF, so kids live longer, but what a life! I lived my whole childhood under a cloud—I was seventeen when my brother died. The world in our house revolved around him—he was mean, nasty and vindictive, and he made sure that it did. I felt hated for being healthy when he wasn't. And the worse he got, the more bitter he was. My parents got the worst of it. He screamed at them that they should never have had him. He said that many times over. Once my sister died, he knew, we all did, that he was going to die too, without really ever getting to live. Can you imagine what all this did to my mother? She carried the gene—it was like it was her fault. My dad—he felt guilty too. He just withdrew, was never there. My mother could never make it to a school program or drive me to Little League. She'd promise, and try, but somehow my brother always needed her. Like I didn't need parents too. I was the healthy one, so I was supposed to look out for myself. I was really angry. And the guilt! I was jealous of somebody who was *dying*. I felt like a monster. I've made peace with my parents, sort of—I see now that they were doing the best they could—but it was an awful way to live. Abby understands how I feel. I want prenatal testing, everything. If there's an indication we'd have a CF child, we've agreed on abortion."

Paradoxically, the availability of abortion has made it possible for some couples who desperately want children and who carry severe genetic defects to have normal families.

Phyllis and Joel Blume came together to Phyllis's first appointment with me. That in itself was a little unusual—I don't often meet the husbands of my gynecological patients at our first encounter unless there's a specific reason, like a baby on the way. Phyllis wasn't pregnant, although, she explained, she was thinking about it.

She said she and Joel wanted to talk to me together, so I invited him in. They were a delightful couple—cultured, well-educated, sweet, and very loving with each other.

"We've always wanted children," Phyllis began. "Several. But I think you should know, our parents are from Eastern Europe, on both sides. So before we got married, we were tested for Tay-Sachs disease. I'm a carrier, and so is Joel. It didn't change our minds about getting married, and it hasn't really changed our minds about having a family. I'm going to be twenty-eight, and we want to get started."

Tay-Sachs is a death sentence. There is no cure, no treatment. Newborns who have it appear normal, but within a few months they begin to deteriorate, losing muscle tone and brain function until they die, usually by the age of three. I wanted to be sure the Blumes knew what could happen. They did.

We talked about the risk of undertaking a pregnancy given their genetic histories. It in no way deterred them. "We're sure," Joel said. "What are the chances—one in four? It doesn't seem right to deny ourselves a baby we want on the chance that it *might* have Tay-Sachs. The chances are better that it won't, right? We like to think we'll be lucky."

Statistical chance being what it is, that bothered me. Theoretically, each baby of parents who carry the gene has a one in four chance of being born with the disease. But that's averaged out over thousands of births. A given couple might have no Tay-Sachs babies—or they might have three out of three. I had to be sure the Blumes understood that, that they weren't being emotional about the facts.

I explained the availability of prenatal testing and, if the fetus proved to have the disease, the option of terminating the pregnancy.

Phyllis looked aghast. "Oh, no," she said. "We couldn't. I'm sure it will be all right." She looked at Joel. "It seems so calculating, so—heartless. We would love it, even if—" She stopped. I could see that the "if" was just starting to sink in— an unconscious baby, a baby who would never smile, or coo, or sit up, or recognize its mother. Who would soon die. "We've never known anyone who—" she began.

"Our families—" Joel said. They stared at each other helplessly.

I knew we would have some counseling to do.

Phyllis became pregnant, right on schedule. She and Joel started out saying that they would take their chances, and if the baby was born with Tay-Sachs, they would love it just the same. But as the pregnancy became a reality to them, they began to understand that the trauma of bearing a child only to watch it die would be devastating to their lives and their hopes for a family.

"These tests," Joel said, "they're foolproof? Abortion—I can see how it might be the only rational choice, but it goes against the grain. Against everything I've ever believed. As terrible as it would be to have a Tay-Sachs baby, it would almost be worse to do away with it and find out that it might have been perfect after all—our child. I don't think I could bear that. I know Phyllis couldn't. We have to be certain."

Certain. As if there were any certainties in medicine. Tay-Sachs is pretty well understood, as these things go. There's a lot of literature. But genetics is still a very esoteric science; geneticists rely mostly on statistics, not clinical facts. I consulted experts in New York and all over the country, one of whom had case information from around the world, especially Eastern Europe. Finally Phyllis and Joel were assured enough to have the necessary test done.

I had to tell Phyllis that the news was bad. She and Joel chose termination.

Less than a year later, she was pregnant again. This time, the news was good. In due course, I was able to hand Joel and Phyllis a normal, healthy son. "We did the right thing," Joel said. "I wasn't sure, you know. But to have started out in grief instead of this—that would have been wrong. What joy!"

Today the couple has three healthy, growing children.

It's difficult for all concerned to terminate a wanted pregnancy because the fetus is doomed, even when the ultimate outcome is a happy one. As yet, though, we have little else to offer parents who carry a bad gene. Ironically, one of the therapies that shows the greatest promise for curing Tay-Sachs and other deadly genetic diseases is fetal-tissue research. With fetal-tissue transplants, those wanted pregnancies, anyway, might be saved. But the antichoice forces have lobbied against the medical use of fetal tissue, because "the thought that some good might come out of an abortion might encourage some woman to have one." And, of course, there's always their position that the "taking of life" cannot be justified by the possibility of salvaging another. Dilemma after dilemma after dilemma.

Fetal tissue, which holds the possibility of cure or at least treatment for diseases like Alzheimer's and Parkinson's as well, is simply discarded. Because of a government ban, medical researchers haven't been permitted to use it. Obviously, forces are at work to loosen those bans. To someone caught in the situation of the Blumes and to many other couples who choose abortion because their fetus is too damaged to live, that sounds more like "pro dead fetus" than it does like "pro-life."

*   *   *

"Doesn't it bother you, doing abortions?" Jessica asked.

"If it bothered me, in the way you mean, I wouldn't do it. Nature provides for more fertilized eggs than can ever grow to be adults. A lot of them are lost naturally—they don't become implanted or the woman miscarries. Every pregnancy is different, every one comes out of special, individual circumstances, and when a woman tells me she doesn't want to be pregnant, I believe her. So I can do it. She has the right to decide."

It's been argued that women should be compelled to carry pregnancies to term *because* each pregnant woman can be considered not one person but two. And surely the fetus, as a person, has the same right not to be aborted as any other person has not to be killed.

Arguably, granting that the fetus is a person, we might ask the question, "Does it have the right to compel another person, its mother, to do something she feels is strongly not in her own best interests, or the interests of her family and marriage or is perhaps even detrimental to her health?" In other words, are the rights of the fetus *greater than* the rights of the mother? A dilemma.

As a rule, no one's rights are automatically greater than anyone else's. Children, though, don't have the same rights as adults, and certainly not the rights to compel their parents to do much of anything. The courts may compel an adult to do something "in the best interests" of the child, of course, but generally adults are left to decide for themselves what the best interests of their children are.

Minor children aren't legally allowed to do a lot of things. Drive cars, sign contracts and so on. The law recognizes that they're not mature enough. But that same law is trying to say that if a teenage girl gets pregnant, she ought to go ahead and be a mother. If she's not mature enough to put a coat on layaway, is she mature enough to have a child? It's worth pondering. A dilemma.

In a democratic society, it's always been deemed best to let people make their own decisions about family matters and reproduction, and to keep government out of it. Controlling a woman's reproductive function in one way—forcing her to continue a pregnancy she doesn't want—isn't really very different from controlling it in another, say, forcing her to have an abortion she doesn't want. Either way, it's a question of who has control—the woman or the government.

"You're really talking about having a choice, aren't you?" Jessica asked. "It's my frog, and I don't want to kill it. I don't want to be forced to do something I don't want to do. And I'm glad they can't make me—because they can't, can they? If I'm willing to take the consequences, I can do what I want."

"As far as your frog goes, yes. As long as you understand what you're doing."

"I know. It's my class, my grade and my frog. It's up to me to decide what to do. I really don't want to kill the frog. But . . ."

I turned to Jessica and wanted to pick her brain, now that she had gotten mine churning away.

"Jess, what about your classmates? Do you think ill of them because they want to experiment and haven't even considered the consequences to their frogs?"

"Well, gosh, it would be better if there were more of us protesting, wouldn't it? We could make more noise. I did try to convince my friend Martha to refuse to kill her frog. Yeah, maybe I was kinda strong about it." She grimaced. "I called her a 'frog killer' and stuff. And said she had no respect for life. Come to think of it, she's still a little mad."

I was going in the direction I wanted.

"Jess, dear, was that right of you? Weren't you trying to force your morals and ethics, your thinking, onto Martha? Did she deserve any name-calling at all? You just used words. But suppose you felt even stronger. Would you have taken Martha's frog away from her—even forced her bodily away from her frog?

What about your other classmates? Should they be allowed to kill their frogs?"

"I did think of setting all the frogs free. Maybe taking them down to the pond. Just to show people I meant it."

"Why didn't you?"

"Well, there's this guy in my class who's a real science nerd, you know—" ·

"Like your uncle."

"Worse. And he's got a chance at a big science prize, and scholarships and stuff, and I could have messed that up. He's a nerd, but even so—"

"But if you really meant it, as you say, why not grab all the frogs and lock the door to the biology lab? Would you be justified in defending the frog tank with a baseball bat, or spilling catsup on your teacher's car to simulate frog's blood? Would you chain yourself to the frog tank so nobody could get to a frog?"

"Hey, wait a minute. I'm talking about me—my frog. No one else's. They have rights too, don't they?"

I was never prouder of my niece.

I thought of that Thanksgiving Day session with Jessica years later when I saw a clever bumper sticker on a station wagon driven by a mother with her five children, a bumper sticker that said it all for me—"Against Abortion? Don't have one."

"I don't know how this is going to help make your decision. Do you?" I asked my niece.

Jessica grinned. "No, I don't know either, Uncle Don, but I'll let you know when I figure it out. I see what you're saying. The most important thing is that I have a choice. I don't have to do what they say, but they don't have to go along with me either. I'm awfully glad I don't have to make a choice about having a baby—that must be an awful bummer. But if I were up against it, I'd sure want to be the one to make the choice. Thanks for taking the time to talk to me."

The call from the dining room said it was time for dessert,

and Jessica's thoughts reverted to more basic needs—she had a sweet tooth to satisfy. She gave me a quick hug and was off.

I sat there for a minute or two after she left. For Jessica and her frog, I had arguments and answers. But there are always more questions. More dilemmas.

6 The Lessons of Darlene Bennett

An earlier-than-usual adjournment of a hospital staff meeting had left me time for a little socializing one evening with an old friend at Burt's, a coffee shop not too far from the hospital, a favorite spot and a welcome change from the institutional food hospitals are famous for. I didn't expect to see anyone else I knew there, but although I was absorbed in my conversation, I couldn't help being aware that a woman at another table kept glancing in my direction.

Doctors with practices in major urban centers—the big towns of America—don't often run into their patients in local pubs, downtown movie houses or big-city department stores on a Saturday afternoon. On those rare occasions when it happens, it's quite a surprise. And then you have to be careful that you don't embarrass yourself—and risk an insult—by not recognizing the patient.

After all, we usually see a patient for a relatively short period of time in an office context. Perhaps she's pregnant—pregnancy applies a special painter's brush to a woman's complexion and her outward appearance. Or she is in the nude, or wearing an office smock. In any case, you're not focusing on her face. Seeing her later on in street wear—maybe even togged out in dressy attire—you get startled and say, Now I know that woman from somewhere. But who is it? You think up all kinds of tricks to get her to mention her name so that you can half pretend you knew immediately who she was.

Then there are those patients—believe me, doctors are only human and some patients are more memorable than others despite what the brochures say—for whom you have instant recall. That's not necessarily because they're younger or prettier or something like that—although it might be. As often it's the opposite—there's been some unpleasantness, some negative aspect to their treatment history.

As I dropped a tip on the table and stood up to leave, I took a good look at the woman across the room. She was definitely familiar—one of my patients for sure. Someone I hadn't seen for a long time. Dorothy? Delores? No—Darlene. The name flashed up in my brain like a neon sign. That was it. Darlene Bennett.

She met my eyes and smiled a little uncertainly, as if she were expecting a brush-off. I went over to her. "Hi—it's me, Dr. Sloan. Darlene, isn't it?" It was more likely that she'd remember me—her gynecologist—than that I would remember her, but she couldn't have been expecting to see me in civvies either. I was giving her an out, just in case.

She stood up. "I thought it was you, but I didn't think you'd remember me," she said. Her voice held an apologetic note.

I was genuinely glad to see her. But even as we greeted each other, with a gentle hug and kisses in the air near our right cheeks, I realized that this was not the Darlene Bennett I used to know.

She had gained weight, maybe twenty-five pounds, and in all the wrong places. Her too-tight skirt spanned her hips in wrinkles, and she'd pinned her blouse closed where it strained across her chest—a good thing, because the button had popped open. Her hair hadn't seen a hairdresser or a colorist in months. Her nail polish was chipped, her fingernails uneven.

Neatness had been one of her trademarks. My first thought was that she had just become complacent, let herself go, but even as I thought it, I felt puzzled—it seemed unlike her. No, it was more than that. It was the look in her eyes, the way she carried herself, the way she walked, the tone in her voice. Almost everything about her was different.

At first, I couldn't recall that many exact details about her. After all, it had been a while, and heaven knew how many patients had passed before me in the interval. But there are certain times, we've all had them, when your sixth sense kicks in about something. I had that ESP feeling when Darlene came back into my life after those five, maybe six years, a feeling that what was about to happen was going to be significant. It was not going to be just a casual, fake nicety, a polite hello and goodbye, or even "Where have you been, and why haven't you been in for your checkups, and what did I do wrong—did I charge too much, or did the office staff act snippy one day?"—things like that. That wasn't going to happen here. I just knew it.

As it turned out, I could have sold my sixth sense to a circus for an evening performance. I would have been putting on a good ESP show for the crowd.

What was it about Darlene Bennett? I let my memory run back through time.

The attractive young woman sitting across from me consulted the list of questions on her lap, like crib notes during a college exam. She smiled and kept apologizing for using them. "I don't want to forget anything, so I wrote it all down," she said. "How do you feel about prescribing birth control for someone who isn't married?" She had already dropped a few hints about wanting to know my opinion of premarital sex. I wondered if masturbation was on the list somewhere, but she'd decided not to ask. This was the Darlene Bennett of a half-decade earlier.

The sexual revolution was in full swing, but attitudes hadn't quite caught up to it yet. I could follow her reasoning: "Nice" girls were supposed to "save something for marriage"—or at least wait until marriage was a dead certainty—and conservative old fogies, like doctors, might still think that. Doctors are authority figures, and although in one way patients want to be told what to do, in another they're often a little worried that they're going to get a lecture on morals or behavior. Or maybe not a lecture but subtle distaste or obvious disapproval. Say, if they come in with a sexually transmitted disease or an out-of-wedlock pregnancy.

When you realize that some currently used and very authoritative gynecologic textbooks—our "bibles"—still speak of a woman's "letting her sexual needs be dictated by her husband's" as the norm, it's no wonder that we still have a generation of practitioners who exert their own morals and ethics on patients. And that sometimes consists of reverting to the days before this revolution took hold. But then again, everything's relative. I guess every generation thinks that they've invented sex. Maybe it's an ongoing thing—it began in the Garden of Eden and never stopped.

In answer to her question, I said I prescribed birth control for anyone who wanted it.

She looked me straight in the eye as she asked each question and continued to watch my face as I answered. With each answer, she gave a little nod, and then went back to her list.

I wasn't Darlene Bennett's first gynecologist, but I was the first one she had chosen for herself. Just twenty-one, she was interviewing me seriously, with perhaps just a hint of flirtatiousness. I was rather enjoying the process. She was so earnest, so healthy and wholesome and fresh-looking, that I felt flattered rather than annoyed that she was taking up so much of my time. She was a spring breeze on a wintry day that had brought me a lot of complaints and a few real problems—and promised, from the look of the other patients in my waiting room, more of the same. All in a day's work, but this was a pleasant diversion.

Newly engaged, Darlene was officially putting aside her teenage visits to her mother's "woman's doctor" and taking on the responsibilities of adulthood. If I passed muster, I would become her GYN.

There have been some times when I've resented being on probation, waiting for a patient's approval. I think my feeling came from the way it was done, rather than from its being done at all. In theory I'm for it—why shouldn't a patient have the right to test out the best doctor for her? She does the same with a dentist or a beautician. Anyhow, I wasn't put off by Darlene.

She was the kind of young woman who only a few years before must have been named "most popular" in her high school yearbook. She had an easy, cheerful confidence, and she gave the impression of knowing what she wanted and how to get it. Her smile alone must have won many a battle for her. I'm sure she was the prom queen, although I never asked. I could tell that she liked her body: She was seductive, in a quiet sort of way. She liked coming on to me, just a little, but she knew where to draw the line. Her flirting never got out of hand. I don't suppose she was even aware of doing it. Indeed, I am sure she wasn't.

After I passed her inspection, Darlene folded her list crisply and put it back in her purse. She had a look of decision in her eye. "Good," she said. "That's it, then. I really would like you to be my doctor. I'm sure we'll get along just fine." She reached across my desk to shake my hand. I had just been hired.

From her first visit on, Darlene came in looking trim and attractive. Her clothes were fashionable, and she was perfectly groomed. Her hair color changed a bit almost every time I saw her, but that day she was a golden blonde, a few shades lighter than her natural brown. She liked herself as a blonde, or her fiancé, Frank, did. I know I liked it. Golden seemed to suit her.

She came to me over the next year or two for checkups or minor ailments, infrequently, as most healthy young people do. Darlene never had anything more serious than a minor vaginal itch or discomfort—the gynecological equivalent of the common cold. My one concern was that we were never able to solve her birth-control needs to her satisfaction.

"I tried the Pill," she said. "It made me fat. I swelled up like a blimp. Really." That could have translated into three pounds of weight to Darlene. She took such matters seriously. "And I was always worrying that I'd forget to take it. And then I've been reading that sometimes it can affect your fertility after you stop taking it. It's not for me. There must be something else."

With each successive visit, we ran down the list of available methods.

"The diaphragm? OK, I guess. To be honest, I'm just not using it much. Frank doesn't like it when he gets started and then has to wait while I get up—oh, yeah, I know I could put it in every night just in case, but it's so messy and such a nuisance. If I use it every night I have to deal with it in the morning when we're rushing around to get off to work. And it's really not all that comfortable, you know?" She curled up her lip as if she had just tasted something slightly rancid.

"An IUD? I've got a friend who has one of those, and she gets such horrible cramps—she says it's worth it not to get pregnant, but I don't know. I guess I don't like the idea of having a thing like that inside me. It sounds awful." More lip curling.

"Well, we use condoms sometimes, if I really insist. But Frank hates condoms. He says they bother him, the way they feel. And you have to admit they are funny looking. I can understand that he might not like to wear them. And then it seems like we can never find them when we're in a hurry. Sometimes we lose interest while he pulls things out of the drawer looking for one. I remember once I found an old watch in the scramble that I thought I'd lost. So I got turned off while he was hunting around, but it wasn't a total loss—the darn thing still kept perfect time."

Her excuses seemed to come from indecision. Every discussion ended the same way: "But we're being careful," she would assure me. And for a while things went along just fine.

It was a few months later that I noticed Darlene's name on my patient roster. Not her time for a routine checkup, I thought;

I wonder what's up. It happens frequently that I lose sight of time and who's due to come in when. I'll see someone after a year or even two and say, "How come you're here so soon? Problem?" Or a patient will come in after a few weeks or months—before I should expect her—and I'll think, Where has she been all this time? So I didn't make too much of it.

A few patients later, Darlene sailed into my office.

She started in with no preamble. "I think I might be pregnant," she said. "I'm only about a week late, but I feel different. Can you tell?"

Given her birth-control history, it seemed like a good bet. I thought she was probably right, but we did the necessary tests, just to be sure. Instant pregnancy tests were not yet on the market, so it was not until the following Monday that I called her to confirm what she suspected.

"Can I come in and talk to you?" she asked. "The sooner the better." We scheduled an appointment for that very week.

It's not unusual for a woman to want to meet right away with her obstetrician—I assumed I was about to take on that role—when she's pregnant for the first time. She'll have a thousand questions, part of that normal anxiety of pregnancy. "Will the glass of sherry I had at Aunt Helen's eightieth birthday bash last Saturday hurt the baby?" "Can I smoke?" "Can I take aspirin?" "Can I take baths, ride my bicycle, eat fish, sleep with my husband?" But somehow—maybe it was something in her voice—I had a hunch it was going to be more than that with Darlene. And I was right.

"I'll be up-front with you, Dr. Sloan. I don't think I want a baby right now. I'm thinking about an abortion," she told me.

"All right, if you're sure. You are, aren't you?"

"I'm not ready for a baby," she said. "I feel like I just got married! I really don't want a baby—well, someday, but not now. I'm too young to be tied down with a kid. So's Frank. We're just getting started, finally saving a little, and everything. It just wouldn't work. Can we get it done today? Tomorrow?"

"Sure, Darlene. How about yesterday?" My attempts at

humor didn't raise a smile. It seemed as if there were none in her.

"Look, it's not as if I'd never considered the possibility that I might get pregnant. Of course I have. And I've always figured this is what I'd do if I wasn't ready. Or Frank wasn't. Dr. Sloan, you don't know Frank. He puts a big priority on being free and spontaneous. A couple of weekends ago he woke me up about four o'clock in the morning and told me to get dressed. He'd already made sandwiches and coffee and packed a hamper and put it in the car—he was all ready. We drove out to the beach and watched the sun come up and ate our breakfast and then came home and spent the afternoon in bed." She smiled at the memory. "That's not the kind of thing you can do if you've got a kid. We're having fun together and we're just not ready to give that up, believe me. Besides, we're saving for a house. It would be good to have the house before the baby, instead of the other way around. The baby would make it harder to save, I know it. Just put us farther from our goal.

"Of course," she continued, "having an abortion isn't such a wonderful thing to be doing, but neither is having a baby we didn't plan on. That's why we were taking precautions—so we wouldn't have one. Just because we goofed up one time, I don't see why we should have to start a family we don't really want right now. That's all."

She seemed thoughtful and serious. As I watched her reflect on her words, my left hand was pushing the intercom to get my secretary to start putting the wheels in motion for scheduling Darlene's surgery. My right hand was marking the chart to reflect Darlene's request for termination. My brain was starting to form the words that would help her understand the procedure, remind her not to eat or drink anything past midnight the night before because she would be having general anesthesia, and let her know that if she was going to be alone, she should plan on public transportation, as I didn't want her driving for several hours, until the anesthetic wore off completely.

She nodded to all of my words and I was relieved that to a person like Darlene, I didn't have to say things twice.

"Let's just get this over with—please," she said.

My office staff scheduled the procedure for the following Saturday, along with several others. This was Wednesday, and Darlene agreed to wait the few days to allow for my schedule and to take advantage of the weekend to rest up afterward. Everything went smoothly—without a hitch in the action. Darlene Bennett got there at nine in the morning and she was home just after noon. I didn't know how she got home. I did not see her after she was wheeled out of the OR to the recovery area— did not see her, in fact, until five years later in Burt's coffee shop.

She didn't miss a beat at work or at play; by Monday morning she was back to her routine. Darlene remembered to call me in two weeks as the first part of her follow-up. That she missed her six-week checkup never hit me until that coffee-shop meeting— nor her missing her semiannuals over the next five years. I guess she was still "being very careful."

I studied the Darlene Bennett who was standing in front of me. Under Burt's harsh fluorescent light, she looked a lot older—or maybe just tired. "Do you have a few minutes? I'd like to catch up with what you're doing," I said. She seemed pleased that I'd asked, although she didn't rush into the conversation.

We sat down and ordered her some coffee. Darlene gave me a rueful smile and gestured to her body. "Look what I've done to myself," she said. "I guess you noticed I let things go a little."

I waited for her to go on.

"Did anyone tell you about me?" she asked. I assumed she meant some of the patients she had referred. I shook my head in a definite "no" and mumbled something about making it a point not to mention one patient to another. Of course, another patient could have volunteered the information. The answer was still no. She had dropped out of sight, it seemed.

"Frank and I are Splitsville—divorced. It happened pretty fast after I had the abortion. Things got a little mixed up and then they were just never the same. He just couldn't handle it, I guess. I don't even know exactly. But I think I blew it. I never told you. I didn't want to. I guess that's why I never came back. It was just too—" She sighed and shrugged.

I know this happens. It's happened to the best of us and to the worst of us. Women can't face their doctors for a lot of reasons, so they go somewhere else. I'd seen it before from the other side—women who came to me for abortions, women who had obviously had gynecological care before, good care, and whom I'd never see again. They wanted an anonymous doctor, a stranger, to do the procedure. Maybe it was hubris, but I'd always believed my patients would come to me with anything. That was the ego of a fledgling practitioner speaking. When you wised up, you learned you were human too, and couldn't be everything to everyone. When I looked back, I wondered who'd want to be.

"What happened?" I asked Darlene.

In the next hour—which felt like an eternity—she poured out the story of the previous five years. I was more than surprised—I was dumbfounded.

"With the Bennetts," Darlene said, "it was babies, babies—right away. I felt like Frank's mother was checking up on me all the time to see if I was pregnant yet. And putting pressure on Frank. Like he wasn't a real man if he didn't get me pregnant on our honeymoon. Like his brother—his kid brother, no less—had a baby in nine months, I think. Close to it. I told him I wanted us just to be together first, and he liked that—I thought he did. But his mother—"

She paused, and then plunged on. "And he didn't want me to use birth control—anything. He said it put something between us, and it wasn't the same for him. The diaphragm? He said he could feel it sometimes and he wanted me to take it out. I never got him to explain it to me. As yappity as he was at dinner and in the car, that's how quiet he was in the sack. A real silent lover. We winged it for a while, but—we couldn't always stop. Anyway, I thought if I had the abortion right away, it would be just the same as not being pregnant at all." Darlene looked down and stared into her empty coffee cup. She shook her head at the offer of a refill.

Why, oh why, I asked myself, hadn't I thought of bringing this all out five years ago? I had looked at Darlene as a mature woman, and in so many ways she was—her career, her marriage, her attitude in general. I had known her long enough, I thought, and I believed I knew her well. I'd just assumed she knew and understood the feelings of her husband and his family, and that if she was asking for the abortion, she must have worked it out. The other side of the coin was that she had indeed known what she was doing and had never shared it with me. That made me feel even worse.

That wasn't all. It was as if, having finally been given permission to talk about the abortion, she couldn't stop. "When I told Frank I was going to have an abortion, he was really upset," she continued. "He wouldn't even talk to me. And then his mother found out, and you would have thought I was the devil. If I was in the same room, she'd just stare at me, or she'd turn her back and stare out the window and cry. And then Frank yelled at *me*, 'What did you have to do it for?' Never 'I'm sorry,' or 'I know this was hard for you,' or even 'How do you feel?' He just—wasn't there."

"Was he at the center that day? I don't remember."

"Well, his body was. He knew I couldn't drive and he was afraid I'd do something stupid. Yeah, he drove me home. In silence. He was my driver, that's all. A regular cabbie."

On any issue, it would be rough to be on the receiving end of this kind of rejection, I thought. But on abortion—devastating. For to some degree, every abortion decision is emotionally painful.

Women learn to nurture as they cuddle their dolls, and most girls grow up expecting to be fulfilled as mothers. Some do it through children, some through nieces and nephews, some through pets. Some, I know, do it through their partners—a big mistake.

Darlene was no exception. She wanted to be a real mother. She just didn't want to feel coerced into motherhood, to be a mother because someone else thought she should be. A little less pressure, a little more patience, and she might have welcomed the pregnancy. A little sympathy, a little support, and she might have weathered the conflicts of the abortion.

As she described it, I felt Frank's betrayal as if it had happened to me as well as to Darlene, but at the same time I found myself feeling something for him too. He had certainly had a right to be involved in making a decision about his wife's pregnancy, and that had been taken away from him—he must have felt it as sharply as a flagrant slap in the face.

The conflict between his family's beliefs and his wife's action had pulled him two ways. He reacted with anger, berating Darlene. The marriage crumbled. In spite of their religious beliefs and their professed commitment to each other, they became increasingly distant; then they separated and finally divorced.

Now, at twenty-nine, Darlene was struggling to finish school and make her own way without Frank or any other man in her life.

"I've gone over and over it in my head," she said. "When I got pregnant, I felt that I was between a rock and a stone wall. I really didn't want to have a baby just because my in-laws thought I should. If I had gone ahead, it would have been for all the wrong reasons. I think I would have been mad at them for the rest of my life if they'd pushed me into it. I didn't feel like I had any choice." Darlene had been caught in a dilemma.

I murmured something that was supposed to be comforting. I hoped it was, anyway.

Darlene went on. "As bad as things are, as bad as they've been, I'd have to do it again. I think I would—I know I would. I couldn't have had that kid."

Somehow, hearing that made it worse. There wasn't anything more to say, except our polite goodbyes and good lucks. We shook hands and Darlene walked away.

I threw another buck on the table to cover the coffee tab and tip and headed out the door. Ill feelings, as yet undefined, started welling up from my toes, clutched at my knees and

stomach and finally hit my brain. I stood there at the curbside
for a moment, feeling sick with failure. I had left her to face the
wrath of her husband and his family—her family then—and
never thought of it. I'd let her make the choice totally on her
own, and the choice she made was a bummer. It was rational, I
thought, intelligent, I thought, carefully reasoned—I thought.
Those were my thoughts. But it failed to take into account the
raw emotions that abortion can stir up, not only in the woman
having the abortion, but in the people around her. And by
failing to anticipate that, I had left her exposed. It was a
bummer, all right—but what was the alternative?

After that evening I had to wonder just how many other
Darlene Bennetts I had treated in good faith. It had seemed right
at the time. Wasn't it? I realized that Darlene Bennett was not
unique; she couldn't be. I must have performed abortions on
who knows how many like her, and never known. Couldn't
have. Maybe I didn't want to know.

A while back, I read about a psychiatrist who discovered that
one of his patients, one he had dismissed as "cured," had—
years later, and after a string of misfortunes—committed suicide. He went back to her file, looking for the ways he could
have missed the signals. He concluded that he had made mistakes, as anyone might, but that on the whole, the emotions are
such a fragile thing that no one could have predicted the tragedy.
Yet he felt failure.

It clouded his entire career. He wrote about all the proud
and triumphant moments he'd boasted of to his colleagues and
congratulated himself on, about the success of his treatments,
the wonder of psychotherapy and the marvel of taking disturbed
patients and guiding them toward emotional health and stabil-
ity. In the bright glare of hindsight, it vanished like a mirage.
He decried the mockery of it all.

Like that psychiatrist, I felt failure. Darlene's case reawakened
the gnawing feeling that we are sending women out without the
necessary supports. It was a big serving of humble pie.

*   *   *

Something has happened to our practices these past twenty years since the Supreme Court gave us Roe and Doe—*Roe v. Wade,* the landmark case that established the right to abortion, and the class-action suit that closely followed it, *Doe v. Bolton,* which set the parameters and threshold of viability. I guess there's good news and bad news. The good news is that we have legal abortion, a safe way for a woman to resolve an untenable situation, and she doesn't have to go through the inquisition to do it—just a certain perfunctory and rather routine counseling session to make sure there are no medical contraindications to what we are doing and to inform her of how we do it. That's the way the law has seen it—as a health concern—and the way most abortion statutes have been written: as the right of a woman to demand the health care she is entitled to as an American citizen.

Then there is the bad news. The question arises, are we taking this thing too casually? Are we being so cavalier about it as to make a mockery of the institution of marriage and the creation and birth process? We spend more time taking out a patient's splinter or doing a Pap smear than we do over abortion, it seems.

There are abortion mills around—good ones, to be sure, but mills nonetheless. I guess that was bound to happen. The abortion centers have sprung up, you might say, because we need them. Our hospitals couldn't handle the load, not even with their outpatient surgical units. And in hospitals, regulations and rules are all-encompassing and onerous. So we have these centers where patients are counseled, but don't make the mistake of thinking it's a thorough job. The counseling is less than might be desirable at times.

But on the other hand, where is the time to devote and the energy to expend going to come from, to allocate "enough" to each and every here-today-gone-tomorrow patient? For someone performing abortions, the volume can be so great it's overwhelming. I've sent out tens and tens of thousands of women, and I know so little about so many of them—most of them. How could I? In a sense, the doctor is only a tradesperson,

a technician performing a task, like any other. To make more
of it would require a glorification of the medical profession that
I'm not willing to subscribe to.

But how about the private patient?

There are many times—frequently, in fact, and to this very
day—when I will get a referral to do an abortion on a woman
I've never seen, will see only for those fleeting minutes of the
termination, and then never see again. That scenario isn't
peculiar to me—it goes with the territory. That is the way it has
to be, and that's bad news, because if we really believe à la Roy
Parker, that every woman has the right to an abortion and a
person she trusts to do it, then we don't give ourselves a whole
lot of time to earn that trust. We may indeed be kidding
ourselves on that one. But all we can do is our best, and wing it
from there.

I keep going back to the insight and determination of Roy
Parker, who insisted that in abortion, the counseling skill was
as important as the surgical skill. The beauty of the service he
provided wasn't just clean, affordable abortion—anybody
could have done that. Many did. It was that he found a way to
make each patient feel she was special, to leave her with the
sense that she had made a wise, reasoned-out decision, and was
doing the best possible thing in her particular set of circumstances.

That's important. We all came to appreciate Roy's insistence
on counseling, and we took it with us back into our private
practices. One of the tenets is, beware the patient who's too
matter-of-fact about her abortion. First, it's a major life decision—there are those feelings of anxiety and ambivalence in
any pregnancy. Second, even though it's statistically safer than
childbirth, it's a threatening procedure. Anyone who discounts
those factors is either immature or so unrealistic as to border
on the neurotic.

Is all this falling into yet another self-serving and self-satisfy-
ing trap? How was I, how can I be, so sure that the host of
women who ran through the almost literal maze of reception,
cashier, counseling session, surgery and postabortal review at

the Women's Center were really in touch with what they were doing? How many of those women were trapped in the dilemma of their moment, went through their own soul searches, ran to our arms and suction machines, and were greeted by people— me included—who were so involved in our own purposes that we never saw them in a true light? Were they given the best? Or our version of the best?

My experience with Darlene let in a flood of insecurities. That wasn't all bad; it led me to reevaluate what I was doing. I had always believed in the woman's right to choose. There was very little I could do to make myself feel more secure about abortion. Anyway, I wasn't the one who had to be secure. It was the women. And they weren't. That was Darlene's first lesson. Abortion tore at all of them—in a special way, because it is a special thing.

Darlene had made her decision purely on reason and intellect—she was too young, too newlywed, just "not ready." I imagine she went through all the motions. And I took Darlene at face value. To be a master detective, to question too aggressively, can cloud the doctor-patient relationship. The authoritarian position of the physician can sometimes be misinterpreted by the patient, to the point of disservice. And remember, I knew Darlene. How about those I meet for the first time?

Darlene had surely suffered. But for every Darlene Bennett, there are many others who never have a serious moment of regret—they've done what they had to do. Every abortion decision grows out of a problem, each one has a different angle, a different hook. And the decision to go the other way could be just as disastrous, only then there would be an unwanted, maybe resented, child in the picture. Makes sense when you say it. The trick is to make sense out of it when you live it.

Most studies find very little emotional backlash; many suggest that after an abortion the majority of women take hold of their lives and move toward accomplishing a goal. For them, abortion seems to provide feelings of independence and empowerment. Darlene Bennett, on the other hand, seemed to have lost her sense of power and independence. She was mired in regret.

Abortion was clearly at the center of her problems, but it was not the abortion itself Darlene regretted. It was, rather, the loss of her husband, the loss of her marriage. Her depression, which is what she was in, was as much a result of the consequences of her action as of the action itself. She took one horn of the dilemma. We would never know what the other one would have led to.

If I had known more, I might have anticipated her reactions. It seems that the women for whom abortion is a bad experience are those who receive the least support from their partners, friends and families. Research backs this up as well. Studies suggest that expected or real disapproval by the important people in a woman's life significantly increases her sorrow and regret.

Certainly one of the things that made abortion so difficult for women in the days before legalization was the guilt that accompanied doing something frankly illegal and often painful, something that sometimes took place in unclean surroundings, something that had to be carried out in secret and kept quiet thereafter. Even now, many women travel to another town or state for care, so their neighbors won't find out what they're doing. Abortion is open and legal now, but to many people—the Bennetts included—that does not make it right.

The anger of her in-laws, the abandonment by her husband—both these things happened to Darlene, crushing her under their weight. Still, she insisted she would do it again. Was that denial? Or did her husband's response to her decision reveal a side of him that made her feel the marriage was doomed anyhow? And what about Frank? I had known him only through Darlene. He became more real to me, a young husband who could not live with his wife's decision about her own body. I guess I had failed him too.

That meeting with Darlene Bennett gave me a healthy dose of humility and a lesson on the evils of complacency—an excellent antidote to some of the ego-driven overconfidence that fuels the medical psyche. It was a stark reminder that if it's done often enough, even a life-or-death procedure can become routine. I was always careful in the operating room; I needed to be equally careful in the counseling room.

Darlene Bennett taught me many lessons. From her, I learned that I have a responsibility to counsel women who come to me for abortion, to be sure they will have the support they need when they leave my office—not to assume it. Even then, some will slip through the cracks. Darlene's story didn't change my commitment to having women make their own choices, but it reminded me that the right to choose includes the need to cry, to regret, to wonder what might have been.

I still think of Darlene. I believe that there is a little bit of her in every abortion patient, and I try to use what I learned to make the way I practice my profession more honest and intuitive. I imagine that I've never done an abortion since that chance meeting with Darlene Bennett without her face coming into view. I hope I never do.

7 From Beginning to End: The Abortion Itself

"Yes, you are definitely pregnant," I said. It's news that can send somebody into raptures of delight or throes of despair.

Patient Ellen Stalisi sat in front of me in my consultation room. A married woman in her early thirties, she might have been plain except for her animation and for her luminous dark eyes, surrounded by an exceptional fringe of black lashes. She had been to me a few times before, for routine checkups, but not that regularly. I hadn't seen her for a while. Ellen treated me as I did my dentist: She waited out minor aches and pains just as I did early toothaches.

Usually she brought along one or both of her children, a boy and a girl, about four and eight. Kids can create havoc in a doctor's waiting room, but Ellen's knew when she meant business—a sharp note in her voice said, "Settle down, and fast," and they did. She struck me as being a cheerful, no-nonsense person. And that was about all I knew of her. Not a whole lot.

She nodded. "I was afraid of that," she said. She fiddled with her purse strap and looked over my head at nothing in particular. "It's not a good time." She gave me a wry smile. "I'll have to think how we'll manage. It's going to be tough."

"In what way?"

She took a deep breath and let it out slowly. "Oh, just about every way. Tony's out of work for six months now. He just picks up whatever he can, piecemeal. I've been working a little part-time down at the mall to help out, and we live upstairs from my in-laws in a house they own, so we don't have a real bad rent problem—they understand. But we've only got two bedrooms, tiny, and it's already not good that the kids are in one. Nicky wants his own room. He's getting too big to share with his little sister."

She looked at me for a sign of approval, and I nodded. She went on. "Before Tony got laid off, we were hoping to get our own place, but no more. So far we're not too deep in debt, with the help we've been getting, and my job, and what we had saved—but that's running out." She shrugged. "It's just a bad time, that's all. We'll get through it. But this will definitely make it harder. Definitely."

She stood up. "I just have to think," she said again. Then she looked me in the eye. "Suppose I wanted an abortion."

"If you think that's what you want, we can talk about it."

"Would you do it?"

"If that's what you want. But remember, Ellen, it's not always the right way out. Sometimes the shot in the arm is done in haste, and you end up with many regrets. What seems like a solution only adds to the problem. It's not something to rush into. Right now, I suggest you go home, talk things over with your husband, maybe your pastor. Then call me, and we can get together if you want to talk things out. Anything at all. You have some time. Not a lot, though—let me hear from you in a couple of days."

Out of legislative committees' discussions of abortion have come some sensible controls, not over the decision-making process between doctor and patient, but with regard to medical prudence. With abortion written into state medical codes, abortion clinics are subject to the kinds of regulations that govern any other medical facility. Because it's an elective procedure, one of the conditions for licensure is that the patient be provided with facts that can lead to her informed consent, and not by people with any sort of political ax to grind, but with honest, neutral advice—and knowledge.

On the evening news we see film clips of antichoice protesters carrying placards with hugely enlarged pictures of aborted fetuses, splashed with red paint to simulate blood. The idea is to create fear and disgust—and it sometimes works. It's an exaggeration to make a point, to be sure. But the point is worth exploring. In truth, in the hands of an experienced and skilled practitioner the procedure is simple and clean, over in minutes. As one counselor puts it, "Abortion gory? You want to know what's gory? Having your tooth pulled. That's gory!"

You never know what kinds of misconceptions people are walking around with. I often think of a case I had back in the early days when we were legal in New York and the rest of the country was on hold. *Roe* and *Doe* were still three years away. I can't remember the woman's name—Susan something—but she came from Ohio. I saw her as a private patient for an early first-trimester abortion.

My first impression of her held up. She was a nice person—trim, attractive, well spoken. Her husband was with her, an attorney, rather grim-faced and stern. He certainly wasn't comfortable with this abortion, but he didn't want the baby either. They had their family, two children, as I recall, maybe three—but enough anyway. He sat in on the counseling session with his lips tight and his nostrils flared as if he smelled something offensive, making his discomfort with the whole idea pretty clear, just on his own moral and cultural grounds. I empathized with his uneasiness. I imagine he wanted us all to disappear, along with his wife's "problem condition."

The nurse came to take his wife down the hall to the dressing room and the OR, and I asked him to wait; I would come out later and speak with him again. But as his wife left the room, he called me over into a corner. "I'd like to have a word with you, Doctor," he began.

They had come into town strictly as an abortion referral, not exactly a great way to get a first view of the Big Apple. I had never seen these people before and would likely never see them again, but at this moment in our lives, they were my patients, and I was their doctor. In view of their tensions, I felt I owed him a hearing.

He lowered his voice to an almost conspiratorial tone. "I know what can happen in an abortion chamber," he said. I imagined he was envisioning me in a suit of armor with a torture mace in one hand and a cat-o'-nine-tails in the other. He went on, "I fully realize the risk." There wasn't any way to respond to that, so I waited for him to finish so I could get to work. More was coming.

"If anything should happen," he said, "you know, if anything like a complication should arise and there is a choice to be made between my wife and my baby, please, please let the baby go and make sure Susan is OK. We have other children to think about at home, you know."

I was totally nonplussed. I tried to keep my composure and not explain to this man the illogic of his statement. We were in a present-day, urban outpatient center, with modern equipment and all the amenities of good medical practice, and with all the needed security that city and state inspection and certification—not to mention my own medical license—could provide.

What was he thinking? I wondered. He had a lot of higher education and some degree of sophistication. But when I perfunctorily assured him that all would be well, and that such an issue was so unlikely as to be virtually impossible, I sensed that my logical response did nothing to allay his fears. He was suggesting that abortion was indeed ugly and evil, a minefield of terrible possible complications, and he was showing his displeasure at being caught up in this unhappy web.

I realized that to many, the parameters of life are drawn with a very diffuse line. "Baby" was the term he understood for a seven-week pregnancy, so he could imagine that a choice "between my wife and my baby" might have to be made. It was that fear and that concern that needed to be addressed. I assured him that his wife would be fine. She would be out in a short time, safe and sound. He didn't believe me, of course, because this was an abortion and I was an abortionist.

The procedure was uneventful. After a few hours of sleeping off the anesthesia, his wife emerged into the anteroom looking very much as she had when she'd left him. He greeted her, and they both left without another word, except a mumbled "thank you." I never saw either of them again.

Three days later, Ellen Stalisi was back in my office. "I've thought it over, and I've decided I want the abortion," she said. "What do I have to do?"

I didn't know Ellen quite well enough to take that on face value, as I might have done for a patient of longer standing. She seemed collected and sure of herself, but I wanted to take her through the counseling process just to be on the safe side. I needed to be sure, in my own mind, that she was not making a snap decision, and that she could handle the ramifications of her choice.

"Have you talked it over with your husband?" I asked.

She looked surprised. "Sure. I wouldn't do anything like this without talking it over with Tony."

The answer seemed so obvious that some people might wonder, why ask the question? But often "yes" isn't the answer I get. Grace Dockins drove two hundred miles to find me, had an abortion, drove home and lay on the living-room floor waiting for her husband. She told me she planned to tell him she had fallen and had a miscarriage. Not knowing her husband, I had to wonder how naive he was, but I guess he lived down to her expectations, because apparently the ruse worked. She gave me the details in a postabortion follow-up phone call.

I don't judge this woman as devious or destructive. On the contrary. I've learned that you cannot walk in another person's shoes, nor can you know what her needs are. In fact, I have found a certain respect and admiration for women who choose to go to what may sound like an extreme to protect themselves and their families. And it is protection that most often motivates a woman to choose abortion. She protects herself and her family from an impossible financial strain, from having to share food, money, love, attention. She protects herself from the burden of an unwanted child and the child from an unwilling and unloving parent. She protects all of them from the fear that those things will happen. Abortion is a true dilemma, the choice between two evils, and the seeking of the lesser of those evils.

I asked Ellen, "How does Tony feel about the idea of your having an abortion?"

"This one, you mean, or abortion in general? Both, I guess—right? Well, in general, he doesn't go for the idea. We're Catholic, for one thing—I guess you figured that out—and it's just not something you expect to do. But he can't handle the idea of having another mouth to feed when he can just about feed the ones he's got. It's not his fault, he's looking all the time, he's a good husband and a good father. He's an auto mechanic, a damn good one. The place where he was working—the city closed the road to repair it, and the traffic pattern changed, and the owner just couldn't make a go of it anymore, so he closed down. It was just bad luck, and Tony hasn't found anything else yet. At least, not anything where he wouldn't have to work for peanuts and take orders from some guy with less experience. He will." But then she added, "We just don't know when."

She was silent for a few seconds and then came back to the original thought. "So—how he feels about it? I wouldn't say he's *for* it—who could be for it? But he figures it's got to happen, because he doesn't see how we can manage another baby. I mean, we can if we have to, right? You can manage anything if you have to, but like I said, it would be tough.

"The truth is," she went on, "he didn't really want to talk about it very much. He's kind of uncomfortable with 'woman stuff' in the first place. You say somebody's got their period and he says 'hush your mouth' if he thinks the kids might hear. The first thing he did when he knew what I wanted to talk about was get himself a couple beers, get up his nerve." Her mouth twitched, and she smiled. "A grown man! He kept calling it 'the operation' or 'you know'—he couldn't say 'abortion.'"

That has happened a number of times—people unable to say the word. Some years ago I had a couple undergoing sex therapy, and the husband was never able to say *masturbation*—even though he indulged. I recalled that whenever someone, man or woman, couldn't say *abortion*. It has a scary overtone for many. It's a violent word for some, and it certainly was for Tony Stalisi.

Then Ellen was serious again. "But anyway, Tony says he's behind me one hundred percent. And he means it. You aren't married to somebody as long as I'm married to Tony and not know when they mean what they say."

"Does he plan to be with you?" I wanted to know just how uncomfortable Tony was and how well Ellen actually knew her husband.

Once again, Ellen was a little surprised. "When I come for the abortion? Sure. Absolutely."

I needed to find out about the rest of Ellen's support group. "You said your in-laws live downstairs. It's going to be hard for you to do this without their finding out. How do you think they, and the rest of your family, will react?"

"I already told Tony's mother. If I do this, she's got to take the kids, so she's got to know. She was upset, she cried a little—but not for herself. You know? For me and Tony, because we have to do this, and it's sad. It is sad. Tell you the truth, I cried a little too. But his mother's OK with it. Tony's papa, I don't know, but she'll take care of him—if he needs to know at all. He's like Tony—the less he knows about women's insides, the better."

"What about your family?"

"I talked to my mom. She's the same as Tony's mother—sorry it has to happen, but she's with us. I knew she would be."

"You mentioned that you were Catholic."

"Yes." Her eyes took on a faraway look. "Of course, the church says it's wrong. But they don't know everything. They say birth control's wrong too, and I don't believe that for a minute. This isn't a great thing to be doing, but I don't think I'm going to hell or anything. And neither does Tony."

"So you're satisfied that it's really what you want to do?"

"Yes. I mean, if we absolutely had no choice but to have this baby, I guess we could scrape by. But life's supposed to be more than just scraping by, isn't it? I want something better for us. So—I'm going to do this."

"Is there anything you want to ask me?"

"It's pretty much like a D & C, isn't it? I've had that."

"Pretty much."

"Then I have a pretty good idea of what I'm in for." She picked up her purse and stood up, reaching out her hand. "Thanks for your time, Doc. It's funny—I thought I knew what I wanted when I came in here, but I'm a lot clearer now. I feel better."

I walked her to the door and told the receptionist to schedule her for the procedure. I would see her in a few days.

Tony brought Ellen to the unit bright and early on Friday morning. She'd stopped in a few days earlier for tests—blood and urinalysis—so now she had nothing to do but wait. She joined several other women awaiting their procedures who were leafing through magazines or just staring at the wall. She sat down and looked around the room. "I'm Ellen," she said to the woman next to her. She said it loud enough that everyone could hear her, and several people looked up. "I guess we're all here for the same thing, huh?" she said. A couple of the women nodded and smiled, responding to her overtures as people usually did—that was Ellen. She talked to everyone. But maybe now she also needed to talk out her feelings of nervousness and sadness, or even guilt and remorse. That was Ellen too.

Ellen volunteered information as though to offer support for some of the others who were not handling the situation as well. I had the feeling that she would have liked to work the room, going from patient to patient, assuring each of them that things would work out. "Look," she might have said, "this is lousy, but what has to be, has to be. If I can do it, anyone can."

That wasn't far from the truth—but only in one way. Ellen

Stalisi was a strong woman. Even if all her veneer had come off, she would still have stacked up quite well against anyone else in the room in the same predicament.

Talking to the others, Ellen restated the reasons for her termination. Maybe she had to hear them again, one more time, for herself and for Tony and for the family. She described her final decision-making with Tony the week before. They were alone for a few precious moments when he was not out hustling for work and when the kids weren't around to distract them. "We figured everything in—how hard it is to find time to do the things we want to do with the two we've got, what we'd do for money, for space, the whole bit. We really tried to think of a way to do it—have the kid. We really did."

It always came down to the same thing.

"Yeah," Tony said. "She comes to me with this, and I think, 'Not in my family.' But the more I think about it, the more I see it's gotta be. I didn't want to be the one to have to say it, but she's right. This is the best way." He told me later he'd been drinking beer that night—or, as he put it, "I had a few brews with the boys"—because he wanted to be able to say he was too drunk to argue, but he knew that just was not true. He could have and would have, if he had really wanted to.

Watching them together, I thought how nice they were— down to earth, likable, wholesome. It was too bad, in a way, that they couldn't have had half a dozen kids. I hoped the ones they had would bring them joy, grow up to be solid citizens with good, healthy habits. Maybe just have a "brew" on occasion.

I left them in the waiting room and went down to the OR to start my day's work.

Ellen Stalisi was so nice—and so typical. She came in all shapes and sizes and from all over. She was one of many. I took something away from each and every one.

It's said that everything is timing, timing, timing. How true. In my medical career, Lady Luck has come into the picture too many times to count. Broke, in debt and raring to go, I had plunged into the abortion business with Roy Parker. But eventually the time came to venture out on my own. After all, that's what I really wanted, wasn't it?

Without the resources to set up a solo practice, I almost literally stumbled into the Fifth Avenue office of a family practitioner, an old-timer whose blend of gentleness and business acumen struck me as wise and good. We became instant friends. The timing was perfect. I was the son he wanted, and he fit my needs as well—my father, my beloved Herman, had recently died at what I'd thought was the peak of good health despite his years.

We split the office costs, which was more than fair—he could have charged me more. I bought myself a small suction unit from a California outfit that had tooled up fast, almost as though they were setting their die for what happened in Albany. American ingenuity had done it again—I bet that the abortion suction-machine business is the one mechanical industry that isn't based in Japan or South Korea or Taiwan. Strictly made in the U.S.A.

I picked up a little secondhand autoclave to sterilize instruments and used my contacts with the suppliers at the women's center to get myself two sets of abortion dilators and instruments wholesale.

I was in business.

I didn't have the courage to add "Abortions Done" to my newly purchased brass shingle. I figured my neighbors in the shadow of the condos of New York's 400 wouldn't appreciate that. And besides, I really didn't need the PR. It wasn't long before the first few people I'd worked with on the frontlines of the movement spread the word that I'd opened up shop. The phone started ringing.

"Are you the Doctor Sloan from Chicago?" I recognized a reference to the Ambassador Hotel meeting.

*   *   *

"Did you do my sister with Doctor Spencer in Pennsylvania?" It was about then that I learned that Doug had passed on. In a strange sort of way, I felt a need to carry on—shades of Doug Spencer. From those early patients, I first heard Doug referred to as "Dr. S."

"Doctor Sloan? This is So-and-So. Doctor So-and-So said to call."

They came from all over—mostly from New England and from Pennsylvania and Jersey and the Delmarva Peninsula, but everywhere, really. It was now all word of mouth.

"Doctor Sloan?" I was waiting to be called "Doctor S. the Second." "Can I bring my woman down on Saturday? She's one of the flower children."

I didn't know what flower children were then. I found out later on. But they knew me. My name and reputation had gotten around to the many, many young people who were a part of the upheaval of the sixties and who had settled down with their spouses or significant others in the hills and small towns of rural New England. Many were conscientious objectors and political renegades who were escaping the threat of Vietnam.

I never learned where they picked up their appellation, but they adopted it as their own. Many came in old rattletrap vans, home as well as transportation for some. Their vehicles were splashed with pastels and decorated with hand-painted flowers, some true replicas of garden blooms and others the products of their colorful imaginations. It was quite a sight to see them pull up under the dour gaze of a Fifth Avenue doorman.

Many—most, even—never asked my fee. They just assumed, correctly, as it happened, that I would charge what the traffic could afford: sometimes money, sometimes barter. But it never caused a problem. Just as my Dr. S.—Doug Spencer—had earlier, I carried on, with no regrets, ever.

And from most, there were gifts. Sometimes in lieu of a fee, sometimes in addition. They all seemed to feel obligated. At first I didn't understand why. I always felt that I was being paid fairly for my services, never that I was being cheated, and I expected nothing more than my fee. But the gifts came anyway.

There were flowers—fresh cut or in pots—hand-thrown pottery, a dozen eggs, slabs of ham and bacon. Or an objet d'art for the office or my desk. Later on came gifts brought in by patients who were referred by others—and who acted as delivery people. "So-and-So wanted to say hello and thanks" was the message, and they would then thrust a little tissue-paper-wrapped package into my hand, the tissue reused from some other gift. Mementos, sort of.

They were so proud of their way of life. After I knew them better and became more than their abortionist, they shared their legal problems with me. Many were with men who were escaping the draft, protesting the Vietnam War. The law was unclear on that at the time. But before they'd share themselves, I had to become a friend and be trusted. Their lives were contraband.

Maybe that was part of it. I realized later on that despite the change in the New York law, the concept of "legal" was still alien to them. They were people who knew the sting and stigma of living outside the mainstream, even though many of them had been born into it. They knew of the back-alley guys, and they knew firsthand a myriad of anecdotes about friends and acquaintances who had suffered "butcher jobs." So here they were on Fifth Avenue, with someone who had a diploma on the wall and washed his hands and cleaned his curettes. But that didn't make it all right for them. Suspicion was still in order until you proved yourself. And then, somehow, I was one of them, linked with them in a kind of honor among thieves.

They'd lived on the run so long that they had no way of grasping what had happened when the New York law changed, and although we now had no need to hide, they hid just the same.

They were grateful that I would do this for them—as people had been grateful to Doug Spencer, but it wasn't the same thing, not at all. He'd been out on a limb then, sawing away, and I'd been out there with him. Now I was legal tender, but they still felt obligated to bring me gifts and home-baked cookies. They were so used to exorbitant and usurious fees from back-alley guys that when the fee was sane and fair, they couldn't believe it was true.

They were all so sweet—the nicest people you'd ever want to meet.

It wasn't long before a nurse called Ellen's name and beckoned her to come along down to the changing room.

Walking down the hall with the little plastic bag provided for her clothes and belongings, she kept up a jabber, but no one brushed her off or said, "Shut up, lady, you talk too much." Ellen was likable. Or maybe she provided a needed distraction. She was shown a private spot and given two hospital gowns to put on—one frontward, one backward—and a pair of outsized paper slippers. Almost as soon as she was changed, the nurse came back, popped a thermometer under her tongue, and took her vitals—blood pressure, pulse and temperature.

Ellen surrendered her belongings, now stowed in the little plastic bag stamped with the hospital logo. Giving up her clothes, her watch and her rings, she said later, made her feel bare, stripped of all her defenses. The stark hospital procedures heightened abortion's bleakness.

She waited alone for a few minutes, although it probably seemed longer. I looked in on her once, between cases, and saw that she was OK, although she was quiet now.

"I hope this'll be over soon," she said. "I don't like the waiting much." Without lipstick, she looked pale and apprehensive.

"Just a little longer."

The anesthetist appeared for Ellen's pre-op interview. Ellen poured out a lot of extraneous information that made it difficult for the doctor to get a word in edgewise, but her talkativeness was chalked up to nervousness—very normal. She reported no allergies or medical problems. Everything seemed fine. The anesthetist gave her a little pep talk and an assurance that everything would go well.

A nurse brought her a sheaf of consent forms to sign—for the city, the state, the facility we were in—and stayed with her to witness her signature. That took a few more minutes.

We were moving along. The anesthetist and I went over Ellen's chart together, checking her blood count and blood type and medical history, to provide the anesthetist with added security. As we finished up, we were told it was a go—Ellen was ready.

There are probably a lot of things in medicine about which I have a laissez-faire attitude. For example, I've always tended to be strict about overtreatment—a tincture of time, and a number of complaints will go away, or if not, you can get by with the minimum. One of my father's many lessons. But then there is the OR—where compromise and casualness are not welcome traits. I'm not comfortable with "dattle do" surgery—"Whatever you got, dattle do."

My travels have taken me through the Eastern European countries, and I saw how they did legal terminations there. The facilities they had were legendary—and well they might be, with abortions easier to get than condoms. One unit in the former Yugoslavia was like a roundhouse—operating rooms surrounding a central control area with the vacuum machinery and suction teams. In each pie-shaped room there was a litter and some medical equipment—crude by our standards, but basic and utile. Hoses, like the tentacles of an octopus, ran from the central vacuum to the rooms in the circle, and the doctors and technicians used them to terminate pregnancies. The suctioned materials were all collected in a central receptacle and disposed of. Practical? Yes. Sound medicine? Not by my standards.

My esthetics were disturbed, but also my sense of Western

medicine. I have never done an abortion, all the many, many thousands of them, when I did not personally and individually examine the extruded tissue. There have been no exceptions. None. Ever. And afterward, each and every bit of that material was blocked and studied by a trained and certified pathologist.

I asked the doctors there what if there were abnormal tissue, and they answered me with statistics—which were and are on their side. We were talking about special tissue, like a rare—very rare—cancer of the placenta. I had to admit that this was an unusual enough event that, statistically, it made sense to wait until the patient exhibited symptoms. It's just that it didn't quite balance with what I consider good and superior medicine. Patients aren't statistics. I look forward to the day when every patient will have the best we can offer—practicality be damned.

Ellen Stalisi's turn had finally arrived.

As I entered the operating room, Ellen was lying on the table, an intravenous drip of sugar water flowing into a vein in her arm. A little exchange of nods with the anesthesiologist told me that everything was ready. Ellen looked up, and I bent over her. "OK?" I asked.

She managed a little smile. "As OK as I'm gonna be."

"You're going to be just fine," I said, and she smiled again, a little nervously this time.

The anesthesiologist was watching. I looked up and caught her eye and nodded once. It was her signal to start pushing the special quick-acting brew of sodium pentothal through the tubing. "Ellen" she said quietly, "would you count for me, backward from ten? Ten . . ."

"Ten, nine . . ." Ellen's voice took up the count. Knowing Ellen, I figured she was trying hard to call out the numbers. Everyone in the room knew that she would never reach seven. Her eyes rolled up; she gasped one long deep breath and fell into a pleasant slumber, one that she would remember as lasting a hundred years spent in the deepest core of the earth.

* * *

One of the greatest traps for a surgeon is complacency about any operative technique, no matter how experienced he or she may be. Abortion is one of those procedures that can cause you to fall into the trap. I always think about that—first, because I've done so many of them, and second, because it's a relatively minor procedure.

I was trained in gynecologic surgery by a doctor in Philadelphia named Louis J. Hoberman, another of the truly unforgettable characters I've run across in my career. He was a huge man, about three hundred fifty pounds, with a heart to match. He had two great loves—teaching students the art of obstetrics and gynecology, and playing the ponies. If a call for him came over the hospital voice-page system, it was from his office—or his bookie.

When you first met him, his bellowing would scare you, but he was all bark and no bite. To new students, he was "Dr. Hoberman." When you were a resident, and "in," he quickly became "Hobey." And when you were graduated—his equal—he was "Lou."

He was the kind of surgical teacher who taught by practice. He always did his best to have the residents, at least those he trusted and liked—which were most of us—do a lot of the case. He would watch and guide us until he knew who were the ones he could confidently hand the scalpel to, slowly feeding us responsibility until we became the surgeon and he became the assistant—although he never stopped watching, and we were never allowed a false move. He was a good surgeon and a very careful one.

But—there was one "but"—we were never allowed to do a D & C for him on one of his elective patients. The D & C was the closest a student came to abortion in those days—we weren't taught abortions. We did D & Cs on the ward patients and in emergency, though, and we thought we knew what we were doing. We figured a simple D & C was a breeze and would have done it to spare him the time and effort—but he always said,

"No way." No matter who we were, even if he'd let us do a hysterectomy, even if we'd taken care of a whole case with him at our elbow, he would always do the D & C himself and make us watch.

Why? Hobey said that we treated D & Cs too casually. We might get complacent and perforate, or something like that. It seemed silly at the time, but now I understand that Hobey was stressing the care we should exercise when treating our own ward patients.

But I always think of that, and I practice it to this day. I'm not as benevolent as Hobey was, although sometimes, with some residents that I trust, I'll let them work on one of my cases. Part of it. But not the D & C. Not the abortion. I do that myself—always. I guess I'm a throwback to Lou Hoberman.

As Ellen lapsed into her sleep, a change in scenery was taking place, like the thirty-second blackout in a stage play. The circulating nurse stepped forward and, timing her motions with Ellen's deep sigh, raised Ellen's heels into the little cloth cradles attached to chrome poles at the foot of the table. This un-scrubbed nurse, the operating-room floater, then picked up an aerosol can containing an iodine solution, which she sprayed liberally on Ellen's inner thighs and crotch area. Next she slid Ellen's now-anesthetized body further down on the table so that her buttocks just spilled over the edge. The table, a marvel of electronics, was engineered to move every which way at the touch of a button. The nurse tipped it into a position that was ideal for Ellen's weight and size. Her part completed for the time being, she stepped back, and I moved in. It had all happened like a well-choreographed ballet.

I looked up to the head of the table and got the final go-ahead nod from the anesthetist, the signal for the procedure to begin. From the sterile tray, I took a sponge stick with a folded gauze pad locked in its teeth, dipped it into a shot-sized cup containing the same iodine solution as the floater nurse's spray and used it to swab out the vagina.

I threw a clean-smelling, sterile sheet over Ellen's abdomen. Careful to touch only the sheet, I lifted Ellen slightly and tucked its folds under her butt, moving her down a little more as I did, and grunting slightly with the effort—she was dead weight. After the sheet came drapes, sort of like triangular pillowcases, wide enough to cover each leg and the stirrups.

Now all that was left exposed to view was a small window-like opening to the genital area. It formed an isosceles triangle with the base across the pubic hair and the two sides meeting at the anus.

I inserted two gloved fingers deep into the vagina and with my left hand on the abdominal wall pressed down firmly toward them. It was a final check to be sure that the size of Ellen's womb was compatible with her prior history and what she had reported about the dates of conception. Even the most skilled and experienced gynecologist could make a mistake trying to assess a tense, anxious patient. Thanks to the relaxation that goes along with the third plane of anesthesia, I was able to get a good reading and feel more secure.

Ellen was about seven weeks along, just as we'd thought. Good.

Using my toe, I hooked a rolling stool under me and sat down. I fitted my foot into the slot over the lever that raised and lowered the seat, and adjusted the seat to my height, the table and the patient's build.

With a weighted speculum, a single-bladed instrument molded in one piece to a lead-filled ball, I depressed the lower, or perineal, vaginal wall. Then I took a second retractor, one that looked a lot like a right-angled shoehorn, and inserted it so it raised the upper wall of the vagina. I then had ample working room and a clear view within.

I identified the cervical os—the mouth of the womb. In childbirth, the cervix can stretch and dilate to ten times its original circumference, and after such trauma it has the ability to revert itself back as though nothing had happened. Well, almost nothing. It's one of the miracles of nature. A feminist friend once told me that if we men wanted to get an idea of how the cervix stretches, we should hook our index fingers into our cheeks, and then try to pull our mouths back over our ears. It was a sobering thought.

I grasped the upper lip of the cervix with a tenaculum, a plierlike instrument. Its right-angled pointed tips sank into the soft tissue of the cervix and held it firmly in place. Remembering the many abortions I'd peformed without the benefit of general anesthesia, I thought about what a luxury it was for both patient and doctor to have safe, quick-acting anesthesia available. I've always been impressed that a woman could—and would— tolerate the kind of pain that has to be involved.

I reached back toward the table again and picked up an instrument called a sound, a simple rod with a rounded end, much like a dipstick used to measure the oil levels in your car— in fact, very similar. Markings on the sound would indicate the depth of the uterine canal. I knew how deep the uterus had to be at each stage of a pregnancy. As I went along, I checked each measurement, each move. Every finding had to match up with what I already knew, or something was wrong. If that happened, I would have to stop and figure out why, maybe plot a new course. It was good to be sure every step of the way.

I guided the sound slowly inward across the two fingers compressing down on the pelvic floor, delicately feeling for the first hint of resistance. This was not the time to force anything toward the upper wall of the uterus. A pregnant uterus had to be respected. The slightest bit of unnecessary pressure would be enough to push an instrument, especially one so pointed, through its wall. When I felt resistance, I stopped and took a reading. Once again, it confirmed what I already knew. Good. It was time to go on to the next step—the dilation itself.

On the tray lay a series of dilators, a graduated, perfectly matched set of tapered chrome rods nine inches long, the smallest, at its widest point, having about the circumference of a drinking straw and the largest, a fat cigar. I'd determined the length of the uterine canal from the sounding, so I knew exactly how deep I could place each of the dilators; from the size of the uterus I knew how wide a dilation I'd need. The rods were arranged in the exact sequence in which I'd need them. As I worked, I could grasp each one exactly in the position in which I'd use it, with no wasted motion. Every step was orchestrated with total precision.

With each plunge of the dilator, I could feel the muscular resistance of the cervical wall guarding the entrance to the uterus. My experience had taught me just how that felt too. Pregnancy causes the uterine muscle to be softer than usual, and too strong a push could force the dilator into a false passage; I was careful to guard against that.

Gradually, the pressure of the dilator forced the mouth of the cervix open. In minutes, I reached the desired dilation and signaled that I was ready for suction.

The circulating nurse moved quickly from her perch in the corner of the room and wheeled the suction machine over to the table. Other than having a smaller motor and glass jars as receptacles to contain suctioned materials, it was very much, in principle and appearance, like the first tank-type vacuum cleaners. Its tubing was clear plastic, like a small-bore garden hose.

The nurse removed the plastic covering from the tubing and handed me the sterile end, keeping the other to attach to the machine. I took a vacuum tip that coincided exactly with the dilator I'd just used and fitted it to the sterile end of the tubing, clamping it in place with a metal adjusting clamp. I slid the tip through the already dilated cervical canal and nodded to the nurse to flip the switch that put the vacuum machine in motion.

The machine whirred, a steady, low-key hum. I watched the transparent tubing to see how much and what type of material was being extracted from the inner cavity of the womb. For each stage of pregnancy, there is not only a proper depth to sound and a proper size to dilate, but also a proper amount of tissue to remove—each week of pregnancy has a known and measurable amount of tissue. Anything that veered from the expected would be suspect.

As suction continued, my eyes moved from the vagina to the clear tubing to the gauge that told me the amount of vacuum pressure being exerted to the anesthesiologist and back to the vagina, an uninterrupted circuit.

When I was sure that the proper amount of tissue had been extruded, I removed the suction tip and the nurse shut off the machine. "Mopping up" began.

I took a fresh sponge stick and used it to assure myself there was no excessive bleeding. There was none. So far, so good. I once again used both hands, one inside and one on Ellen's lower abdomen, to be sure that the uterus was firm and well contracted—a safeguard against hemorrhage and a key to a successful procedure. All was well there too.

I signaled the anesthetist that I was moving toward the finish.

Now I took a curette, another rod-shaped instrument, this one having a leaded handle at one end and a pinky-ring-sized loop with a rather sharp edge at the other. Inserting it through the cervical opening, I gently applied the edge of the loop to the inner surface of the womb, systematically covering each area, making sure no remnant of the pregnancy was still there. There is a special feel to the clean surface of the muscle wall within, and a special sound dubbed in gynecologic lore the "cry of the uterus." When the womb "cried," I felt secure that no speck of unwanted tissue had been left behind; even a tiny bit could cause bleeding and wreak havoc for a patient in days to come. I was careful that wouldn't happen to Ellen.

The procedure was complete.

The nurse placed a small sanitary napkin at the vulvar entry. She then slid Ellen back up the table, eased her legs from the stirrups and crossed them at the ankles. Ellen was ready for the recovery room and two hours of monitoring.

In the recovery room, Ellen was quiet—a bit more, I thought, than just coming out of the anesthesia would account for. But when she heard me speaking to the nurse, she opened her eyes and smiled at me, a warm, beckoning smile. She always seemed to feel that her friendliness would be returned, and I think it usually was. It was by me. I went over and took her hand.

"You're doing great," I told her. "How do you feel?"

She was still groggy and unfocused, but she smiled at me. "I'm glad *that's* over," she murmured. Behind those words I could hear the unspoken ones—that the pain of the decision and all that went with it were in the past. As much as they could be.

Time—and energy spent elsewhere—would be the greatest healer. Ellen would be fine. Her support system would stay intact; Tony was waiting outside. For all his rough edges, his lack of a fine gentleman's manners, he came through as gentle where Ellen was concerned.

Her stay in recovery over, Ellen wobbled a bit as she made her way back down the hall to the changing room. In a few minutes she was dressed, her hair combed, a little lipstick on, back to being herself—almost.

The recovery nurse had told Ellen not to leave without seeing me first. I caught up with her as she was coming out of the changing room and took her to a little office area nearby, where I sat her down at the desk. I asked her a few questions to be sure she was alert and OK, and made sure she had urinated—a nice sign of the body's returning to normal after anesthesia.

I reassured Ellen that everything had gone well. I told her that the amount of tissue I'd taken out had exactly matched what might be expected for seven weeks of pregnancy, that there'd been no surprises. But, I explained, as a further check, a pathologist would go over everything, so we'd be doubly sure she was OK.

I gave her a list of written instructions, and, to be on the safe side, I stressed a few points. "Use common sense," I told her. "You've had anesthesia. For the rest of the day, at least, don't do anything foolish. Don't drive a car, don't climb a ladder, don't lift the kids. In the next few days, if it doesn't feel like the right thing to do, don't do it."

She nodded. "OK, Doc."

"You can shower, but no tub baths for a week. Nothing in the vagina for two weeks. This is important. No douching, no tampons, no soaking in the tub. No sexual contact." The integrity of Ellen's uterus had been violated, and the cervix needed time to shrink back to its naturally closed state. With a dilated cervix, Ellen had an open pathway to a sterile portion of her body. Anything that got into her womb through that opening could cause trouble. Semen especially. In the context of the sterile condition of the uterus, semen is contaminating—dirty. It can cause a raging infection, one that's easy to prevent with just a modicum of prudence.

Ellen nodded again.

"And no gymnastics or calisthenics for two weeks either," I added.

This brought a smile. "No cartwheels, huh? I don't think you need to worry, Doc," she said.

I smiled back. "Do you have any questions?"

She waved the printed sheet. "No. I think this'll do it."

"OK, then. You know where to reach me. Don't hesitate to call for anything that seems out of the ordinary, anything you're uncomfortable with at all."

"I won't. Thanks."

I walked her back down to the waiting room and Tony.

We met again for a brief minute as she was leaving. She was perkier than she'd been earlier, although still very quiet for her. I walked a few steps with her and Tony as they headed toward the exit. "I'm taking a long nap," she said to him. "Your mom can have the brats for the rest of the day."

"Sure," said Tony. "You got it. No sweat."

She leaned against him as they waited for the elevator, and he patted her a little awkwardly on the back. I had no doubt that she would be herself in the morning—all over again.

I learned something from Ellen Stalisi, something that as an abortion counselor I take to every session. What is done is done—but in another sense, it's never done. The importance of what has happened remains, even for women who have been through the procedure and say they would do it again, and again, and again. The sting is there. I could see it in her eyes.

8 The Two Faces of Larry Porter

Larry Porter* and I went way back—to medical school, in fact. I was a few years older than my classmates, and Larry seemed more mature than the rest of the crowd. Although he was several years my junior, we became friendly—even more so after we both chose to specialize in gynecology. We didn't socialize much. Larry kidded me about my "freewheeling bachelor life," and I gave him what-for about his being an "old married man," but I counted him and his wife Dianne among my closest friends just the same. I didn't hang out at the Porters' very much, but I felt I was always welcome there.

Our choosing the same specialty was strictly a coincidence. We never discussed it, it just happened. Whatever got us to that point had apparently transpired before we met. Larry often remarked that we thought alike, and we did seem to—at least as far as medicine went. Maybe his sense of social justice wasn't as highly developed as mine, but I didn't expect it to be— everybody couldn't be Herman Sloan's kid. Larry was a good listener, and he had a sense of proportion. I had no doubt that his feelings of social responsibility would ripen along the same lines as mine. Why shouldn't they?

One thing that made it pleasant at the Porters' was Larry's relationship with Dianne. This was no retiring little wife staying home with the kids. She was bright-eyed and outspoken, earthy and vital, his peer and partner in every way. She was a very attractive woman, and she enjoyed flaunting her good looks—

160

not obtrusively, just enough. We all liked each other. The three
of us had many a happy time together.

Dianne and Larry were on a kind of ten-year plan. They had
married very young and had two sons right off the bat, but
Dianne had managed to finish school, and in addition to full-
time mothering, she had a career of sorts, free-lancing as a
jacket designer for one of the big New York publishing houses.
She kept herself busy and made her fair contribution to the
Porter family budget. Larry was going through training and
planning to set up his practice. They were right on track.

Dianne was delighted when Larry chose gynecology. She was
a self-described feminist, and she saw Larry's choice as a
validation of her beliefs. She considered herself to be his inspiration. "Larry's going to be great," she said. "He won't be one
of these OB-GYNs who put women down. He'll take his patients seriously." She grinned and hugged Larry's arm. "I plan
to make sure of it!" The two seemed to thrive on each other's
support.

When I hit New York again after my residency, Larry and
Dianne were still there. It was natural to pick up the friendship
where we'd left off, although my political interests and activities
didn't leave me much time for a social life. Politics and lobbying
for legislative change weren't Larry's things, but when we talked
about what I was doing, he was interested enough. He supported my causes with a few bucks every now and then, and
even did a little extracurricular work for me when I asked him.

When the women's center was recruiting, I offered Larry a
chance to come on board while he was getting his own practice
off the ground, but he already had a quarter-time hospital job,
and he decided to stick with that. He came to the center and
helped out a few times—he was a skillful-enough abortionist—
but basically he didn't want to put in the kinds of hours there
that a permanent affiliation required. For one thing, Dianne
had always stressed the importance of his spending time with
her and the boys, of not being an absent father, and he made it
a priority in his life. No argument there.

Larry may not have liked the rough and tumble of politics the way I did, but he enjoyed arguing its theory, especially the feminism Dianne was into and abortion. Whenever we got together, with or without Dianne, that's one of the things we often batted around. We played devil's advocate with each other on many occasions.

"*Roe v. Wade* is the most important rights decision to come out of the Supreme Court in this century," he said. "Potentially, it affects over half the population. It's a big step toward granting women their full constitutional rights, which, I'm ashamed to say, we've never really done. Do you realize," he went on, "that with *Roe v. Wade,* we're about to see the first generation of American women who can actually control their own reproductive function? Decide whether to bear children or not? It's amazing when you think of it. Not more than a decade or so ago, there were laws in this country against married couples' using birth control. Birth control! That was the Dark Ages. Keep 'em barefoot and pregnant! What a policy for the government to get involved in!"

And Dianne would chime in, "How can women be full participants in American society when we aren't even permitted to control our own bodies? When we're routinely excluded from jobs—even job training? Half the time women can't get into medical school or law school because they 'might' get pregnant. Do people think that's equal protection under the law? It's nobody's business but the woman's—hers and her doctor's. That's what makes *Roe v. Wade* so brilliant—it finally recognizes that women have rights."

Larry would finish the thought. "When a woman comes to me for an abortion, I take care of her. And if a woman comes to me with her tenth pregnancy—well, we do get them on the services sometimes—and if she wants the baby, I'd take care of her too. That's what choice is all about, isn't it?"

Larry seemed to live his philosophy. I saw him in action often enough to know. He brought sensitivity and gentleness to his dealings with patients, and he was well liked on the hospital abortion service by both his patients and his colleagues. A fair share of his private practice was abortion as well.

Dianne went to work for a major school-book publishing firm full-time when the boys reached junior high, and her career was going well. She had worked her way up to director of design and production, a job that had previously been held only by men. Larry was proud of that. His practice was thriving too. They had paid off Larry's medical-school debts and even bought a house. They, of all the people I knew, seemed to have it all together.

If I noticed that Larry was looking glum, I didn't pay much attention until one night when we were both working late and I joined him at a table in the hospital cafeteria, where he was picking at a Danish.

"What's new?" I asked.

"Dianne's pregnant. Can you believe it? Damn, damn, damn."

The damns stopped me from proffering congratulations. I looked at him quizzically.

He ran a hand through his hair. "Oh, God. I'm too old for this," he said. He stood up, picked up his tray, swept its contents into the trash and left the room without another word to me or anybody else.

I sat there chewing on the conversation, if you could call it that. I figured that by "this" he'd meant the pregnancy. At forty or so, he was really just hitting his stride as a physician, so it couldn't be professional doldrums. Dianne would be about thirty-eight—shades of my mother. A little past her gestational prime, maybe, but not a vast age by a long shot. Not even old enough to have this baby be considered a monument to middle-aged fertility. When Larry and I had started out in this business, thirty-five was "elderly" in obstetrical jargon. But as we got older and technology progressed, "elderly" came to mean later and later. No one knew where it would come to an absolute, it seemed.

With their other two children so much older, I wondered idly why they'd want to start another family—well, maybe raise the baby-sitters and then have the baby. It had been done before—by my mother, for one. Who was I to say?

A few days later Larry drew me into an empty examining room. "You ought to know," he said, "that Dianne and I are at each other's throats over this—this pregnancy."

I was shocked. A rocky spot, sure—most marriages have them. But this seemed to have gone to extremes. Larry used expressions like "breaking up" and having "had it."

"We agreed when we got married. Two. That would be it. Whatever they were. We had our two, and we were done. Now she wants to change the rules. Says she's always wanted a girl, and this might be her last chance. She's absolutely irrational on the subject." Frankly, he didn't look too rational himself. His eyes were hard and bright and his face had gone livid, just talking about it. "She's determined to see this pregnancy through, in spite of—I don't want it. I don't want any part of it. Two are enough. I'm not starting over. We've been all through it, and she will not budge."

"It's her choice, Larry. You've always said it was for the woman to decide."

"Choice! I know all about choice. It sounds good. You make it sound good. But you're not saddled with an unwanted pregnancy, twenty years of another kid!"

"If it's what she wants—"

"What *she* wants! How about *me*? Isn't it my life too?"

"It's her body." I was playing devil's advocate with Larry again.

"Right now. But in just a few more months, it's going to be my bank account, isn't it?"

"You can afford it. So can she, if it comes to that."

"You think kids get cheaper as they get older? I'll be in my sixties before this one is out of college."

This wasn't getting us anywhere. Everything I said he managed to twist to make it seem—to him—that his situation was somehow unique, unlike any other we had ever heard about. Of course, it wasn't any different. It was just that none of the questions—Whose body is it? Whose choice is it? Who should make the decision?—had answers that he liked when it came to him.

The next few weeks crackled with tension. Unable to get his way with persuasion, Larry finally blew his stack at Dianne, pouring out a torrent of the kind of words that don't easily retract. He only succeeded in entrenching her more deeply in her position. It was a standoff.

Dianne was reaching her point of no return, and Larry knew it—only too well. The battle raged on. I tried to talk to Dianne, but she wasn't having any of my talk. She couldn't be sure that I wouldn't side with Larry. I wasn't taking sides, but she didn't know that. How could she? As Larry's friend, I had no standing with her, and I wasn't her doctor. She was squeamish about seeing so close a friend as a GYN and had settled in with one of our more distant colleagues long ago. No reason to change—and no reason to listen.

But I was friend to both. I was older and considered wiser if only for that reason. Not that it did any of us any good.

Then nature stepped in. Dianne started to bleed.

Maybe she could have kept the pregnancy, maybe not. Maybe she was just worn down with fighting over it. Acting on her own, she asked for, and got, a D & C. It was really a termination at that point. She knew—we all did—that she did it sooner than she had to.

Larry had won. And, eventually, Larry had lost.

He was enormously relieved. You could see it immediately in his face and his personality. In a day, he went from rage to denial—he could forget the whole thing. He was his old, exuberant, upbeat self again. It was over. It had never happened. There had been no dissension, no fighting, no rift in the marriage. Everything was back to normal, just the same as it had always been.

But not for Dianne. She had thrown away a wanted pregnancy, experienced the death of her hopes. She would not or could not let it go. The gulf between them grew wider, until it couldn't be bridged.

*   *   *

I'd always considered Larry Porter a pro-choice feminist, and he'd considered himself that too. For a long time after all this happened, I tried to dismiss him as a hypocrite, but I could never find it in me to tar him with that brush—not completely. He had wanted a choice too—did that make him a sexist? Feminist, sexist, pro-choice, antichoice—it's not so simple to sort out. The lines of demarcation just aren't that clear.

Pro-choice feminists, like Dianne and, for that matter, like Larry's idea of himself, generally believe that women must be in control of their own bodies. That's how they themselves put it. That doesn't imply that they're pro-abortion. Nobody, in my experience, is actually pro-abortion, in the sense of considering it a higher good than a pregnancy. But they see it as, at best, ethically neutral and, at worst, a necessary evil—the essence of the argument being that only a woman can get pregnant, and therefore only she should be able to decide whether to bear the child. It's a pro-woman stance, a statement of power and independence.

But not everyone who is pro-choice is a feminist. There are pro-choice sexists too. I wondered if I ought to lump Larry in with them. The pro-choice sexist sees women as slightly inferior material, prone to getting themselves pregnant at inopportune times. The pro-choice sexist is saying, in effect, "I give you the choice to abort, because it's your body and your problem. We can have fun in bed, and if a pregnancy happens that we don't want—or that I certainly don't want—I will preserve the right for you to abort. Lucky you." How was it once put? "I take away the baby carriage, but I want to leave the playpen."

Maybe the most honest of the lot are the antichoice sexists, the believers in male superiority. It's the "men are better suited hormonally and temperamentally to rule the world and make the decisions" school of thought. Basically, they just don't want women to have the power to make choices of any kind— abortion is just one example. They're consistent, at least. It might be tempting to say that a lot of politicians fall into this category, but it's sufficiently widespread that you can't make blanket statements.

That leaves the antichoice feminists—the "feminists for life," as if other feminists weren't. They make some interesting points, though. Their position is that choice and abortion are in reality sexist, because they absolve men of responsibility for the products of their philandering. As long as society remains permissive, boys will be boys. The only way to get them to grow up is to remove the "easy out," and make them responsible for the pregnancies they help to create. Then and only then will there be equality. And there's also the antichoice, yet feminist, doctrine that says women are superior to men because they can produce life, and the male establishment shouldn't be allowed to brainwash them into obliterating that distinction.

Antichoice feminism has a pretty impressive list of founding mothers speaking for it. Activist Elizabeth Cady Stanton said in 1878 that abortion treats women like chattel or property. In 1869 the suffragist Susan B. Anthony urged prevention and not "execution." The woman, she said, was guilty if she committed the deed, but "thrice guilty is he who drives the . . . women into the crime." And in 1875 Victoria Woodhull, the first woman to run for president and an avowed supporter of women's rights, socialism and free love, said, "Every woman knows that if she were free, she would never . . . think of murdering [a child] before its birth." Woodhull, a true feminist, knew even as she argued against abortion that women were not free. But it's a chicken-and-egg argument. Without freedom of choice, how can women be free?

And who knows what Margaret Sanger, the "mother of modern birth control," would support now. With her propensity for promoting the sterilization of the unfit, you might expect her to be stumping for safe, legal abortion in the ghettos today, true to her eugenic principles. Except that Sanger was radicalized when, in her job as a public-health nurse, she watched a woman die from an illegal abortion. In a sense, her fight was as much antiabortion as it was pro birth control. Where would she be on this issue today? We'll never know.

Of course, when these women were formulating feminist theory, abortion was at least as risky as childbirth, and both were chancy at best. Who knows what side they'd come down on today? Nowadays, the notion of antichoice feminism seems oxymoronic to many. The debate rages back and forth.

I tried to reach out to Larry Porter, but his attitude just wasn't something he wanted to discuss. The intellectual side of it was obvious to both of us—it must have been embarrassing for him. But the emotional side was another question entirely. He wasn't entirely a hypocrite. He believed everything he'd ever said. For someone else.

If a couple with such a hard-line difference had come to him with the problem, Larry would have told them that the issue might be too great for their marriage to overcome—the alternatives were work it out or split. Now he sat in front of me unable to work it out and unwilling to admit that it was going to cost him his marriage and his way of life. "Should I be condemned for the way I feel about this?" he asked. It was a rhetorical question—he didn't really want an answer. But if I had responded, I would have had to agree with him. No, he shouldn't have to accept a pregnancy he felt was too much for him to bear, or, for that matter, any major structural change in the relationship that he considered a betrayal. No one should. I saw anguish in his eyes and heard it in his words, and I tried to identify with him. It wasn't that difficult for me to do.

One thing the antichoice folks have got right—those million-plus fetuses that end up in OR suction tanks didn't get into women's wombs by themselves. I've never seen a case of immaculate conception yet, nor heard of any—not since the first and only one, at any rate. But antichoice men—whether religious right or civil libertarian or in between—even when they're willing to take on the financial responsibility, fail to address the issue that they're not carrying the pregnancy, not running the risks of childbirth. No man has ever risked his life to have a baby. The best he can do is secondhand—risk his partner's. Anatomy and physiology are two things he can't control.

Men and abortion—it's an area we don't pay half enough attention to. Men are fifty percent of the problem and so far aren't making much of a contribution to the solution. Larry Porter agonized over it; so did Frank Bennett, Darlene's husband. So do a lot of others. But agonizing isn't going to make it go away. That women have seized this issue as a feminist prerogative and shut men out makes a lot of men very uncomfortable, for one thing. It's at least partly a power issue, but it's also an emotional one.

Maybe instead of attacking women who seek abortions— women who are really victims in many ways—the antichoicers ought to direct their energies toward the men who got them there. After all, it takes two to tango.

Men exert pressure on women in all kinds of ways, subtle and not so subtle. "Date rape," in the jargon of the Now Generation, may say it all.

When Terry came to me for an abortion, I couldn't believe what I was seeing on her chart: twenty-four years old, no children, five previous abortions. This would be her sixth. It seemed reasonable that the counseling session ought to focus on getting her to set her sights on some reliable birth control, so that the next time she became pregnant, it would be because she wanted to. For the moment at hand, I had before me a woman who needed an abortion and someone she trusted to do it. My long-range goal for her was contraception.

It wasn't hers.

"Me and Arnie have been together since I was sixteen," she said. "He won't use that birth-control stuff, and he won't have me using it either. No telling what it might do to you, Arnie says. Mess up your insides, or something. Doctor, I got to do what he tells me. He's a good man, and you know they're hard to find. He's got a good job, and he's good to me. I don't want to mess that up."

Listening to her, I thought back to my experience when I was a third-year medical student in Brooklyn, and we were each assigned, as part of our training, a whole family. We acted as their doctor—examined the kids and the adults both, took care of them all. Anyone in the household. It was only for a few weeks, but depending on the situation, you could get to know them very well. I developed a real feeling for "my" family—the mother, Dorothy, even invited me to dinner with her crew. This was my introduction to the field of social medicine.

There were thirteen children, all living at home, from late teenagers on down. Their father, Bunky—a nickname for Brandon—was rarely around. He was holding down two jobs to try to make ends meet. Dorothy was in her late thirties, and she had been pregnant so often that she could not remember the last time she'd had a period. She almost literally went from one pregnancy to another.

I suggested a tubal ligation after her next delivery. It seemed so logical. Why hadn't they thought of it? Surely, someone had given her that option in the prenatal clinic.

She shook her head. "No!" She was adamant.

In my naïveté, I asked her why not, and she explained. It was because of her husband. Not that he needed more mouths to feed. Far from it. Artificial birth control was against his cultural beliefs. But more, her continuous pregnancies were a way of assuring him that she was faithful. Her power of fertility was his—a way of assuring her fidelity.

"Bunky knows I'm all his if I can't be foolin' around with no one else." For Dorothy, intercourse was just about an automatic conception.

Somehow, I came to understand what at first seemed like foolish, even destructive, thinking.

Like Dorothy and Bunky and many similar to them, Terry also rejected the use of adequate birth control. We spoke of the risks involved in multiple abortions, of the fact that every form of surgery is a risk, no matter how minor and even in the best of hands. She realized that, she said, but she had no other choice. "I'm not scared," she told me. "Only sad."

"Why sad?" I asked her.

"Because it's my baby," she said.

It's never simple. But when it comes to a choice between the man and the pregnancy, many women yield. They do what the man wants. They often want their marriage or their relationship more than they want the unknown, unimagined baby.

Men like these husbands, you might say, aren't very well educated, very aware. But Larry Porter, with all his privilege, his education, his sophistication, his understanding of the medical and political aspects of choice—was he really very different from them in his desire to control his wife's reproductive decisions?

Barbara and Jim came to me for an abortion on referral from Barb's gynecologist. They were significant others in a secure, long-term—and unmarried—relationship. The only child of divorced parents, Jim was determined never to marry. He was convinced that he and Barbara were solid as a couple and that a formal ceremony would just get in the way. "Look at all of our friends," he'd say to Barb, as he called her. "Half of them are already divorced or in the process of splitting. We're just great together the way we are. Let's not rock the boat." Barb, deeply in love, agreed.

Jim's parents and stepparents accepted the couple's decision without much difficulty. Barbara's family, a bit more traditional, raised the marriage issue over and over, until they finally realized they were beating a dead horse—the two were not going to wed.

Barb and Jim led busy, active lives. Jim was a talented and successful ad executive with major clients and a liberal travel budget. When the couple merged their assets and bought a co-op apartment, Barb quit her job at a major New York hospital and used her experience along with her master's degree in social work to set up a private practice that afforded her the leeway to travel with Jim. They enjoyed life and each other. So far, Jim's strategy seemed to be working.

Jim felt about children much as he felt about marriage—in a word, no. He had made childlessness a condition of the relationship, and Barb agreed—a little reluctantly at first, but without reservation in the end. She started out in the relationship on the birth-control pill, and being basically honest and committed, she was a diligent pill taker.

When Barb approached thirty-five, she brought up the question of continued pill use. "We've been talking about my having a tubal ligation or Jim's having a vasectomy, but they both seem a little drastic, if we don't have to," she told her GYN. "What have you got?"

"It would probably be a good idea to switch," he told her. "You say you smoke a little socially, and risks for smokers on the Pill do go up. You're almost thirty-five—your fertility will be starting to wane. If you want to get off the Pill, there's a new IUD on the market with a ninety-eight percent protection rate— very nearly as good as the Pill."

Barb decided to give it a try and had the IUD inserted the next week.

It was late the following summer that Barb came to me.

"We've got a time-share in the Hamptons," she explained. "We were out there for a long weekend, just relaxing—I guess that's when it happened. Two weeks later, I missed my period, but that's happened before, and it was nothing. Then I missed another one, and I figured I'd better see. I'm pregnant."

She told me about her situation, her arrangement with Jim. "When I found out, Jim wasn't there. I was alone. I glanced in the mirror, and—I couldn't help it—I was smiling this silly, smart little smile. I'd always wondered with the Pill, if I missed one, would I get pregnant? Or even if I took it religiously, could I be in that two percent failure rate, how would I feel? Well, I felt—proud of myself. And then I realized—no way is Jim going to change for this. He's never veered from the 'no-baby' rule, even a little, and I've never seriously thought of asking him to.

"I wondered—my parents were really upset by our living

together at first, but now they've come around, and they love Jim like a son-in-law, and he loves them. He's closer to my folks, in many ways, than he ever was to his own parents. I couldn't resist thinking maybe I'd tell my mother, and she and my dad could put a little pressure on him for me. But right away, I realized I couldn't go behind his back like that—what a betrayal that would be. I could never do that. So I kept it to myself for another day, just to think."

The next evening, she met Jim downtown for dinner with one of his clients. "Abortion and pregnancy came up in the conversation—in a casual way, but it really got to me. I tried to pretend that I wasn't personally involved, but I had to clamp my mouth shut and swallow hard not to blurt out that I was pregnant. I knew I had to do something—soon."

That night in bed, she let it all out. Jim gulped. He described to me later how he had felt.

"For a minute I couldn't breathe. I had this sick feeling in the pit of my stomach. All I could think was that I was going to lose Barb. I couldn't imagine a life without her. There is nothing in my whole life that is important to me that Barb has not been a part of. Nothing I have in my life is meaningful but what Barb has shared with me. But—" He stopped and closed his eyes, struggling with remembered emotion. "It was like drowning. I think my whole life passed before my eyes," he said.

He wondered how Barb would deal with an abortion. It had never come up; they had never dreamed they would face it. They were both so sure that they would always have excellent birth control—which they did. But excellent isn't perfect. It was Murphy's Law: If something can go wrong, it will, and usually at the worst possible moment.

Holding each other that night, they agreed that their commitment and pledge to each other was intact. Barb asked Jim's forgiveness.

"For what?" he asked.

"For being dishonest, just this one time."

"What are you talking about?"

"I can't tell my mother and dad about an abortion. They

don't know I'm pregnant, so I don't want to hurt them by telling them this—they might never be able to deal with an abortion. We have them this far. They've accepted my 'living in sin'—it's still a little sin in their eyes. But not abortion. We'll always have to hide this. We'll never be able to tell them."

Jim said he felt a kind of mingled pity and regret, a great sympathy for Barbara's concern over being "dishonest," as she had put it. He tried to find words to soothe her discomfort over this lie of omission to her parents without patronizing. It was something they would both have to live with until time did its healing.

The abortion came and went. Jim and Barb are as strong as ever and her mother and dad are none the wiser. We talked all this over again in a postabortion counseling session that was also, coincidentally, their tenth "anniversary." I reminded them that of all the things they have in their lives, putting aside the question of their health, which is not under their control, the most vital and significant thing is their relationship. Nothing can compete with it—not their parents, no matter how close, or their friends, their finances, their careers—nothing. With their health and each other, they have a chance at happiness. They can work and succeed elsewhere, in their careers and their daily lives, but without their relationship being solid, no wealth, no career, no success will be meaningful.

They nodded their agreement.

Unlike Larry and Dianne, Barbara and Jim used abortion as a means of survival for them as a couple. Together, they made the decision that their relationship was of greater importance than her ever-present though apparently controllable desire for motherhood. For Barbara, the worst of it was the "dishonesty" she felt at having to keep the episode from her parents. There's a Freudian dictum that might apply here: You are as sick as your secrets.

You are as sick as your secrets—of course, to Freud, the key to treatment of a neurosis lay in uncovering the hidden fact that lay beneath it. Once you are aware of that, you can dismiss it or deal with it as you see fit. It is the harboring of the guilty secret that causes the problem.

Barbara chose to keep the secret to maintain the most important thing in her life, her relationship with Jim. For her, it was well worth it. And she came to see that a "lie" of omission is not the same as the one that you tell to gain a dishonest end.

But Barbara's dilemma points up the unique and uniquely troubling place that abortion holds in our minds. She could tell her parents that she was living with Jim, cohabiting outside of marriage—to their eyes, living in sin. Of that, she said, tell them and be damned. But this, at all costs, she would hide, and she did.

Jim and Barbara were able to meet their crisis because, in a way, they were prepared for it. As the one who felt most strongly about preventing a pregnancy, Jim had taken an active role in the decision-making about birth control, and when the worst happened, he took his share of the responsibility, offering comfort and support. I've got to ask myself why Jim's attitude, which seems not heroic but only decent and sensible, should make him stand out so.

Somehow, men have just got to get used to not entering the bedroom without the guaranteed knowledge that they are going to practice good contraception, to pledge that they will not be careless in that regard; that they will not play around in adultery; that they will not rape or date rape; that they will not sleep around, period. A tall order? In the current state of male-female relations, unfortunately, yes. The assumption that birth control is the woman's problem alone and a smoldering resentment that women like Dianne Porter dare to assert themselves as full-fledged individuals give a lot of men plenty of reason to behave as irresponsibly as they want to.

Even men who ought to know better, who ostensibly like and respect women, frequently don't "get it." As one man summed it up: "The Pill was the best thing that ever happened to men.

After the Pill came along, you never had to think about birth control anymore! Do you realize what a nuisance that was—always having to worry and be prepared?"

The funny thing was, he was talking to a woman. Yes, she realized. She was using a diaphragm.

And what if a woman gets pregnant anyway? The law is going to have to be there to mandate child support to adulthood, and overcome the regrettable fact that in as many as seventy-five percent of breakups, the father walks away and reneges on his kids. It's a sorry business. If pro-choice feminists don't want to listen to men on this issue—well, most of them haven't got much reason to.

It would be far easier for us all to say why try to change human nature? "Men are men, and boys will be boys, and the only difference is the price of their toys," as the saying goes. Give everybody equal rights and let them do as they please. But apart from the cynicism involved in that attitude, it's antifeminist, antiwoman. Everybody gets to play, but only women bear the burden. We're back where we started, and no better off.

By the time Larry Porter realized what was happening, it was too late. Too much had gone down between him and Dianne. He knew it would be wrong to patronize her; no mink coat or island vacation was going to buy her back. Communication? There had already been too much anger, too many words spoken in resentment, too much exposure.

The marriage was over. Larry and Dianne divorced. None of their friends thought it would come to that—but it happened. Can a healthy relationship break apart over one issue? Except for adultery, I doubted it then, and I do now. But if there was anything else, we never knew about it. If there was, they hid it well.

You might think that Larry would have been aware of the pitfalls. After all, he was a doctor, wasn't he? But that doesn't

make anyone immune to sexism. Maybe the opposite. Medicine—at least established medicine—has a long sexist history to
answer for. Women, and a few doctors, are just now waking up
to the fact that most of the drugs on the market today have been
tested solely on men. There are no clinical studies that tell us
how women react to them, but doctors prescribe them anyway,
as if women were just ersatz men. And there *are* studies to
suggest that when a man goes to a doctor with chest pain, he
gets a stress test and a cardiac evaluation; when a woman goes
in with the same symptoms, all too often she gets Valium. That
still happens. In reply to the question "When will the pharmaceutical industry perfect a male birth-control pill?" one professor put it this way: "Not as long as drug company CEOs are
men."

The multibillion-dollar plastic and cosmetic surgery industry—comprised almost totally of elective procedures—has
sprung up to "help women feel better about themselves." Its
focus is almost entirely on women's appearance, their beauty,
their looks. The virtual epidemic of face lifts, breast augmenta-
tions and liposuctions in the past decades attests to women's
dissatisfaction with their bodies. Cosmetic surgery says, "Your
most valuable asset is your appearance. Losing it? Never had it?
We can make you beautiful. We surgeons, we men, can provide
you with fresh currency—a new face, a new body. One that will
appeal to us."

Not enough people ask why women feel so dissatisfied, or
who, exactly, is setting the standard and putting such a pre-
mium on physical attractiveness that a lot of women don't feel
like worthwhile human beings if they don't measure up.

We gynecologists aren't much better. Not so long ago, con-
ventional wisdom had it that menstrual cramps were all in a
woman's head—she didn't like being a woman, that's all. Ditto
hot flashes. Everybody "knew" they were a figment of the
imagination of neurotic menopausal women, until quite recently, when lo and behold, researchers "discovered" that what
women have been describing for centuries really happened.

It can't be pure coincidence that the three surgical procedures most frequently performed on the female patient are hysterectomy, abortion and cesarean section—all of them assaults on the uterus, the maternal end organ. Somehow, it seems that the manipulation, removal and "cleaning" procedures that the womb is subject to arise from an attitude that it's expendable—what one feminist friend of mine calls the "We Don't Have It You Don't Need It" school of medicine.

Some quality doctors and some prestigious medical centers have been known to suggest cesarean section to pregnant women as a routine alternative to vaginal delivery—they offer the convenience of scheduling and none of the bother of going through labor. It's all under the guise of resulting in healthier babies—no rough trip down the birth canal, I suppose.

Hysterectomies are touted as a viable elective method to get around the "drudgery" of menstruation and the "rigors" of childbirth. The "useless uterus syndrome," or "UUS," describing a woman over thirty-five with her childbirth plans complete, has often been listed as an indication of elective hysterectomy in more than one gynecologic medical center. The only winner is the doctor's bank account.

And what can we say about abortion?

Abortion is, by almost any standards, a violent act. All surgery violates the integrity of the body; purely elective surgery seems particularly gratuitous. On the positive side, it gives women the means to decide their own fates and control their own reproductive lives. But it also puts more of the weight on women's shoulders, allowing men and society in general to literally scrape and vacuum away their responsibilities.

Abortion reform grew out of the successful women's movement. The turnaround in thinking about abortion that occurred in the sixties and seventies paralleled the entry of women into the marketplace. Even though they're still a long way from economic equality, in the last decades women have advanced in jobs, wages, politics and the like, in numbers that amount to a revolution.

I guess there had to be a backlash. By the eighties, we were seeing scare stories about career-woman burnout, a marriage-able-man shortage and an epidemic of infertility caused by delaying childbearing too long. Watch it, ladies, if you get too pushy, bad things will happen to you.

Many men do feel threatened—no question about it. There is a sense in some circles that women need to be put back in their place. And with a rise in reports of wife-beating and violent rape, a lot of people are getting the uncomfortable sense that it's dangerous out there. Women can't take care of themselves—they need big, brawny men to protect them.

We have a society that confuses sexuality with violence—the "She asked for it" defense still works in rape trials, the pornog-raphy industry is booming and young men still insist that it was OK for five or six of them to have sex with a woman they had first rendered semicomatose with liquor because "she con-sented." Sure, guys.

Abortion fits this picture too. An abortion clinic is bombed. Nobody was killed? The authorities shrug. There's not much active investigation and very little prosecution. We're inured to violence against women. What is it but sexism run amok?

A lot of people—both male and female—are vaguely uncom-fortable with the idea of women having equal rights with men. There is a fear that, given power, women will abuse it. By, for example, having abortions for what Justice William Rehnquist, in his *Doe v. Bolton* dissent, called "convenience, whim, or caprice." It's a deep distrust of women and their motives in general, and the old question of who holds the power.

The antichoice factions are making good use of the general-ized fear of powerful, independent women when they champion "fetal rights." We're seeing instances where women have been arrested and charged with such crimes as "delivering drugs to a minor" because they allegedly were guilty of substance abuse while they were pregnant. Some states have deliberated on the advisability of making "adult beverage" drinking or taking street-type drugs while pregnant a felony.

It's interesting that a lot of this is happening in places where it's almost impossible for a pregnant woman to get treatment for her addiction while she's pregnant or, conversely, to get an abortion. We really don't know how many women are being intimidated into not aborting and then go on to have a cocaine-addicted or brain-damaged child or a child with fetal alcohol syndrome. We do know that their access is severely limited—at least sixteen states already have restrictions on funding that effectively prohibit abortion for poor women, the people least likely to be able to scrape together the money to get private care.

And then there's the movement to have legislatures exclude pregnant women from those eligible to sign living wills, so they cannot reject the use of life support on comatose newborns. It's the woman-as-container syndrome, which views women principally as the vessel that carries another person.

Most people are disturbed by the idea of a pregnant woman doing things—like drinking and taking drugs—that will damage her fetus. They assume that she "chose to be pregnant" and therefore should eschew behavior that might harm the developing pregnancy. But they're making a big assumption. Did she, in fact, choose? In what sense? The women who abuse drugs or liquor, at least who do it to the extent that it takes to do serious harm, are in deep, deep trouble. Is throwing them in jail the best we can do? The insidious thing about fetal rights and fetal-protection laws is that they pit the woman against her fetus—divide and conquer. It's a clever political strategy, but, particularly in this situation, a cynical and cruel one.

We've all read about cases where hospitals—or worse, if that's possible, strangers with a cause—go to court to force protection of the fetus over the wishes of a family. In one recent case on New York's Long Island, a pregnant woman in a coma from a car accident became the object of a court battle when activists from a antichoice coalition brought an injunction against the abortion that had been recommended by her doctors and was being sought by her husband. The injunction only delayed the inevitable—the court found for the husband, and the abortion was performed. Shortly thereafter, the woman began to emerge from her coma.

The judge in this case strongly criticized the complainants for their unwarranted intrusion into the private lives of the family. But the law from courtroom to courtroom is capricious. It could have gone the other way, and while the dry legal debate dragged on from court to court, the woman could have lost her chance to survive, not to mention the prolonged anguish inflicted upon her family.

As the rights of the fetus rise, the rights of women decline. The fetal-rights movement says that the fetus has to be protected from its mother. In a clash of rights, its rights should prevail. The pro-choice feminist says the bottom line is this: Is the pregnancy wanted or not? That is the question that has to guide every decision to protect both the pregnancy and the mother.

Dianne Porter wanted her pregnancy. When she decided to abort, in a sense, she yielded to Larry, but at the price of the marriage—to keep that would have meant denying too much of herself. For Larry, she'd been too forward, too much of an independent woman, too outspoken about her rights, and that, even more than the abortion, was the crux of the matter. By the time Larry caught on, there was too much water under the bridge.

Larry got visitation rights with the boys: every other weekend, half their school vacations, two weeks in the summer. He has a live-in girlfriend, but not always the same one every time I see him—he's the freewheeling bachelor now. He always compares his women to Dianne. She has her career; if she is in a relationship, I don't know about it. They've both had to live with the loss of their marriage. Larry tells me that he thinks of it every time he counsels another abortion patient.

9 *A Study in Contrasts*

Where we parted ways, I really don't know. I do know that in my quest to understand the full meaning of abortion in my career, I had to try to understand my friend and colleague, Dr. Bernard Nathanson. As much as any of us, he had been a part of the struggle to win abortion rights for the women of America.

Those were my thoughts as, almost two decades after our parting, I visited Bernie in his office on New York's fashionable Upper East Side. I was surrounded there by his well-deserved icons. On the walls, his face beamed with pride in a trio of enlarged photographs: Nathanson and Ronald Reagan, Nathanson and Mother Teresa, Nathanson and His Excellency John Paul XXIII, the Vicar of Rome. A framed original *Doonesbury* comic strip, with a message signed by cartoonist Garry Trudeau, showed a caricature of Bernie introducing a pregnant woman to her "baby"—a tiny dot in the middle of the large screen of an ultrasound imager.

Nathanson is proud of the cartoon. "It's meant to poke fun at me, of course," he smiles, "but it's not malicious. I asked if I could have it to take a place with my other mementos."

I looked around for the VCR monitor that patients have described as standing ready to play a continuous-loop version of one of his best-known contributions to the abortion debate—*The Silent Scream*. The short color film purports to show an abortion from the point of view of the fetus. It is one of the cornerstones of the so-called right-to-life movement.

Before *Roe* and *Doe*, before the change in the New York State

182

statutes, even before I got involved in abortion politics, Bernie Nathanson was in there fighting for reform. Like a lot of doctors of his generation and mine, he had dealt with the results of back-alley butchery and had both seen and felt the wrenching guilt and emotional upheaval that followed illegal abortions in the fifties and sixties. He wasn't someone who could sit passively by and watch things happen. Not Bernie. He was in at the beginning. I was looking forward to reminiscing with him.

I'd first heard his name soon after I got back to New York from Philadelphia and Ashland. With my interest in Planned Parenthood and NARAL and reform, how could I not have? He was an outspoken and effective proponent of legal abortion. When I got my chief to agree to send me to Chicago for the strategy meeting on abortion reform, he told me, "Keep an eye out for Bernie Nathanson.

"You're almost certain to meet him," he said. "There's a whole New York contingent, I understand, and he's one of its shining stars."

Sure enough, when I located the delegation from New York, Bernie was at its center—the acknowledged medical leader. We met and talked for about half an hour. In a way, he was welcoming me aboard. He was established on the scene, and I was a relative newcomer. He made me feel that he was happy to see another doctor joining the battle. We liked each other.

He was in his very early forties at the time, my chronological peer, and successful—he gave that impression, anyway. In an atmosphere that tended to get hot and heavy, with a lot of passionate reformers and angry activists yelling and jumping around, he managed to seem above the fray—calm, rather elegant, kind of aloof. He always spoke in a soft voice, but one that got attention—you had to quiet down to hear him, so you did. And he had a talent for getting people to come along for the ride. The night I took the microphone and spoke out publicly on abortion rights for the first time—would I have done it if Bernie Nathanson hadn't said, "Come on," walked me to an aisle microphone and thrust it into my hand? Hard to say.

Up to the time he got into abortion reform, it had been pretty much the province of the activists—Planned Parenthood, the National Organization for Women and other feminist groups, former flower children from the sixties who'd had their own horrendous abortion experiences—people the politicians in those days didn't feel they had to take very seriously. As a respected gynecologist and obstetrician, Bernie brought the cachet of organized medicine. He was authoritative and sure of himself, even a little arrogant—a lot harder to ignore. On abortion reform, Bernie was the right man at the right time.

The Reverend Howard Moody still greets visitors at his office in the Judson Memorial Church in New York's Greenwich Village, where he's been since he arrived there as pastor in 1956. Moody's quarters were not as unfamiliar to me as Bernie Nathanson's—I had been there before, although not for many years. Cluttered with papers and books and as comfortable and well used as an old shoe, the room looked and felt descriptive of its tenant.

Moody came to New York via the Big D (Dallas, Texas, where he grew up a seemingly traditional Southern Baptist), a military stint and Yale Divinity School. When he landed at the Judson Church, he'd found himself a home. Since the 1890s, under old Judson himself, the church has been known for its activism, especially in providing health care to the poor.

Now seventyish, Howard Moody has spent virtually his entire career at the Judson, becoming as much a part of the place as its namesake. He's a relaxed, tweed-pants and fisherman's-sweater kind of guy, a little more grizzle in his crew cut than when I first knew him, but still maintaining the erect carriage of a U.S. Marine—which he proudly was. A man who had seen a lot of action in World War II, he wasn't afraid to risk a few skirmishes over abortion—or anything else, for that matter.

Rambling back through the history of the abortion-rights movement, Moody didn't remember being in Chicago. Indeed, he remembered being left out—a church budget doesn't allow for much out-of-state travel, then or now. But like Bernie Nathanson, he was in at the start.

Like many of us, he got into the abortion business almost by accident. He was new to New York and new to the Judson when his predecessor at the church called from his Florida retirement retreat to ask a favor: Would Moody help to arrange an abortion for a woman "in trouble"? A "name" was needed.

"It was early fifty-seven," Howard explained, "the woman was an older lady, had some teenage children already and just couldn't afford this child. She had had an affair, as I remember. So I got a friend in the church, and we saw a doctor—terrible. We wouldn't send anybody to her. I got hold of a woman in the church who was in show business, and she knew the route to contact someone. I really got involved after that."

Howard made it sound like the sort of thing any decent person would have done. I was reminded of Doug Spencer, who used to say, "I always thought a doctor's job was to help people, that's all." Howard believed it was a pastor's job too.

At first, it was one, then a few more. And then the abortion movement, as he put it, "took off." A reform bill in the New York assembly got as far as the health committee. Howard Moody recalled, "A few of the ministers got together and talked about strategy—what we could do. Some ministers met with Larry Lader." He was referring to someone we both were familiar with—Larry was one of the key figures in NARAL and a force behind the Chicago meeting.

Lader wanted the ministers' group to go public and kept nudging them. They kept meeting, maybe once a month, having conversations—theological, cultural, all kinds of stuff about what the abortion issue meant. And then, in the spring of 1967, the Health Committee of the New York State Assembly met again on abortion reform, and again, the bill died there. It never got to the Assembly floor. No wonder we were all so pessimistic about the future of abortion reform in New York.

"We said, enough! Let's do something," Howard recalled. "So we pulled together a group of ministers—twenty-six of us. We called ourselves the Clergy Consultation Service on Abortion—CCSA." The group helped women with problem pregnancies do whatever they wanted to do, including having the babies.

Moody went on, "We had a debate on the name. People didn't use the word 'abortion' in public conversation—it was verboten. I told them, Let's not do that. Let's take that word out of the closet and use it!"

They didn't hide their light under a bushel, these clergymen. Howard explained, "We gave the New York *Times* an exclusive, and we had a front-page story as a kickoff—[explaining] exactly what we were going to do. The whole thing started out of this discussion group."

Chinese revolutionist Mao Tse-tung once said that every change that ever took place in this world started from a few people getting together in a room to kick around an idea. Thus a movement that shakes the world is put into motion. The CCSA was evidence enough of the wisdom of Chairman Mao's words.

"Not all the ministers went along with us," said Howard. "A lot of them wanted more theological discussion, not to do anything. I had a few Catholics I trusted, and we had a Catholic woman or two—"

"Rabbis?" I asked.

"A few."

Those guys were a tough little ecumenical council, all by themselves. Howard was proud of the group he'd put together.

How did a bunch of New York clergymen go about finding a nationwide network of reliable abortionists? A young woman named Arlene Carmen had come on board at the Judson Church as Howard's right hand. She made the CCSA part of her work there.

"Arlene and a few other women from the church would go and seek out a doctor, and Arlene would pretend she was pregnant. She would go all the way up on the table, right into the stirrups"—he said it with more than a hint of pride, and I have to admit I was impressed as well—"checking them out to see if there was anything in their mannerisms, their language or in the way they dealt with women. If they would pass the test.

We went to West Virginia—all over—to set the criteria as to how doctors treated their patients.

"We set a price, something everyone could afford. We exerted our power. We had one guy who wanted five hundred or even more, and I said too bad, women can't afford that. He was stubborn, all right. We turned off the faucet. He called me and said he would comply." He spoke as if he had enjoyed putting the screws to the gouger.

If not actually as illegal as hell, it was all pretty irregular.

"Were you scared?" I asked.

Moody reflected. "Yes, but I didn't know enough to be really scared. What I knew—when people asked the D.A. what about these illegal clergymen doing this terrible thing, he'd say, 'No comment.' We had great advice: Act as though you are right and doing nothing wrong. So when an extortionist called me, and wanted lots of money for his payoff, I called the D.A. and told him. I just acted as if, well, he's the extortionist. We were doing nothing wrong. And they helped us." The memory evoked a smug smile.

After Chicago, Bernie Nathanson and I used to cross paths fairly often at meetings and such. We had the same priorities, so I was not surprised that he was at the New York capital the day of the Albany watch. When he saw me, he took me aside and asked what I thought our chances were.

"Not very good, I'm afraid."

He critiqued my assessment with a superior smile. I was too pessimistic by far, he told me. He sensed it was our day. He'd been in touch with someone in the legislature who suggested that a one-vote switch would do the trick. That's why he'd come up—he wanted to be in at the moment of triumph.

I didn't take him too seriously.

Of course, he was right. It did take only one vote. But Bernie didn't hang around to celebrate. Afterward, he—along with Larry Lader, the PPH folks and some of the other prime movers—rushed back to New York in time to do an evening TV news broadcast. We were all luxuriating in our triumph.

Howard Moody saw it all, knew everyone. He'd sent people to "that guy in Pennsylvania" from the first.

"Maybe while I was working with him," I said. "It's a—"

"—small world." We finished the phrase in unison.

By the midsixties, the CCSA search had turned up many names. "We sent a couple of people to monitor them," Howard said. "Or as many as we could. I learned about them from the women who came back. Those who were praised deserved a visit from Arlene. There was that guy down south working out of a hotel in downtown New Orleans who used potholders on the stirrups to pad ladies' heels. A nice touch." Howard was quite impressed with that.

Potholders on the stirrups—I've always used them. Now that I think of it, where did I first see them? Doug? Roy?

". . . He treated them like human beings. Rave notices. I went there—I was impressed. A little crazy, as I learned later on, but that didn't matter to me. We sent lots of women.

"As soon as the law changed, we really got mobilized. When I heard 'Want a clinic in New York?' I said, 'I'll tell you what— if you set up a clinic, I'm gonna look it over.' " Rev. Howard Moody didn't want the CCSA to be tied to any one service, because then they would have a vested interest. No—he wanted us all to act on our own, and he would inspect us as he did the others. If we passed his and Arlene's test, we would get the referrals.

"I told them all—if they set it up, and they had the right kind of place and the right kind of price, we'd refer. The women's center was really organized and ready to go."

I said we'd been ready to go two weeks early, and he laughed.

The tariff was important to the CCSA. When the New York unit was getting under way, Howard was adamant. "How much would be fair?" he was asked.

"Will one twenty-five do it for you?"

"One twenty-five it will be."

It was as simple and as quick a negotiation as that. We all went to work.

The CCSA had spread around the country. There were still doctors in other states willing to work. But because the women's center was there, neat and clean and—above all—legal, the clergy decided it was almost foolish to go elsewhere. Moody ended up on the board of directors, a kind of silent partner.

My path was crisscrossing Bernie Nathanson's and Howard Moody's even more than I realized at the time. At the height of our political upheavals at the Women's Center, it was Bernie who came aboard to bail us out. He was a cut above. The paycheck was secondary to the burning need to keep abortion safe and legal—a motive we shared back then.

We were all still quite new at this legal game. The New York switch had taken us all by such surprise, despite the optimistic rumors, that our excesses of enthusiasm had brought growing pains. We needed the discipline that Nathanson brought.

Some of the staff felt a little miffed at Bernie's disdain of their motives, what they called his "arrogance." But under his administration, the center kept rolling, and that was what counted. Those who didn't like it accepted it or moved on. And Bernie brought respectability, as he had to the reform movement earlier. He was what the doctor ordered—a good "front man."

In the New England Journal of Medicine, one of the foremost medical journals in the country, he published a definitive report on the 26,000 abortions we did in that first year. New York City statistics overall showed a total of 165,000, which had to be shy of many; not everyone reported scrupulously. The article proudly demonstrated the safety of the abortion procedure. There were no deaths, and an extremely low complication rate as defined by any medical standard. As a safe, acceptable medical procedure, abortion had "arrived."

Those first years passed quickly. None of us took the time to look at our watches or our calendars. I left the unit in 1973.

Bernard Nathanson left not too long after. We both went on to our many pursuits and interests in OB-GYN—after all, abortion was only one part of our work. Leaving seemed a natural step in our professional growth. I wanted more variety, a chance to know my patients, and a way to put my gynecologic and psychiatric training to use. As for Bernie, I didn't know why he left—it didn't concern me.

In that East Side office, under the peering eyes of President Reagan, Pope John Paul XXIII and Mother Teresa, Bernie Nathanson told me that he had been at a moment of transition. He was solidifying thoughts and honing feelings about life that were no longer compatible with abortion and the abortion trade.

Bernie and I had come to a parting of our professional ways.

Today, Bernard Nathanson is a medical jewel in the crown of the antichoice movement—a similar position to the one he held for pro-choice years ago. I knew about that, of course, but I decided to hear it from him. After almost twenty years, I wasn't entirely sure how Bernie would receive me, but I should have known better. We were and are members of the same profession, and we belong to the same organizations. Our mutual respect had not changed. I wanted to use Bernie Nathanson's thinking to better understand my own.

We remembered the old days with some fondness, although he dismissed his earlier activism with a wave of his hand. "I was young, revolutionary—it was 1967 with a spirit of change, Vietnam, the sexual revolution. I was swept up and I wanted to question authority. Abortion fit right in.

"I'm not doing penance now. I acted out of conviction then," he went on. The change had come after his days at the Women's Center, when he came into contact with new technologies that, he said, brought him new awareness. "I saw and realized—the techniques that showed me the fetus . . . it was a whole other world." He became convinced that he was on the wrong track about when life began. With the aid of high-resolution sonograms and sophisticated fetal-monitoring equipment, he heard "the silent scream."

"When we see a patient who's pregnant, we don't say, 'My, what a lovely zygote you're having,' " he pointed out, using the medical term for a newly fertilized egg. "We say, 'You will have a lovely baby'—at any stage of the pregnancy."

Yes, I've done that. And yet, do I believe it's a baby? It's not the baby I'll deliver, months down the line. "But what changed?" I asked.

"Abortion changed." He went on. "Social engineering changed. And social engineering follows verbal engineering . . . We have to have the right words to tell the patient. It's not a zygote. It's a baby."

Howard Moody looked thoughtful. "Bernie Nathanson. He worked with us. We liked him because he never considered money a priority. It wasn't an issue. When we had licensing problems, we went to Bernie.

"We all knew him. He was a person who always needed to be on the outside. He really tackled the job. And when we gathered around him, he wanted to be on the outside again. It's hard to believe that he was converted by the pictures he saw. He had to have seen them before—had to. Obstetrical training, med school? I have a hard time with that one. I came to count on Bernie—"

Like Howard Moody, I was wrestling with it too. Perhaps Bernie was trying to say that the emotional reality of abortion hadn't hit him until then. That I could understand. But if he was saying that he didn't know that a fetus had little hands and little feet and a heart chamber and so on at six or eight weeks, then I wonder. I knew that in medical school, the first time I glanced through an embryology textbook. What was new?

* * *

A big part of the pro-choice/antichoice debate hinges on the questions of rights and life, two issues that are really one issue intertwined—the rights of the mother versus the rights of the baby. When is it a "baby"? Where does it all begin?

The antichoice stance is to say that it's a baby from the moment of conception. It's a "person," or it's "human life." But most people understand that what we have at the moment of conception is not a living, breathing, thinking, feeling, acting "human being," just as an acorn is not an oak tree, or grapes are not wine—not yet.

A single fertilized egg may someday, through the miracle of cell division and differentiation, become a person. But a person at the instant the sperm and egg meet? That's something else again. It's a question that lies at the heart of the whole issue.

The fertilized ovum—the embryologist's term for the combined egg and sperm from conception to the end of the first week—normally contains the forty-six chromosomes that determine all that a full-grown human person will be. In it are the materials to become a person, through the marvelous process of genetic chemistry. It is what happens between the first union—the zygote—and the millions of cell divisions later that will decide what that person-to-be will be, if it is to be.

Along each of the forty-six chromosomes in the fertilized ovum lie the genes, tiny bits of cellular material that transmit information about what a person will be. These tiny, self-determining particles are the messengers that carry heredity. The tip of your grandfather's nose, your great-grandmother's long fingers, your father's tendency to freckle or burn in the sun—or not—all come to you through the genes you receive.

Genes are arranged in a specific order on each chromosome. Before a chromosome splits, each gene divides, and one daughter gene goes to each of the daughter chromosomes. Why "daughter" instead of "son"? At the onset of the fertilized ovum—it's not even an embryo yet—all creation is female. Even if it's carrying the Y chromosome that determines maleness, the ovum or even the early embryo—which emerges in the second week—doesn't "know" what it is yet. In the jargon of the geneticist, it's undifferentiated, just waiting for the Y chromosome to make its move. Not until the seventh or eighth week, almost the end of the embryo stage, does the Y chromosome, if present, manifest itself, making the undifferentiated embryo a differentiated male.

Probably the first question we ask about a baby is "Is it a boy or a girl?" It sounds like a simple question, but like everything else about us, our maleness or femaleness is complex. Every human being has six different kinds of sexual differentiation—chromosomal, genetic, hormonal, anatomic or genital, gonadal and social. Ninety-eight percent of the time, all of those factors are the same, or compatible, in a given individual—all male or all female. The rest of the time—two percent of the population—there is some kind of incongruity between at least one marker and the others. It usually isn't obvious. We often don't find out, if at all, until later on in life when infertility or some other problem drives someone to an endocrinologist.

A good deal of what we know about brain differentiation in humans comes from experimentation on the laboratory rat, which is a unique animal because its brain remains undifferentiated for seventy-two hours after birth. In those three days, manipulation of rats' anatomy and body chemistry in various ways results in their becoming quite confused sexually. The research demonstrated how different biological influences work to shape the individual and continue to do so well after the embryonic stage—right up into early infancy. A lot of the things that make us who we are, at least medically and biologically, aren't determined at conception.

The Supreme Court's *Jane Doe* decision made viability—the ability to sustain independent life—the determining factor in legal abortion. The *Doe* decision was limited by the *Webster* case, which states that life begins at conception. Does "life" begin at conception? In what sense? That's another idea that bears exploration.

In one way the notion that life begins at conception is unarguable. In a sense the fertilized ovum is indeed "alive." A fertile woman's eggs are alive, and so are a man's sperm—alive, but not viable unless certain conditions are met. It's possible to take the argument back one more step and say, "Yes, and since they're alive, barrier-type contraception should be outlawed too," but most people accept the idea that birth control ought to be a private matter. Even there, however, the line is hazy. Some methods of birth control may work by blocking implantation after conception has occurred. Are those methods "abortions"? Are they "killing"?

To add to the controversy, some say pregnancy does not begin at the moment of conception, but rather, with implantation, which is not a moment at all, but a process that occurs over time as the fertilized egg attaches itself to the womb. It's estimated that only one-half of all fertilized eggs make it through the implantation process; the others simply wash out of the woman's body. She conceives, but she is never pregnant.

There is a pending case in Tennessee, in which a couple undergoing in vitro fertilization are divorcing, with seven of their frozen embryos in a laboratory awaiting implantation. The couple sued each other for "custody" of the frozen embryos; the judge has awarded the "mother" the seven "children." It remains for the court to decide on the final disposition of the embryos.

If the woman chooses to have two or even three of these embryos implanted and carries them to term, what happens to the other four? Would it be murder to destroy them? To let them die? This kind of "murder" is being done all the time, in every in vitro laboratory in the country.

Suppose the "father" had been awarded custody of the seven "children." What was he going to do with them? Does he have the right to simply hold them hostage, so to speak, in a frozen state, forever? Is that "preserving their right to life"? Or would he try to find a woman who wants to have his first wife's child in preference to her own, thus adding the problem of surrogacy to the stew?

As the argument currently stands, there's a fair amount of popular support for the idea that "life begins at the moment of conception"—as if it's something that could be decided by a vote. But even if life does begin then, does that necessarily mean that the ovum or embryo is a "person"? A "human being"? Many people have an innate sense that it is not. "Personhood" implies not only the physical attributes of a human being—hands and feet, a beating heart—but also thinking, moral reasoning and emotions, for which the embryo has no capacity. Do these things, though, somehow exist in all embryonic and fetal life? Is it always necessary "to see something to know it's there"? Political cartoonist Trudeau was twitting Bernie Nathanson about this very issue when he drew that single dot to portray a "baby."

What actually *is* there? Cells divide. They keep on dividing until a person emerges. Each cell has to make up more cells that eventually cluster into the various organs and parts of the body. It is not enough to make a nose and a leg and an eye and a stomach. Somehow each cell has to "know" what its job will be and go to it. The cellular process has to be orchestrated.

This role has been assigned, officially, to the nucleic acids that make up the basic materials of the chromosomes and transmit the hereditary pattern, DNA and its messenger RNA. But that too may be misleading. Even the DNA and RNA, which are making the various cells into the necessary organs and parts, have to get their instructions from somewhere. Each cell, with its chromosomes and genes and their DNA-RNA structure, "knows" what to become, but it has no idea of where to go and what to do until the next set is made. Thus, the first set depends totally upon the succeeding sets of sets, and so forth.

An analogy has been made to house-building. We have lumber and windows and doors and pipes and wires but they are not a house until an architect comes along and tells the contractor, the carpenter, the plumber and the electrician where to put them. But the comparison isn't a perfect one. What happens in cell division isn't the same as putting together pieces to build a house. The architect's blueprint tells us where everything will go in the house. It's all there on paper and can be done an infinite number of times over—always the same. Not so with the ovum. As Oscar Hammerstein II wrote, "There is nothing like a dame"—or any human. If there is a preset pathway or blueprint, we have yet to find it. DNA? RNA? We don't know.

As the cells of the human divide and divide and divide, they take the DNA and RNA message from the next cell set and from preceding cells and do what they have to do, and the organ systems are formed. Each cell made is not sure yet what it will be until the next cells are formed. A blueprint for a human doesn't exist.

It is precisely this random chance formation that makes each person different. Even identical twins are not exact clones. They may come from the same egg and have the same genetic makeup, but they do not have the same fingerprints, and there are many other things in their bodies that are different too. They look very similar, true—but they are individuals. Close friends and family can tell them apart easily. Genetic material by itself does not a person make. Not by a long shot. The embryo is not the same as the person it will become.

But person or not, an embryo is human life, isn't it? Here again, the answer is, that depends. What, exactly, do we mean by "human"? Isn't there a difference between "human cells" and a human being? Even those who argue that embryos should be protected because they're "human life" don't go so far as to call them "human beings"—in the full sense of the word.

What, then, does it take to make a cluster of cells into a human being? How does it happen?

The first system formed is the nervous system, the neural tube and the spinal cord with the bulge at the top that will eventually become the brain.

Over the next few weeks, all the systems are forming. After the neural tube come the internal skeleton, the mouth, the jaw, the pharynx and then the lungs, the heart and blood vessels, the colon, or body cavity, and, at about the same time, the meta-nephros—the rudimentary organ that will become the kidney and the renal system. Then come the limbs, and finally the genitalia.

The earliest anlage, the foundation of all that the organism will become, starts with the neural tube that appears in the first month. Not until the second month are brain cells seen. In the third month, nerve cells appear in the periphery of the forming brain and go on forming through the fourth month. By the fifth month, the brain is functioning, but on reflex only. There is no central control.

The cerebrum, the largest and highest part of the brain and the one that gives rise to the thinking function—and makes it all happen—is the last to form. In the cerebrum—integrated with the other parts, of course, but essential—are housed the breathing center, the cardiac center, the sleep center, the swallowing or deglutition center and, we now think, the sex center, the possible answer to the question of where and what is the libido. The appearance of the cerebrum is a milestone, because without the brain centers that control the basic life functions such as breathing and heartbeat, no life can be sustained.

When does the brain come to fruition? When is it able to function as a brain?

The consensus of perinatologists and fetal neurologists is that the mature brain is not seen in its developed state until the sixth to seventh month. Independent life before twenty-four weeks of gestation is not viable on that basis, despite reports of exceptions. It was on this basis that the Supreme Court set twenty-four weeks as the limit for elective abortion in the Jane Doe case.

As Bernie Nathanson remembers it, the *Doe* decision was a kind of a coin toss. When we were in medical school, it's true, textbooks set the age of viability at twenty-eight weeks, although that doesn't mean that any twenty-eight-weekers survived. At that time, back thirty or even twenty-five years ago, babies that premature were doomed. It wasn't until the late seventies, in the right hospitals, that neonatology got to a point where twenty-eight-weekers had a real and measurable chance.

But those same obstetrics textbooks made twenty weeks the cutoff for abortion, which, by Bernie Nathanson's interpretation, meant that it was the recognized point of theoretical viability. So the difference between twenty-eight and twenty weeks was split, and the "authorities" picked twenty-four.

But that version defies history. In fact the court heard hours and hours of expert testimony on fetal brain development and based its decision on a medical definition of "independent life."

Even after it has a mature brain, though, the fetus's nervous system is far from complete. When is that fully formed brain able to provide connections to arms and legs and the peripheral nervous system? These systems arise even later. And later still comes the connection to the limbic system, the system that connects the brain and the central nervous system to the emotions. They may not be until just before birth, or even at the birth moment itself.

Is referring to the fetus as a "baby" a case of assigning to the embryo or fetus characteristics that we have as born human beings, but don't have while in the womb? Quite possibly. It's an emotionally potent, but not scientific, argument. *Silent Scream* showed the reflex movements of the fetus—true. But reflexes aren't feelings. Indeed, reflexes, by definition, are something that don't require thought. And thought doesn't occur in the early stages of fetal development—not at twenty-four weeks or less. Certainly not in the first trimester of pregnancy, when close to ninety percent of all abortions are performed. There is no thought; no brain connection; no system to provide the fetus with feeling, emotions, pain, cold, heat; no mind demanding information or facts. The acorn is not a tree. The grape is not wine. And by the same token, the embryo is not a sensate human being.

What seems to be happening, then, is the assignment of potential to this group of cells—traits that in fact are not there at all. Not yet. The potential of the embryo is in our own minds. We give it characteristics of personhood, just as Jessica endowed her lab frog with human rights and feelings because she felt for it as a living thing. Can mere "potential" hold us in the grip of such emotion as the abortion debate engenders? Watch an infertile woman grieve every month for the "baby" she has lost by not conceiving. The "baby" is neither conceived nor real, but the feeling is, as anyone who has seen or felt it knows. Does wishing make it so? Alas, no.

What is a human? Not simply our cells, but the way they are put together, along with the how and why of our experiences and thoughts and feelings. Until and unless we are capable of brain function, we're not fully human, at least not in most people's eyes.

Humans are unique in both obvious and subtle ways. We are the only biped mammals—the only ones that stand upright and walk on two feet. Even close relatives like chimpanzees habitually go on all fours.

Karl Marx, a student of anthropology and comparative anatomy as well as politics and economics, was one of the first to point out that when early people stood erect and let their skulls drop forward, they gained room for the forebrain to develop— the cerebrum, the seat of our powers of thought. Comparatively speaking, our brains became enormous; much larger animals such as the whale and the elephant have far smaller brains than we do.

That same shift in posture also created room along our necks that made it possible for people to develop voice boxes and vocal cords, also comparatively larger. Thus we became the only animals who can communicate with words. Parrots can screech and mimic, lions can roar, dolphins can transmit messages with squeaks and squawks, but only humans have true language.

The late Alan Barnes, MD, former chairman of the department of gynecology at Johns Hopkins University and later chairman of the medical board at women's center, pointed out the price we pay for being bipeds. With tongue in cheek, Dr. Barnes wrote that although thought and speech may make humans superior animals and give them the means to rule the world, nothing is without cost. We are the only animals that suffer to any degree from low back pain and fallen arches, varicose veins and prolapsed pelvic organs. And though pound for pound we have the strongest legs of any member of the animal kingdom, we're plagued with gimpy knees and pulled muscles. Furthermore, our legs may be very strong, but horses and cheetahs and most other lower animals outrun us easily.

With all these woes, you might wonder why we don't just drop down on all fours again—especially if your back's been acting up lately. What's in it for us poor bipeds? Barnes had an answer for that too. We're the only animals to face our partners during sexual intercourse. That may be reward enough.

After *Roe v. Wade* made abortion legal essentially "on demand," there was, in Bernard Nathanson's words, "no counterbalance. I had not seen the other side." Now he did. "It overwhelmed me, and I began to question." His resignation from NARAL came in 1975; by 1976, he had decided that he would no longer perform abortions under any circumstances. He wasn't unusual in this. Far from it. Many, many doctors have chosen not to do abortions for religious and ethical reasons of their own—a valid personal decision.

For a time, that decision not to perform abortions stayed between him and his conscience. Then, as he tells it, "Back in 1979, I was not strongly pro-life. I had a stereotypic view of the other 'lifers.' But I was wrong, as you may have been. The pro-life people called me. I saw an organized moral stance . . . I saw solid and reliable platforms. Not disposable, but solid.

"I am unhappy in a world where I set my boundaries. I am not capable of setting boundaries and values. We must take the values we have received from antiquity and use them and apply them. We have discarded them."

But what of the people who will suffer because of the moral absolutism of others? The Nathansons and the Sloans of the world, I insisted, had to answer to them.

*   *   *

Howard Moody seemed quite prepared and willing to play devil's advocate. We imagined an extreme case—a disabled mother with a heart condition carrying a damaged fetus, a baby that could not hope to live for more than a few hours or days outside the womb, one with no brain or kidneys, or with its organs outside its body, the woman taxed, physically and emotionally, by the continuation of the pregnancy. Exaggeration to make a point? Yes. But not a rare example. Cases like this occur daily.

"No abortion even then?" I asked Dr. Nathanson.

Even then. In a world of moral absolutes, there are no exceptions. Some people are comforted by absolutes, others find them profoundly disturbing.

We might ask what right a disabled woman, alive with her disability, has to deny her unborn child the same rights she was granted. She has, in one view, the responsibility to give birth to the defective baby, nurture it, house it, pay for its upkeep and watch it live whatever its life span may be, at whatever cost to her own health. One school of thought is that this should be required. Another says let each of us decide.

Wouldn't such a woman be making a decision out of her own experience? The unborn, being unborn, will never know. And the woman, adult and aware, would indeed understand the act—a truly informed consent.

In Bernie Nathanson's world of absolutes, the baby should be born, at whatever cost. "Suffering and dying are not the worst things in life," he said. "This may sound cruel. But they are ennobling and can even enrich. It can be the richest experience of life. To deliberately excise all of the values we are given in order to avoid suffering is something that in the end impoverishes us. We are never supposed to be perfect."

Was abortion to him, then, I asked, a kind of eugenics—a way of excising the "worst" or getting rid of the "troublesome"?

"It's more," he said. He explained abortion in the context of our social existence as symptomatic of the evil in the modern world. Drugs, crime and pornography are all manifestations of the same evil—instant gratification, too much license. He described his unhappiness with a society that permits people the latitude to make such mistakes. One that gives them freedom of choice. "The woman will be made a better person by the ennobling role of suffering," he explained.

But, I wondered, who has the right to assign this ennobling role to anyone else? Who's doing the suffering—when have these women been "ennobled" enough? For some, for all too many, that reward will clearly never come in this life.

The ennobling role of suffering? "Good Catholic theology," said the Reverend Howard Moody.

Shouldn't this philosophy be taken to its fullest element and stretched to cover both sides of the issue? If suffering is ennobling, is one kind better than another? Who says abortion is "easy" or "instant gratification"? For the woman who suffers guilt and anguish, it can surely be a painful experience. Can't she be ennobled by that too?

Bernie, Howard and I all came up with one shared theme. We thought of Buddha's three noble truths, circa 500 B.C.: "The first noble truth is that all beings are subject to suffering. No one escapes . . . suffering is universal. The second noble truth is that the cause of suffering is ignorance and ignorance of oneself is the greatest ignorance . . . The third noble truth is that ignorance, the cause of suffering, can be overcome."

I found we still had much in common.

*   *   *

Any true believer has a right to argue for a religious belief or a moral stance. Every religion has a right—a duty, even—to instruct its adherents in the tenets of the faith, to try to make them follow its precepts. But first, admit that those tenets are religious. In a pluralistic society such as ours, should anyone be forced to live according to the religious beliefs of someone else?

The state's interest? The Constitution is clear on separation of church and state. In order for the secular courts to take an interest in the question of when life begins, it must be a scientific argument, not a religious one.

The Reverend Howard Moody was warming to the debate. "Abortion reform didn't introduce abortion to America. People were getting abortions. You just needed a lot of money and needed to know the right people."

"Are you at peace with it all?" I asked him.

"I am at peace. We lost ministers—the pictures got them. And lay people—that constant drumming home of 'life.' The issue of reproductive ethics will break open in the nineties. Abortion—in a sense, its technology has changed the debate. Do you keep pushing back viability? Do abortion after viability? Between conception and birth we all of us become anti-abortion, at some point. There's a commonality that all of us have with the lifers. At some point—maybe two weeks before birth, but we all have a point.

"There are ethical and moral issues. Total pro-choice? Does that mean amniocentesis, and you're not going to have that blue-eyed boy baby—let's get rid of it? Genetic engineering, pregnancy policing, morality—these are the issues of the nineties. And who's being policed? It's the black and Hispanic women, the poor women. How come the rich women who drink every day—no policing there. Here we are, persecuting women who are in public hospitals, drug addicted, and they have no place to go. There is the hypocrisy.

"We get it all bass-ackwards. We don't care whether she had prenatal care—or anything like that—except that she personally doesn't beat the child in her uterus. Abortion has not gone away and people are not going to let it go away. Yes, I'm comfortable. I'm saying that we all draw the line, and I draw my line arbitrarily: at birth, or the first breath.

"You can't say what about the day before. You don't know. That arbitrary line-draw—it's up to you. But I am at peace . . ."

It is clear that Americans are going to have to find a way to live with the moral ambiguities of abortion, a dilemma that is apparent from surveys that say most people feel simultaneously that abortion should be allowed and that it is a kind of "murder." That's a tough one to sort out.

One route that's been suggested as a sort of compromise is "permit but discourage," which would emphasize the teaching of values and ethics, but continue abortion as a legal right. This approach says we should attack the root causes that drive women to abortion—unequal opportunity, ignorance, sexism, a society that turns a blind eye to the needs of women and children, the poor, the mentally and physically handicapped—rather than abridge the legal rights of women. That seems to satisfy the United States Constitution and yet might soothe those who cannot come to grips with the abortion process. At first look, I thought that no one could argue with that approach. End abortion by eradicating its causes and reducing the need, if there were such definable things, and not by denying women their constitutional rights. I could live with that.

"Pie in the sky," declared Bernie Nathanson. "There is this argument that we should set a limit, as a compromise—find the limit, some time limit, at an early enough time that will be acceptable."

"Permit but discourage" is, to his thinking, just another name for choice. And choice permits no compromise. "The choicers are intractable," he said. "They want full rights and no restrictions." There's something to this, I suppose, but as Nathanson understands it, groups like NARAL want "abortion to nine months. This is *The Man of La Mancha*—the impossible dream," he insisted.

I'm not really sure what "abortion to nine months" means. After twenty-four weeks, the fetus is clearly becoming viable, and abortion is approaching the impossible. It's a delivery then. How could such late abortion be done? Only by intrauterine destruction. What would come of such "abortions"? Is this an exaggeration meant to inflame? Out of the nearly 1.4 million abortions performed in 1988, only about a dozen were reported as having been performed in the third trimester, presumably for desperate reasons—a nonviable fetus, a dying mother, or both. And that was a typical year. Can it be that the two sides in this battle are entrenched over something that has only a one-in-a-million chance of occurring, and then in name only?

"At some point," the Reverend Howard Moody reflected, "we—all of us—become pro-life. It's a question of where you draw the line."

A lot of people who accept the idea of abortion in the early weeks of pregnancy begin to get uneasy about second-trimester abortions, which are problematic for some doctors too. Who's having these more difficult and dangerous procedures? Anti-choice propaganda would like us to imagine that women who wait past twelve or fourteen weeks of pregnancy are lazy or indecisive or frivolous or uncaring. The reality bespeaks desperation. A lot of later procedures are done on young girls too ashamed and frightened to tell anyone, women who have been unable to get information because of federal gag rules, women whose earlier procedures were canceled because of pickets or protesters, women who—because of Medicaid and other governmental restrictions—can't get the money together in time.

Second-trimester abortions may be a shame, but whose shame are they? That of the women who seek them? Or ours?

Aristotle said that every event grows out of a condition, a situation and a cause. So while the cause of an unwanted pregnancy—a couple's indiscretion—may seem obvious, the situation—that moment of passion and sexual drive—and the condition—a reaction to socioeconomic plight or just a state of being human—also play a role. We have to accept all three if we're going to understand the whole picture.

The burgeoning technologies of pregnancy have created an even greater burden of responsibility for parents-to-be. Amniocentesis allows us to test the amniotic fluid for defects; chorionic villus sampling analyzes a snippet of the early placenta in women at high risk for genetic problems; the alpha-feto protein, or AFP, test identifies fetuses with neural-tube defects such as spina bifida and anencephaly or brain absence; and high-resolution ultrasound shows structural defects. Isn't it wonderful that we now know these things? is only half the story. The other half is, What do we do with the knowledge?

"Take Down's syndrome," offered Howard Moody. "Not what it used to be." He's right. We no longer routinely hide Down's babies away in institutions—a good thing. But that puts a greater—maybe a lifelong—burden on the family. Moody takes it one step further. "If a baby has six fingers, does that mean we abort? The blue-eyed boy or the sex-preference question scares me. That may be a slippery slope to eugenics and the Nazi stuff."

We're all in danger of the slippery slope that caused Howard's uncertainty. Yes, there's a slope. But all of us must find for ourselves a place on that incline and slide no further. I'm not comfortable with the idea of "abortion" in the ninth month. I

draw my line, and beyond it, I'm as "pro-life" as Bernie
Nathanson or Howard Moody or anyone else.

But up to twenty-four weeks, before presently accepted viability, according to the laws of the land, a woman has a right to
decide for her unborn, because the unborn, until that viability,
has no capacity to decide anything. Someone might easily argue
against her—show me a loved and lovely Down's baby, and
make the point: Who are we to decide? But who are we to
decide for the woman either?

It's been argued that if it's wrong to kill a baby on the day
it's born, it's wrong to kill it the day before, and so on and so
on and so on, back to conception. That's a slippery slope of its
own. Because while philosophers argue, women are the ones
running the risks of childbirth and being saddled with unwanted
children. Where's the justice there?

If there is absolute right and wrong, there is no slippery slope,
because there can be no compromise. As Bernie Nathanson put
it to me with great conviction, the pro-choice faction "doesn't
understand how deeply entrenched we are in the way we think.
It is not an ethical reverence for life. God is God. You don't
negotiate with God."

Is life sacred? Most thoughtful people would agree that it is. But
what do we mean by that? Sure, there are people who mean all
life—who won't eat eggs or wear leather shoes or fur coats or
swat mosquitoes or step on a cockroach. But most of us, when
we say life is sacred, mean "human life." Some of us include
our beloved pets as well—certainly to the degree that they seem
to those of us who are owners to love us and to respond to our
love.

For the most part, we can draw a distinction between human
and lower-animal life because we've come to accept the idea
that only humans are higher animals. Humans think; feel
sadness, passion, desire, joy; have memories; relate to family

and friends; have expectations and goals and ambitions and hopes. Our lovemaking is based on libido, not estrus.

Technology with its sophisticated machines has blurred the line between life and death just a little. People used to be dead when their hearts stopped beating and they stopped breathing, but now it seems we can almost routinely bring them back—at least for a short time. Some doctors won't write or respect a DNR, a "Do Not Resuscitate" order, as long as there's any hope of rekindling a spark of life.

But death happens anyway. People ask doctors to write DNRs for their loved ones and let them "die with dignity." When someone stops doing all the things that make him or her "human"—thinking, feeling and so on—and when the higher brain waves stop, we let them go. We respect the family's DNR and let nature take its course.

One of the most tragic, surely, of all birth defects is anencephaly, when babies are born without a developed brain. Death comes, often within hours, because these babies lack the cerebral cortex necessary to support life, to keep their hearts beating and their lungs taking in air and all of their other vital systems functioning.

While the country watched, the Florida parents of a newborn anencephalic girl who was still breathing sought to have her declared brain-dead, so that her organs might be used for transplant to save other babies. In this case, the court found that the baby did not meet the criteria of brain death. Yet in no sense could it be said that she was "fighting for life." Without a brain, she could never think or feel or have goals. At best she was in a kind of limbo between a life that consisted only of biological functions and a true death in which all those functions had stopped.

Once the absent skull is covered up, it's difficult—some would say impossible—to look at a newborn, ostensibly sleeping, and say, "It's dead, let's take its organs." We're hard-wired to feel protective of baby things, from mice to whales, our own kind not the least. But many medical ethicists, doctors and parents of anencephalics—the people who have actually lived through the experience—feel that an exception should be made for these cases, because the only comfort to be had from the tragedy lies in having a bit of the baby live on in others.

During the courtroom arguments in the Florida case, one doctor said, "What makes us human is what goes on upstairs in the brain, not downstairs in the brain." And many parents of such babies agree. Without a functioning brain, there is no "person" there to protect.

Even people who claim that a fetus is a person admit that the fetus has no thoughts, no emotions, no memory, no hopes, no ambitions, no passions, no libido, intentions or goals.

Why, then, is the life of a fetus so sacred, even to those who would allow a DNR order for any other kind of human life? They share every characteristic with the brain-dead. It's not enough to say, along with *The Silent Scream*, "I felt the pain of the fetus." Pain? Maybe. But can it be pain as we know it? The peripheral nerves are not there, so the pain, if present, can't be felt. And even pain is not the same as thinking, feeling emotions, having goals. Pain alone does not make us human.

Why should the "pain" of a fetus that cannot feel it count for more than the suffering of an adult woman? Is it because she should pay the price for her roll in the hay? And why should the "silent scream" of the fetus weigh more heavily than the piercing wail of an abused or hungry already-born child? More of our children live below the poverty line than any other single group. What do our priorities say about us?

Perhaps the fetus is sacred because there is the assumption, the hope, that it will someday be a productive person. It is, in itself, the goal of the pregnancy. But isn't the whole question of "When does life begin?" basically more religious and philosophical than scientific?

*   *   *

Howard Moody told me, "It's a question of where you draw the line." The people who draw the line at conception are imbuing the conceptus with a soul, something that can't be rationally verified. Like other kinds of belief and unbelief, the notion of the moment at which life begins is simply not arguable. It's one of life's imponderables.

As Bernie Nathanson and I talked on, philosophy and politics took over. I asked if a large part of the attraction of the antichoice movement lay in its absolutism.

"We trash life," he said, "and it is not meaningful anymore. Values are whatever the situation requires. No boundaries exist any longer, except for religion. Everything is compromise. We are supposed to trade off and yield to our needs." He'd stressed boundaries again. The freedom to make decisions about right and wrong, to make the close calls of individual conscience or moral good versus the lesser of two evils clearly made him uncomfortable.

And for the women who must give birth to unwanted children that they have no money to support? "There are three thousand private organizations and homes that offer full care. They'll take the baby, raise it." No problem.

But today women keep their babies. Only six percent of children born out of wedlock in 1989 were placed for adoption. The rest? Who knows? Sociologists are pointing out a phenomenon of the nineties, the "no-parent" family—children who have neither father nor mother, children being raised by relatives or paid foster parents, arguably the most abysmal program yet devised by social agencies, children for whom the concept of a loving home and family is as imaginary as a fairy tale.

I had to be impressed with Bernie's consistency, though. Most comfortable in a world of absolutes, he deviated not one whit from total "pro-life." He would not for any reason whatsoever perform an abortion, not even to save a woman's life, if that concept were presented to him. The trade-off of saving one life at the expense of another was totally alien to him. Capital punishment under any circumstances is repugnant to him. War is death and has no place in his thinking. He is opposed to the "right to die"; he excepts only personal self-defense. "You take a life only to defend your own," he said. Anything else is "murder."

To call abortion "murder"—what does that mean? We accept capital punishment, we accept war. There is nothing more Machiavellian than our accepting the possibility of nuclear holocaust, but almost every president who's ever mustered up the troops has enjoyed soaring—if temporary—popularity. Dissenters get shouted down. We like a little war, especially when the power's on our side.

And in the abortion wars, who has the power? Who's making the laws? Not the women, surely. Yes, there are women against choice. But in the end, they have no more say than any other women. It's the men who make the laws and vote on them. And they make these laws to control pregnant women, who are going through risks that they will never experience—and can never experience.

We have to draw the line somewhere, perhaps. But must we do it by denying women their rights? It's a dilemma of its own. What right has anyone—anyone at all—to stereotype or to trivialize the needs of women?

Is it only a rights question? Howard Moody expressed a problem, as many do, with total choice—the idea of abortion for no reason at all, or for reasons he considered frivolous, if, indeed, that happens. Frivolous to whom? Yet, as he said, "The woman has a right. We have to raise the question . . . where do we draw the line? Time? The child to be?"

*   *   *

It was noteworthy to Howard Moody that after *Roe* and *Doe*, women still came to the CCSA, "and they were not interested in getting an abortion, but in having a baby. The family wanted an abortion, she wanted the baby, time and time again. We had them all, we took them on and we did the same. He said you do what *you* want, it's your choice. The guy may not want it, you do. It twists around. I would always take the woman's position against the family." The CCSA became associated with the concept of choice—choice to abort, choice to deliver.

Moody paused again to reflect. "We might lose *Roe v. Wade*. You know there are a lot of states where you can't get an abortion—rural areas. Eighteen percent of the counties have abortion, and half the hospitals don't do abortion. We think *Roe v. Wade* enabled everybody—that's just not true. The poor have never been able to get abortions. We blocked them with the Medicaid thing, the black and the poor women. Rejoice over *Roe v. Wade?* The poor never knew it!

"So we haven't really arrived. It won't make a lot of difference to them if we lose *Roe v. Wade*. A lot of folks that needed abortion didn't get one. We couldn't help them. And if they were poor, we didn't help them much at all."

He sounded so much like my socially conscious father that I had to smile. But he's no extremist. His position is not so far from that of many mainstream Protestant denominations. We've come to associate antichoice with religion, thanks to the orthodoxy of the Vatican, the religious right and antichoice activist groups like the "Lambs of Christ." Nevertheless, many established churches today, while deploring conditions that give rise to unplanned pregnancies, support a society in which a full range of reproductive choices is available to all women and not merely a luxury for the economically advantaged. That includes abortion, which many faiths believe can be at the same time a sad and unfortunate decision and a moral and necessary one.

*   *   *

Howard Moody summed up his lifetime of activism. "Abortion—this is probably the single most important thing I have ever done. I don't know of any issue in this world that affects the life of women so specially."

I leaned back on the sofa in his office and leaned back into my memories. When I went to Doug Spencer and did what I did, I felt the same way about myself—nothing I could do would be more of a help to women than this. That's why I did it, why I had to do it.

If Howard Moody has any reservations, they're about his not going far enough toward helping the poor and disadvantaged. "It kept you humble," he said, "that what you did was great— you, me, all of us—but don't forget what we didn't do. And when we could do it as a nation, we didn't."

He thought for a moment. "Life is a complex issue. Conception is life—let's say that, finally, take that approach—and yes, you're taking it away. And then we have to develop the rationale for the taking of it, as we develop the rationale for taking life elsewhere—in war, in capital punishment."

Does he have any regrets?

"Regrets? About our stand on abortion?" Howard Moody looked me in the eye. "No, no, no. Only for the ones we didn't get to help—and for them, our work is in front of us. We have picked up the gauntlet. We have to carry it through to the end."

I left my reunion with Howard Moody, replaying his words in my head. I held his statements up to Bernie Nathanson's, turning them over in my mind. I thought about my two old and respected friends from the early abortion reform movement, now seemingly so far apart.

My head swam with it all. When I went to see Howard Moody and Bernie Nathanson, I'd expected discussions of theology and social medicine. I'd had them. But from whom?

Howard Moody, the minister, had spoken of unresolved

social problems, of the failure of the richest country in the world to look after its children, its poor. To Howard, the government regulations that deny poor women access to abortion were a symbol of how we have lost our way socially in a world of money-making and warfare, a sign that we've forgotten how to care for our neighbors. "You and I," he'd said, punctuating his words with his finger, "still have to find a way to deliver our medical knowledge to the people who need it most. We have our work cut out for us."

To Bernie, the medical doctor, abortion was proof of how far we've strayed from the will of God. For him, the world of abortion revolved around the dicta of Mother Teresa and the Holy See. "You don't negotiate with God," he said. True enough, I suppose. But to take an absolute position and call it God's—how can he be so sure? I'd always believed fallibility was inherent in the human condition. Bernie had invoked God as though he knew what He wanted.

Were my old friends somehow a microcosm of the ways the issue of abortion has twisted us around and pulled us apart as a country? And with the division so great, is there a hope of reconciliation?

Bernie Nathanson and I have the same pedigree, so to speak— by age, by interest, by training, by profession. And it landed us on two different sides of the same question. Why? I still don't know.

10 *The Politics of Abortion*

Downtown Brooklyn. North Philadelphia. Ashland, Pennsylvania. Chicago, Illinois. Roy Parker. Women's Center. CCSA. What has all that meant? Was it all just serendipity? Sometimes it seems as if abortion has dominated my whole professional career—from the backroom days to the private clinics and hospitals. I've performed abortions at all stages on women of all ages and stations of life. I've heard as many reasons for choosing abortion as I've met women who have had one. And I'm sure I haven't heard them all.

Abortion has a life and a politics all its own.

Although both the American Medical Association (AMA) and the American College of Obstetricians and Gynecologists (ACOG) seem to have sidestepped the real issues of the abortion question, they are on the public record: They are pro-choice. Early abortion is still ten times safer than childbirth, so from a purely medical standpoint, choice is the position that gives the doctor the greatest latitude to do what's best for the patient. But when it gets down to cases, there's nothing to stop individual doctors or hospital boards from playing politics and branding the doctors who do abortions with the Mark of Cain.

As much infighting, controversy and political maneuvering go on within the sterile walls of the medical world as on the floor of the legislatures or out on the sidewalks in front of abortion clinics. And it's often as ugly as it can get. The term "abortionist" still carries a heavy weight. We've made it legal, but we haven't made it respectable—not quite. I learned that lesson early. It was my education in hospital politics.

215

*   *   *

I guess if it weren't for abortion, Tom Gresky* and I would have gone through our whole lives as acquaintances with a subtle respect for each other's skills, nodding as we passed each other in the hallway or on hospital rounds. He had preceded me at County General*, but when I was a newcomer there, he wasn't exactly the old man of the staff.

Recalling my lunchroom anthropology session, I looked at his lumbering gait, long square face and tufted dark hair and typed him as an orthopod—he looked so bony himself. But he was in fact second in command of neurology—and a well-respected member of the medical staff. Since junior staffers usually use peers instead of the old guard for any necessary consultations, we never had any shared patients. Dr. Gresky—I used his title when the rare opportunity came along to address him directly—was not exactly the friendliest guy in the world, but then again I didn't know him well enough to judge. I guess I just figured we wouldn't cross paths that seriously. I also thought he didn't know me that well.

I was wrong.

The Albany watch was behind us. Medical services, clinics, the health departments and the hospitals were gearing up for what was to come. I'm sure that most clinicians had no real idea of what New York was going to be—the abortion capital of America for the next three years or so.

Activist groups—NARAL, NOW, PPH and their counterparts—were arming for the next campaign. The hard-fought battle to bring abortion out of the closet and the back alley was won, and now they all felt that the logical next step was to make sure hospitals were going to provide the women of the state and their patients in general with the facilities required by law. Medical care was to be delivered on demand, and abortion was now under the medical code—it fit right into that category.

My reputation had preceded me. It was almost a given that I would be involved in abortion at General, and setting up a service was the right thing to do for the community. So when the hospital balked at giving anything more than lip service to the neighborhood for which they were responsible, I took to the media to criticize.

Apparently I touched a nerve in a few of the staffers. What had been a friendly "hello" and a shared cup of coffee suddenly became an icy stare or an abrupt nod—sometimes even a total cold shoulder. I had expected it from some, was surprised at others—but I took it all in stride.

Gresky's reaction, though, was above and beyond the call. That puzzled me.

Tom Gresky was no dummy. He was well qualified in his specialty. I grew aware that he was outspoken about many hospital practices. He wasn't afraid to go up against anyone, and he was often right. He was well thought of for his candor. We might have become buddies, but for abortion.

By training and experience, I was the logical choice to head up the new abortion service. So I was surprised to learn that Gresky was opposing my appointment with snide remarks about my experience as an "old-time abortionist." I was actually a little flattered. I didn't realize I was that famous—or infamous, as the case might be. I was prepared to take that in stride as well and let things cool down. They never did, with Gresky.

At first I assumed it was Gresky and the church, that his traditional devotion to his faith had made it difficult to accept someone with my background. Then I attributed it to his being too straightlaced, too wrapped up in the cloak of medical traditionalism, too elitist. At the time, that was enough of an explanation for me.

It all came out over coffee and a Danish late one afternoon with Moe Robbins*, director of the hospital laundry service and a real hospital old-timer—he predated Gresky by a decade. We'd become quite friendly and shared many a rap over politics, women and hospital gossip. He started dropping some pretty broad hints, as though he wanted to make sure I knew the reasons behind Gresky's animosity—of which he was aware. Moe was in on everything. As he used to say, you'd be surprised what you got out of emptying the pockets of the doctors' uniform coats before you loaded them into the washer.

After that, it didn't take much sleuthing to find out what was behind Gresky's overreaction. Pretty quickly, I found a skeleton in the ER closet—it wasn't even much of a secret.

Well before I'd joined the General staff, and a couple of years into a politically correct marriage, Tom Gresky had worked his way into the affections of the head X-ray technician, an involvement that soon led to a politically incorrect pregnancy. All the players were medical types, though, and if they couldn't look after their own, who could, right? It was decided that an abortion would cover things up. A "Saturday-night special" was arranged. But something went wrong. The tech ended up hemorrhaging in her own ER, and the cat was out of the bag.

I guess it took a lot of fancy footwork to get around that one, although Gresky somehow managed. His marriage and his hospital position survived intact. Time was the healer, and Tom's secure hospital position made it all but forgotten.

Until I came along.

When I came on board, Albany was a year—and a millennium—away. I hadn't exactly listed Doug Spencer on my professional résumé or asked for his letter of recommendation. Why push? The rest of my curriculum vitae was enough to get me staff.

Gradually it all fell into place. For Gresky—maybe it was irrational, but it made a kind of twisted sense—the very word "abortionist" made him feel exposed and dredged up old memories that he had hoped were all but forgotten. I know now they were—for everyone but him. He struck out in anger—an anger that he perhaps extended to anyone and everyone associated with terminations. I couldn't be denied the position on the strength of my qualifications, and he knew it, so he fell back on what he hoped was tainted enough, distasteful enough, ugly enough to sway the board against me—the label "old-time abortionist." He was hoping it would scare me away.

I felt as though I were living through a grade-B movie or a weekday TV soap. I didn't know how to use Moe Robbins' story—or even if I ever would. Eventually logic and reason prevailed, and Tom was subtly pressured into letting his vehemence fade away. My appointment was approved.

Over the next few years, before Tom's tragic fatal heart attack and my leaving General, our relationship consisted of polite nods in the elevators and hallways. Knowing what I know of the rest of Tom Gresky, I regret I was never able to be his friend.

First-trimester abortion is considered "minor" surgery in the lexicon of the gynecologist, in that it does not require incision or suturing of a body cavity. But it's subjected to a scrutiny far beyond its nominal status. Several years ago, a research study exposed the way health professionals look upon abortion by comparing two procedures that are so similar as to be virtually identical—first-trimester abortion and the diagnostic D & C, dilation and curettage. The latter, now done routinely on an ambulatory basis, is considered one of the most valuable diagnostic and therapeutic tools in the armamentarium of the gynecologist, as evidenced by its frequency.

The project examined the emergency-room records of several cross-section hospitals to see if there was a pattern of care for women who came in with complications following abortion as compared to the D & C. The researchers allowed for any patients who had problems such as any gynecological pelvic pathology or unrelated medical problems like asthma, heart trouble and diabetes that might bring a patient back to the emergency room after surgery for reasons other than those directly and solely related to the procedure itself. They were therefore looking only at first-trimester abortions and D & Cs with no extraneous factors that could affect the findings. The study was well conceived and well executed. What they found was startling.

With rare exceptions, the abortion complication was treated with greater concern and a more extensive evaluation, including lab testing, sonography and X-ray, and—usually unnecessary—additional surgery. The ER services admitted the abortion patient with a much greater frequency than the D & C patient, even when their complaints were the same. The postabortal woman had more consultations, longer hospital stays, a higher rate of social service intervention and, most alarmingly, subsequent emergency hysterectomies, a very rare event following complications in the postdiagnostic D & C patient.

The researchers concluded that there was an obvious built-in prejudice against the abortion patient, partly due to ignorance on the part of the ER and hospital staff, and—I suspect even more—partly out of a regressive attitude toward the abortion patient and her doctor. There seemed to be a need to punish both.

My own personal experience has been similar. During my hospital duty covering the ER as a consultant to the teaching service, I have noted that the resident or ER duty officer will show a greater concern when a postabortal patient walks in and will ask to do more—whereas the complication in a diagnostic D & C patient with similar complaints will be minimized and treated with a calmer or more laissez-faire approach.

Melissa was a nineteen-year-old woman whose cousin, a long-standing patient, asked me to see her as a favor. Melissa's mother was estranged from the family, and Melissa had turned to her cousin in desperation, although the move was certainly warranted by the closeness of their relationship.

At my exam, I noted that she was about sixteen weeks' pregnant—later than I had been led to believe, but having agreed to help, I accepted the case. I arranged to have her admitted to a hospital ambulatory unit for a termination.

The residents seemed pleased to have me do it. It was a rare chance for them to assist at a second-trimester suction abortion. With the proper lab tests and admission procedure completed, I took the residents through the termination step by step. We finished about ten in the morning. Everything went well, and I left routine orders for Melissa to be discharged that afternoon—three to four hours later. That was it, I thought.

Early that evening, the resident on duty called me.

"Your AB patient is complaining of dizziness and weakness," he said. "She has some bleeding. I'd like to take her up for a sonogram and get some blood work, so if we need to do a transfusion—" If a transfusion were to be needed, it would be a first.

"How badly is she bleeding?"

"Well, not very much, but—"

I knew the resident on duty well enough and had come to respect his objective and clinical evaluation of a problem. He detailed his "not very much" in clearly understandable medical terms—we both spoke the same medicalese. He had examined the patient, albeit without my knowledge or instructions, so I was able to question him closely.

Once I do a procedure and there are no complications at the time, I can be pretty sure of the risks later on. My experience has given me a great deal of security and I am quite familiar with what can go wrong and what likely will not. He hadn't found anything out of the ordinary. I decided she was reacting as expected.

"She's OK," I said. "Send her home—no problem."

Again, I thought that was the end of it. But the resident, behind my back, then consulted with the chief of the service—my superior, in a sense, but very much my chronologic junior and someone with very little abortion experience, by choice. Without my knowledge or consent, my discharge order was cancelled, blood counts and X-rays and sonograms were ordered and my patient was held overnight.

She was fine—as I knew she was—and she went home in the morning. That was that, as far as patient care went.

But protocol? Out the window. The resident and my chief had acted contrary to good and usual medical ethics and courtesy. My patient's care was usurped by a subordinate and a superior without medical credibility, and moreover, without my knowledge. It soon became obvious to me that they had reacted—nay, overreacted—without my consent, and at the patient's expense, to abortion. They were both showing their discomfort with midtrimester termination.

We all parted friends, but it gave me pause.

That resident was one I thought of highly—he was relatively mature for his years and level of experience. He knew me. He knew of my experience. His knowledge of postop D & C complications was sufficient to enable him to recognize that the bleeding and the patient's other complaints were well within the expected norm for the procedure. That is, if he were being objective. Had it been any other type of surgery, his adherence to protocol and courtesy would have been exemplary. We would have shared in the patient's care. But he could not overcome his built-in prejudice against abortion, even though he professed to have no religious or ethical scruples against it. It was a purely emotional reaction.

This resident, I sensed, wanted to learn. Most of today's student gynecologists aren't trained to do abortions, any more than I was, in my day. I had to cut my eyeteeth in Doug Spencer's office, not in my own training program. I understood it then—abortion was, in a sense, illegal. Our opportunities and exposure and our need were rare. But why now?

We have modern and well-monitored residency programs today that strictly outline the requirements for training in cesarean, vaginal hysterectomy, infertility, forceps delivery, endocrinology, perinatology, sexuality, oncology, every facet of care. Indeed, for proper accreditation, there must be demonstrable proof that every program has qualified, board-certified clinicians to do the teaching. But abortion is not included. Whatever training the resident of today gets in this area, it's on his or her own. To this very day.

It it's not lack of training that discourages doctors, it's the bureaucracy. Besides the usual hospital paperwork, a doctor is required to complete special government forms for every abortion. According to the accepted medical code, this is supposed to be a medical procedure, private, between doctor and patient.

That was the clear message of *Roe v. Wade*. Why, then, are we required to submit special forms on abortion? For the statistics?

That defies logic. Modern computer technology can provide hospital statistics—number of procedures, sequelae, whatever—in a minute at the flick of a modem. But this is more than that. The information requested includes such things as race, ancestry, birthplace, maiden name, marital status, education level and home address. We are told it is "confidential," but such information is readily accessible to those who want it. And the big question is, why do they think they have to know?

Despite *Roe v. Wade* and its clearly defined constitutional outline, abortion is scrutinized as no other medical procedure. Furthermore, things are getting worse, not better. One in-group joke has it that it's better to complete the red-tape forms prior to the procedure than afterward, because in the few minutes it takes to complete the abortion, another piece of documentation may have been added to the growing pile.

Abortion is obviously treated differently by everyone, including all governmental agencies. Maybe especially by the governmental agencies. The feds, as well as the state and local agencies, it seems, can't help meddling in human reproduction, even when their policies are shortsighted, pointless or downright counterproductive.

The developed nations have a shopworn theory that all the Third World needs is adequate birth control—limit the population, and prosperity will ensue. The problem is that such thinking contradicts history and geopolitics, and when it doesn't succeed, we blame the victims—those "ignorant natives" won't do what's good for them. Or we fire the agency head and find a new dreamer to try to convince the starving masses mired in poverty to control their fertility. It's all pretty silly. More, it's cruel.

In fact, we've got it exactly backward. There is one means and one alone that curbs the birth—and abortion—rate to acceptable levels: a rise in the standard of living. Birth control naturally follows.

Some twenty-five years ago, a leading population control

think tank instituted a campaign to convince Indian men to agree to vasectomies. They offered any and every man who would submit to the procedure a fancy portable radio as an inducement. The radios were shipped by the boatload and stacked on the docks of Indian seaports—where they corroded and eventually were discarded. Surprise! Virtually no one wanted a radio badly enough to make the deal.

What does an Indian man—who works sixteen hours a day in the fields for little pay and whose only hope for a secure old age is to father enough sons to support him when he can't work anymore—want with a portable radio? It was a question nobody had thought to ask.

In 1974 the first World Population Conference was held in Mexico City. The conferees issued a statement, which the United States delegation supported and signed, rightfully linking population and poverty, and making population control— of which abortion was a part—a priority. But a decade later, with Ronald Reagan in the White House, the federal government reversed its position, saying that population growth was "a natural phenomenon" and the solution to world poverty was free market economies. As a sop to vocal antichoice forces, the administration had agreed that it would not support abortion, including referral and counseling services, in the undeveloped world.

Although there was no evidence that population planning funds were being used for abortions, the United States made financial aid contingent on the agreement that no U.S. assistance would be used for abortion, even in countries where abortion was legal, birth control was inadequate, the birth rate was out of control and the mortality rate of children was at shameful levels.

The effect was chilling. Clinics in countries like Bangladesh and India curtailed their abortion services for fear that U.S. observers might not believe that American funds weren't being used and would cut off all aid, thus putting essential gynecological and prenatal services in peril. Even in countries like Turkey, where abortion is quite legal, clinic nurses and counselors stopped discussing abortion—withholding information that legally, ethically, morally and medically they should have been providing.

The upshot of all this? Abortions have increased, not decreased. But there is a problem: The increase in abortion is due to illegal, back-alley jobs. The World Health Organization (WHO) estimates that around the world at least 200,000 women die each year from septic abortions. And we're letting it happen. A crime? Surely. But not the only one. How about the fact that we're letting the antichoice faction run our foreign policy?

World health journals have been printing articles about the scandal of unsafe abortions in the Third World for many years. A report in the late eighties estimated that each year there are between thirty and thirty-five million legal abortions worldwide. The number of illegal abortions, based on our knowledge of deaths and other complications, adds millions. The total must be near the fifty million mark. Very likely more.

Sepsis—severe infection caused by unsanitary conditions—is the most common problem, not only in the back alleys, but in the clinics too, where sanitation standards leave much to be desired. And then there are the many incomplete abortions, where tissue left behind results in overwhelming infection, and where the massive antibiotics needed to treat the infection are usually not available, leading to "life-saving" hysterectomy, which may be fatal in itself. Many women enter the operating room strapped to a hospital litter but leave concealed in a wooden box.

Finally there's internal damage done by inexperienced practitioners—damage to the vagina, the cervix and other organs. It's a desperate situation made more desperate by lack of funding for even the most basic amenities. Except more wooden boxes.

So we keep going back to the same tired solutions—sex education and birth control. Or to what one first lady might have advised: "Just say no!" Sex education in schools? What schools? Education classes in the town hall and local meeting places? What meeting places? Group discussions at church socials? What church socials? If there were schools and jobs and any kind of security for their futures, people would not feel the need for outsized families.

U.S. monies for family planning abroad are dispersed through the Agency for International Development (AID). Not long ago, they allocated $200,000 to a Catholic-based organization to teach the rhythm method of birth control and sexual abstinence to African natives. The greatest part of the funds was earmarked for Zambia, where Human Immunodeficiency Virus (HIV) disease and its clinical syndrome, Acquired Immunodeficiency Syndrome (AIDS), are rampant, along with illegal abortion.

WHO estimates that well over three-quarters of the women and couples in the most undeveloped countries have no access to birth control at all. Nothing. Is it any wonder women turn to anyone who promises to "help" them? In Ethiopia, twenty-five percent of all maternal deaths are abortion deaths—and because of underreporting, Ethiopia's statistics are considered falsely low. The numbers are higher elsewhere. There have to be many thousands of Ethiopian women whose deaths go officially unnoticed. Worse, when a clinic does do a dirty abortion and the woman dies, the authorities don't report it for fear of losing funds. Not only that, there's a resistance in the clinics to helping women who are the victims of botched abortions, for fear that too will disqualify those clinics from getting the almighty U.S. dollar. "Don't touch abortion" gets around. More wooden boxes.

One U.S. policymaker, speaking against funding Third World clinics that mention abortion as an alternative, said that not having the freedom to abort would be "a good thing" for people in underdeveloped countries, because it would force them to practice better birth control. The truth is the opposite— cruelly so.

And while we try again what's already failed—if you do the arithmetic—illegal abortion worldwide kills a woman every two minutes. Around the clock.

*   *   *

In 1966, the Romanian government banned all abortion and modern birth control. The ban failed utterly in its purpose—to raise the birth rate—but the policy continued in force for twenty-three years.

A patient from Romania gave me a firsthand account of the hellish conditions for women under the Ceausescu regime. Illegal abortionists, she said, were rife. It was not unusual to find women who had had a dozen or more illegal abortions. Having survived, they counted themselves lucky.

Conditions were worse than primitive. I was told of a woman abortionist who worked out of an apartment in the suburbs of Bucharest. She used a kind of homemade curette that sounded like a long-handled spoon with a sharpened edge. There was no suction. No anesthetic.

The vast majority of these kitchen-table abortions were incomplete, of course. And then, with the woman hemorrhaging or burning up with infection, there was the problem of finding a sympathetic doctor who would not notify the police—penalties for "abetting a crime" in Ceausescu's Romania were severe. A lot of doctors and nurses did help, though. The woman abortionist my patient described was never arrested.

The rate of maternal mortality was horrific. And the policy had other consequences as well. Infants whose mothers had not wanted them and could not afford them were abandoned by the score at orphanages, where they were warehoused like so many machine parts.

After Nicolae Ceausescu's downfall, Romania made abortion available up to the twelfth week in its hospitals and began working to introduce modern methods of contraception. According to the World Health Organization, maternal deaths from abortion fell more than sixty percent in one year. Sixty percent! In one year!

What can we learn from Romania? A lot. Outlawing abortion by no means stopped it. A woman determined to end a pregnancy will find a way to do it at whatever cost. Legal, safe abortion saves the lives of women who would otherwise die. And, the observers noted, simply making birth control available was not the answer to unwanted pregnancy, for reasons as complicated as the human psyche. Outlawing abortion doesn't automatically make people "responsible"—or, heaven knows, abstinent. If we can draw any conclusion, it's that legislating against abortion has never succeeded—anywhere in the world. We must find other solutions to our problem.

What's good for the world is good for America, I guess. The Title X regulation making clinics that mention abortion ineligible for federal funds—the infamous "gag rule" upheld by the Supreme Court in the *Rust v. Sullivan* (1991) decision—seemed to grow out of the same logic that brought us our foreign policy.

Maybe the Title X gag rule wasn't an assault on free speech. In deciding its constitutionality, the Supreme Court, anyway, seemed to think it wasn't. But it did put doctors in a double bind—break the law or abdicate their responsibility to their patients. Although very infrequently, abortion is sometimes the best route for the woman's health. Title X restrictions prevented many physicians from sharing that alternative with their patients. Responsibility to the patient went by the wayside. Belatedly but wisely, the administration realized that gagging doctors was a mistake—as well as unenforceable. Some alterations were made.

The gag rule was new to us. As Americans, we're not used to being told there's anything we can't say, and we don't like it when we are. But in Guam, a U.S. territory, it is—and has been for some time—unlawful for doctors or anyone in a public meeting even to mention abortion as an alternative. As a test of the law, an American Civil Liberties Union (ACLU) lawyer publicly read aloud the telephone number of a Planned Parenthood office. Now she's fighting her arrest and conviction. Perhaps it can't happen here, but it's getting uncomfortably close.

Loosening the gag for doctors may have been a cynical move

because at most places doctors don't do the counseling. For the most part, that job belongs to nurses and social workers. What about them? They too have a responsibility to their patients. And ungagging doctors really doesn't do much for the woman who's trying desperately to locate abortion services by telephone in a town two hundred miles from her home. Hot lines suddenly turned cold.

There is a bottom line. Who's using the clinics? We know who's not using them—women who can afford private health care. As my father told me long ago, and as Howard Moody reminded me, there have always been abortions for the well-to-do. And there always will be. The *Rust* decision disproportionately affects the minorities and the poor—the people who can afford help the least and need it the most.

Perhaps the most vivid example of government's turning a blind eye and a deaf ear to public need has been the denial of Medicaid funds to women on public assistance who seek abortion. "Sure, it's your right under the law, but we won't pay for it" smacks of "Let them eat cake" all over again. The poor and the disenfranchised suffer first. As Howard Moody said, it's just another example of how we fail the poor in this rich country of ours.

The majority of abortions are done on young women under twenty. They are the ones with the fewest resources. Often they are alone, with no husband and with little in the way of a support system. It seems gratuitously mean-spirited to target them with a regulation that effectively prevents them from exercising a legal right.

But mean-spiritedness often seems to prevail when it comes to sexuality in the young. Recently a chapter on sex and contraception was deleted from a government publication called *Taking Care of Your Child*. The new publication appeared just about the time the Centers for Disease Control (CDC) was issuing new statistics on AIDS in teenagers—in people under twenty-four, it's now the sixth leading cause of death. And on the same day came the estimate that forty percent of American children now live below the poverty line, thanks in large part to the alarming rise in single-parent families. The bureaucrat responsible for dropping the chapter said it might "cause some people to be offended." More offended than they would be if their child died of AIDS or unwittingly became pregnant?

In the last few years, there's been no abatement in the demand for abortions; the number is holding steady. But despite what the medical and psychiatric communities know about the safety and sequelae of abortion, and despite the AMA's firm stand on the side of choice, more and more MDs are dropping abortion from their practices. Only eighteen percent of all the counties in the country now offer abortion services of any kind. A change of heart? Hardly. ACOG finds no decrease in the number of gynecologists who support the right to abortion. But a lot of philosophically pro-choice doctors are giving up abortion because they are getting bounced around in unpleasant ways.

Moral suasion is one thing. But increasingly doctors are being subjected to such pressures as death threats and bombings or other kinds of violence as well as harassment of their families and disturbances in their neighborhoods. Their medical practices, their personal safety and the security of their families are at stake. Who can blame them?

The newspapers and the TV evening news chronicle demonstrations in front of clinics where abortions are performed. Occasionally we see people being hauled off to jail for trespass or some other minor offense. What happens to these protesters? Mostly nothing. It's their "constitutional right to protest." But what they're doing is blocking women from exercising *their* constitutional right to a legal medical procedure. It may not be a coincidence that the protesters' practices have been more and more tolerated by the law enforcement authorities since President Ronald Reagan took the oath of office in 1981. Permissiveness often filters down from the top.

It's tempting to speculate what would happen if, instead of white antichoice demonstrators, clinics were blocked by a black or a left-wing activist group. Would the police response be as nonviolent? Or would the rubber hoses and nightsticks come out?

The demonstrators do get arrested sometimes. But the "pro-life" activists who bomb abortion clinics often get off scot-free. NARAL and the ACLU have been trying to institute suits against various law enforcement agencies, claiming that they just haven't been doing their job and trying to force them to do some serious investigation toward bringing the bombers to justice. In one Midwestern city, a NARAL rep was asked by a government attorney, "What do you expect, when you are inside that building killing babies?"

So far, no matter what the antichoice movement has hurled at pro-choice—bombings, violence, denial of federal funding, Title X regulations, court decisions and state laws that chip away at women's rights—abortion remains as popular as ever. There has been no decrease in numbers, although many rural areas have been hurt. It appears that the right to choose whether or not to bear a child is so precious to women that they simply will not let that freedom go.

If *Roe* and *Doe* are overturned, what then? We see women banding together around the country to practice the techniques of "self-abortion" just in case they should need it, and I've no doubt that plenty of back-room guys are honing their skills right now, getting ready to make a killing—no pun intended.

Eve had been my patient for about ten years. Now in her early thirties, she was a bouncy brunet with energy to spare. She needed it—when she first started coming to me, she was heading for a career in retailing and studying for her master's in business at night. Then she'd decided ready-to-wear wasn't for her and had taken up cooking—she called it "culinary arts." The last I'd heard, she was trying to get a catering service off the ground—always a chancy venture, and especially so in an up-and-down economy.

A glance at her chart told me I hadn't seen her for nearly two years—a bit of a stretch. She was usually more prompt. The last time she'd been in, she'd complained about money—mildly, I'd thought then, but I wondered now if she had been trying to beat my price. I made a mental note to talk it over with her.

She looked a little nervous when she walked in. I chalked it up to embarrassment over her tardiness, maybe the fear that she was going to get a lecture about neglecting her health. But it turned out to be more than that.

"I have to tell you something," she said.

I waited.

"About six months ago, I was pregnant, and I had an abortion."

Planned Parenthood—or someplace like that, some clinic—leapt to mind. Maybe she'd been more worried about money than I'd known. Or could she be one of the ones who went elsewhere to avoid facing me? But Eve? No way. Others, maybe, but not her. She was very outspoken and alert and straight on. She had told me right out—no beating around the bush. What, then?

"I—I didn't go to a doctor. Or a clinic. I went to someone else. Someone I'd heard about."

An illegal abortionist? In New York? In this day and age? I was appalled and struggling not to let it show on my face. "Tell me about it," I said.

"I don't know how much I can tell you. I mean, I know I can tell you, but I promised them—they made me swear I wouldn't tell anyone who they were."

I could respect that, but I needed to know more. "Them?" I asked. "More than one?"

"Yes—well, I guess I can tell you this—it was a couple. A husband and wife. They were very nice."

"What did they charge you?" I wanted all the details.

"Oh, a couple of hundred bucks, I guess." From her offhand response, I gathered that money had been secondary. The difference between what she paid and what I would have had to charge was not that great, and she must have known it.

I kept probing. "What kind of facilities did they have?"

"It was in their home. In the kitchen."

Oh, no, I thought—next she's going to tell me they did it on the kitchen table. But no. They had something like a Barcalounger that they raised up to where they could do their job. The husband and the wife worked together, they both did some of the scraping.

"The room was all white," Eve described. "The windows were painted over with white paint, and everything. It looked clean enough."

Clean enough—not immaculate, I thought. "You know there was a risk anyway, don't you?"

"Of course. I'd heard all the horror stories. And after all, I'm not stupid," she said. I let that one pass, and she continued, "If I'd thought either one of them was a butcher artist, I'd've left on the spot. But they really were nice. Kind of middle-aged and homey—he wore thick glasses, but not scary or anything, and she had on running shoes." A high recommendation, apparently. "And they were comfortable with each other, like your aunt and uncle. I was scared, sure—but not so much that I was afraid to go through with it. I'd've been scared anywhere."

I kept trying to fathom her motives—what would drive her to do such a thing? But I couldn't come up with much. "Suppose you got pregnant again. Would you do it this way another time?"

She stopped to think. I sensed that she was ambivalent. "I hope it doesn't happen again," she said finally.

I hope so too. But I wouldn't put it past her.

I didn't want to grill Eve about something she clearly couldn't put into words, maybe hadn't even consciously thought out, but I got the notion that, maybe along with the anonymity of going to strangers, somehow she felt more comfortable about the "homey" atmosphere in the abortionists' kitchen than she would have in a sterile clinic. Even in New York City, with clinics galore and coverage for the poor in city hospitals, we still see several botched cases a year in the emergency rooms, women who turned first to old-time abortionists, the people who did their mothers and elder sisters and aunts. Old habits die hard, and there's an ingrained distrust of the medical profession in many a woman.

The public sees doctors as conservative and establishment—and they're not all wrong. To do their job, doctors have to be authority figures—bold, sure of themselves, even cocky. A little bit of that can be a good thing, although it doesn't always make us likable. But there's another side to it—when you have to be sure of yourself, it's dangerous to be too far out on a limb. Putting individual doctors on the defensive is an effective tactic for antichoice.

As doctors back off, run scared and decide not to do abortions, patients are not at all sure where they stand. I see it in my own practice. A long-standing patient will come to me, pregnant, with a story. She's taken an antihistamine or caught the flu or had a dental X-ray—something that would never harm a fetus—but she thinks, um, for medical reasons, uh, an abortion. Would I send her to someone? She seems surprised when I tell her I will, of course, do it; she is entitled to it under the law. I remind her of my obligation as her doctor.

Keisha was the daughter of one of my patients. I'd treated her grandmother and her aunts, so I'd watched her grow up, although I'd never seen her professionally. One afternoon she came to my office with her mother. She was about nineteen by this time, a tall, leggy, attractive young woman with a chic Afro. "A long drink of water," as my mother would have said. We got into an update-on-her-life conversation, which was how she happened to tell me about her abortion the summer before.

"I was working upstate, and I got involved with this guy—it was dumb, but I got pregnant. I mean, we both knew it was just a summer thing, that we weren't going to see each other again. Well, I asked around and got the name of a doctor there who did abortions in his office. It wasn't that expensive, a few hundred bucks, and we could get that together between us. I mean, the guy was all right, he just wasn't the love of my life. So I made an appointment.

"The people in the office seemed real nice, so I was kind of surprised by this guy. He kind of leered at me, you know? But at the same time he really had an attitude—like I was dirt or something. I thought, was it 'cause I'm black? But I think it was just him.

"He said, 'Get your things off and lie down.' And I'm thinking isn't there a gown or something? He was standing right there. So I asked for someplace to change and he said, 'Do it here. We have to get this over with.' But he gave me a sheet to wrap up in, which was clean, at least.

"When I went to put my feet in the stirrups, my legs were too long. And while he's adjusting them, he's making these cute little remarks about my legs and my nail polish. I'd already paid, and I wanted to get it over with too, or I'd have been out of there, I swear. I was that angry.

"It hurt—a lot. And I could hear the suction thing—it was real loud, and it was like it was sucking out my whole insides. I kept asking questions, and the whole time, he didn't say one thing. Just ignored me."

It seemed like an eternity, Keisha said, but it was probably only a few minutes until the doctor told her he was done.

"When I got up, I felt sort of faint, and there was blood running down my leg. I showed him, and he said it was nothing. But when I went to get my clothes, the blood was getting on the floor. And he said to me, 'You're dirtying things up. Get back up here.' He did some more stuff, and I heard the machine again. It didn't hurt as much, though, or maybe I was just so out of it I didn't care."

He gestured to her to get up again, and this time he gave her a sanitary napkin. "You know how to use these things, I suppose?" he sneered.

Keisha's mother caught my eye and shook her head. "She's quite a girl, isn't she, to do something like that? She didn't tell me a thing until it was all over." She turned to Keisha. "But it better not happen again."

Keisha shot back, "Don't worry about that—it won't. If I ever get pregnant again before my time, I won't get an abortion—I'll jump out a window."

As they were leaving, I said to her, "I'm sorry you had such a bad experience."

"Oh, it wasn't so bad, I guess," she shrugged.

Not so bad? I figured that her relief that it was over and done with was more important to her than anything. But I had to wonder—couldn't it have been less unpleasant? How much of that doctor's insensitivity was due to his personality, and how much was due to abortion?

It isn't only doctors who give women the business about abortion—it's the whole hospital system. Indeed, disdain over abortion is a reflection of the sexism that is part of our culture. Why should we expect our health-care system to be immune?

The patients on any hospital's obstetrics service are generally the easiest ones to handle, needing a minimum of nursing and only rarely intensive care. Obstetrics has been labeled "the happy specialty," with very little major pathology or, by nature, sickness, except in that small minority of high-risk patients.

We bring women in, get them delivered and send them home. Often, they even take care of their own babies. Our purpose, along with nursing, is just to be on the alert, to avoid or prevent or to handle crises. Yet the women—or their insurance carriers—pay what anyone else pays. So obstetrics serves as a real cash cow for the hospital. All the same, though, neurosurgery, general surgery, cardiology, orthopedics—you name it—get special floors and bigger budgets and more attention. Maternity services notoriously depend on donations and private grants more than on hospital budget committees.

Why? Well, for one thing, obstetrics is all women. It's part of that subtle prejudice among medical people, the one that can be counted up in so many D & Cs, cesareans and hysterectomies—millions of uterine invasions. Can we perhaps conclude that women in hospitals have to bear the same sting of sexism that they feel in the rest of their lives?

Women's medications have the same sorry history. The birth-control pill, known to the trade as an oral contraceptive agent, or OCA, is a case in point. It was finalized in the decade of the fifties and hit the market around 1958 or '59—a ten-milligram pill then. In the past thirty-plus years, it has been reduced in strength to less than a third of a milligram, one-thirtieth of the original dose. Through trial and error and mass tryouts on Third World women—on whom just about all such experiments are carried out—it was discovered that lower doses were just as effective. Well and good. Just as effective, and yet it's the exact same drug. Changes in its chemistry have been so minor as to be insignificant, even including the new breakthrough pills that are in readiness for the decade of the nineties.

When we complain about the cost of medications, the pharmaceutical industry always cries "research" and points to the costs of bringing a safe drug to market—safe, that is, to the first two worlds. But here's an agent that has required little added study and no more major expense. Additionally, the pill itself is smaller—the woman's taking less of it.

But in the thirty years it's been on pharmacy shelves, the price has just kept spiraling upward, well above the allowance for inflation and market fluctuation. What other medication in the history of pharmacology can make that claim? The drug industry has used investigative and development costs, the demands of the Federal Drug Administration (FDA) and marketing expenses to justify high profit margins. None of these allowances make sense when it comes to OCAs. Subtle sexism?

More, the record of the industry on birth-control research is abysmal. Forget male contraception—remember, research boards have chairmen, not chairwomen. Women in most European countries seem to have more to choose from than American women. Is "safety" the only factor at work here? That new low-dose pill on the market in western Europe, with a small, albeit significant, change in its biochemistry—finally some research—has reduced the negative side effects of its use to the barest minimum without affecting efficiency. Delays in its introduction into the American market are due to court battles over patent rights and infringements—big business. In the meantime, American women wait.

It seems almost like a built-in prejudice against women and their needs.

The most dramatic controversy in the war to win medical rights for women is the one around RU486—a new female drug to pick on, and an abortifacient to boot. Approved in France in the fall of 1988, it's been used by thousands and thousands of women there and across Europe with few problems—and those certainly all within acceptable levels. It also shows promise as a treatment for brain and breast cancer, endometriosis and glaucoma—but that's "beside the point" to those who oppose it.

Why has the introduction of RU486 been so delayed in the United States? Could it be a fear of giving women a choice, the fear of unleashing women's sexuality by making it too easy for them to avoid the consequences? There's an attitude at work here—one that says, "If she can avoid pregnancy, how will we know whether or not she's 'pure'?" It seems that somewhere in our Puritan hearts, we Americans still aren't sure that women can be trusted, and it seems safer, somehow, to keep them from having access to a full array of rights. To give them their due, though, the antichoice forces' stand against RU486 is consistent with their beliefs about the onset of life.

But also, if surgery weren't involved and abortion weren't clearly distinguishable from a heavy menstrual period, the antichoice argument would lose much of the clout that comes from grisly pictures and the specter of crushed fetal heads—the second-trimester abortions that make so many people squeamish. There would be no "silent scream." Everything would take place in the privacy of the woman's home, well before seven weeks. There wouldn't be any abortion clinics to picket, no spot on the six-o'clock news.

*   *   *

If young residents-in-training aren't learning to do first-trimester terminations, imagine how much more they're not learning to do the more difficult and problematic second-trimester procedures. During Melissa's surgery, I had many more than my assigned assistant looking on. Curiosity ran high.

Second-trimester terminations are tough all around—tougher on the patient, tougher on the nurses, tougher on the doctor. It's no accident that they are associated with greater morbidity and mortality—more complications, more deaths. Experts are still debating on the best methodology for the second trimester, and each method has its downside.

The old-fashioned way, by hysterotomy, or a surgical opening of the uterus, has been discarded as unnecessary and too drastic. Surgical risk and a prolonged recovery time have relegated it— with rare exceptions—to antiquity. It was replaced in the early abortion era by the saline infusion, or "salting out"—an injection of a highly concentrated salt solution into the amniotic cavity. The procedure is biochemically simple, sound and effective—the fetus and placenta are destroyed and nature then takes over with an expulsion by labor.

A similar, more recently accepted method, recommended in the standards of care issued by the ACOG, is the serial introduction of a potent lipid, or fat, natural chemical agent called prostaglandin in the form of a vaginal suppository. Also used as an adjunct to RU486, prostaglandin acts by being absorbed through the vaginal mucosa, or lining, and induces the uterus to contract violently enough to throw off its contents. The rest of the termination is exactly as though saline had been used. It's a toss-up as to which one is less complicated. Both have their pros and cons.

Then there is the so-called D & E—dilatation and evacuation—the application of the suction method to later pregnancies. The dilators and suction tips have been made available in larger sizes. All very convenient—I guess.

As the pregnancy advances, the idea of abortion becomes more and more repugnant to a lot of people, medical personnel included. Clinicians try to divorce themselves from the method.

In a saline or prostaglandin abortion, the doctor administers the agent to the patient and the wait-and-watch period is a labor process, which is not predictable. It may take several hours or even longer; up to twenty-four hours is fairly common. The care of the patient is usually left to specially trained nurses and abortion technicians.

There is a distinct advantage for the abortionist, who doesn't have to be around when the fetus, macerated and lifeless, is expelled. The doctor is then summoned for the check-out process, to assure that the abortion is complete and the patient can be safely discharged to follow-up care. With the D & E, as with any suction procedure, the materials passing through the suction tip are easy to see, and at that stage, the clear polyethylene tubing and the translucent plastic cannula are of a large enough bore to allow you to identify what you're seeing. In fact, it's medically required that you do so, to confirm that the abortion is total and the uterus empty. Out pass the limbs, the intestines and the various internal organs. Most important, it is imperative for the operator to be convinced that the skull tissue has passed, this being the largest part of the fetus formed at that stage of the pregnancy.

Want to do abortion? Pay the price. There is an old saying in medicine: If you want to work in the kitchen, you may have to break an egg. The stove gets hot. Prepare to get burned.

Now consider the patient. During the saline or prostaglandin technique, the woman must go through the labor process, awake and aware enough to know what is happening. The D & E, at least, spares her being the witness to a most traumatic and unpleasant moment in her life. She is under anesthesia, asleep. I've had cases where I would have liked to do a D & E for that reason alone, but most hospitals have not budgeted for the purchase of the necessary equipment. Those I have done were with improvised equipment that made the procedure longer than it had to be. I had to become a "dattle-do" surgeon.

It is almost as though the patient is being made to submit to further punishment—by saline—for her part in her unwanted pregnancy, and the doctor is being spared.

But most patients who have second-trimester procedures aren't "choosing" them in the sense of preferring a later termination to an earlier one. They're caught in a bind, like Melissa, with no one to turn to, or with no money and no knowledge of where to get help, or they're coping the best they can with painful dilemmas and personal tragedy.

Celia and Gary, a devoutly religious couple, had first been referred to me by another patient when Celia was in her late twenties. In accordance with their fundamentalist beliefs, they had been closely chaperoned before marriage and were virtual strangers on their wedding day. But they had grown to love and respect each other as though their courtship were like any other.

Large families were the order of the day in their tightly knit religious community, and there was a good deal of pressure from peers and relatives to get the production line started. When the babies didn't put in their expected appearance, the couple came to me for help.

It hadn't taken long to find the source of the problem, and even though we had religious strictures to work around—timing is essential when you're trying to achieve conception—Celia soon became pregnant. Happily, she and Gary were parents within the year.

Sometime during the next two years the twins were born. At almost seven pounds apiece at birth, they were very healthy babies. I figured that as this was a contemporary couple, they might decide to limit their family to three. But Gary's traditional faith exhorted him to "be fruitful and multiply." He wanted as many children as he could handle—or she could. And Celia did have a strong, healthy body.

By the time she became pregnant for the third time, Celia was thirty-nine, and the subject of genetic testing came up as a routine matter. She cocked an eyebrow at me and shook her head.

"I see no reason for that," she said.

I made sure she understood the ramifications of her decision—which, being bright and well read, she in fact did. She already knew that the risk for genetic defects is statistically higher after the age of thirty-five, but not that much greater for someone like her who has a history of healthy pregnancies. She was not worried, she said.

"Besides," she asked me, "if something were wrong, what good would it do for me to know? Abortion is out of the question. We accept whatever God sends us. It is what we believe."

Nevertheless, on her next visit she expressed some concern and an interest in hedging her bets. She admitted to me that she was still thinking about having the amniocentesis done anyway.

"I keep wondering," she said, "if I shouldn't try to work something out about the amnio. Just do it, and not tell Gary. To ease my own mind, without worrying him. Perhaps it would be a good idea. But there is a risk to that too—oh, I know, a small one—" She gave me a wave of her hand. "I think of it, but if it came out badly, we would still have to have the baby. So it would serve no purpose."

I agreed with her and even encouraged her in that direction. I expected that to be the end of it. But it wasn't.

Planning for routine prenatal care and delivery, I went through the customary blood tests, those I do for every patient. Within a few days, the results were back. One of the tests, although by no means diagnostic, was suggestive of an infectious organism, one that could have serious fetal implications. It was rare in Western culture, but not impossible—unsuspecting people have been known to pick it up on vacations. It doesn't seriously harm them, but when it infects the fetus, the results can be devastating.

Having done the test, I couldn't ignore it. We had to proceed, and quickly. The clock was moving inexorably ahead. I needed to pass my findings on to Celia and Gary, clarify the issues with them and have them make yet another informed consent. Then, if they wanted the amnio, I would have to arrange it, get the results and, if necessary, schedule and perform a termination before it was unsafe or too late. I just kept hoping my screening test was invalid—but they had to know the odds and the risks. I had no idea then which way they would go.

I broke with routine and got Celia on the phone. As gently as I could, I explained the situation: The test might or might not be accurate, and only amnio could tell.

"I'll have to talk to someone at the church and call you back," she said.

The next twenty-four hours were spent in harried phone calls as Celia tried to work her way through the labyrinth of religious and secular law, medical technology and emotion that she now found herself caught in. One religious scholar said absolutely no, another said perhaps. A third advised her to seek yet another authority. Finally a call to an elder across the country produced at least tacit permission to proceed with the amniocentesis.

Perhaps most difficult of all was telling Gary. Celia considered and then dismissed keeping the test secret from him "for his own good." I assured her I would keep her confidence, although I urged her against any form of deception where Gary was concerned. "I could never deceive him, not even to spare him," she admitted.

In spite of his reservations, he came with her for the amnio. It was painful for him, but he did not want her to face the procedure alone. He knew he'd be needed.

As we proceeded, I hoped and even prayed a little that the original result would be wrong, and this would end the suspense. But it didn't. My worst fears were confirmed—the infection was verified in the fetus.

Knowing what was to be, I was expecting to schedule Celia for a termination. But she hesitated. "No," she said. "No abortion."

"Why?" I asked. I had understood that it was all cleared; that there would have been no amnio without permission to proceed if the results indicated a defective fetus.

"It is not that simple," she replied. Although she had found a scholar who agreed, she had found no one in her own community who would give her an unqualified go-ahead. She would have to decide now if she could live with that.

The next day—forty-eight hours since that original suspicious test had come back—Celia called me. "We have decided we cannot go through with it—the abortion, that is," she said. "We're going to have our baby and pray for the best." I tried not to let my uneasiness filter through the phone wires. Celia knew I was feeling some of her pain.

Celia and Gary were scheduled the next day for her regular checkup. Anticipating that, I set my sights toward the delivery and the management of any emotional backlash that might follow. Hoping for this baby to be born only mildly affected by the disease, I had to prepare for what might be. It was still possible all would be well, although not likely.

Almost as soon as they stepped through the door to my prenatal exam room, Celia began to talk. They had once again called their elder, an eminent religious scholar and authority, and he had agreed to sanction the termination. They had decided for the good of their existing children and the well-being of their family to proceed with the abortion.

We were getting down to the wire. I admitted Celia to the hospital and performed an abortion by saline injection later that day. It was all over in the next twelve hours.

I secured Celia, wrote my postop notes and orders and went out to find Gary. He chose not to be with Celia for more reasons than one—religious, moral, philosophic. I understood them all. He was nearby, in the waiting salon.

"Celia's fine," I told him. "She came through it well. She'll be going home in the morning." When he nodded absently, I guess I couldn't stop myself from patronizing, just a little. I took his hand. "You made the right decision," I said, taking yet another page out of Roy Parker's book. "I know it's been lousy, but the worst is over. I'm just glad I could be here to help. I know this was quite a trauma for you."

"I don't need that kind of help from anyone," he said gently, but in an unmistakably firm tone. "Please understand. I know what you are saying, and I am grateful that you were here for Celia. I appreciate all that you have tried to do for us. But there would have been no trauma, as you put it, one way or the other.

Neither way was good, but one way is not better than the other
one." He gave me a quiet smile. "I am a religious man," he
said. "I believe in my faith and in my God. I had no problem,
either way." For Gary, all that had happened was not a tribula-
tion. It was God's will. He was at peace. Some of it rubbed off
onto me.

I walked away from Gary realizing at once that yet another
patient had given me a lesson in life. I saw a strength and a
maturity in him that was so precious and so rare. I saw that
abortion, a quick fix to some, a convenience to others and a
means of survival to many more, had that common theme—it
was a dilemma to all. Gary and Celia were the exceptions that
proved the rule.

When I released Celia the next morning, I was still thinking
of Gary's words. She must have known all along what he was
thinking. Would she feel guilty about having imposed her will
on him to find a solution she could live with? I wondered, but I
didn't ask. It's something that time will tell.

Celia was one of those patients that I would especially have
liked to spare the seeing. I had to tell her, "It will be the worst
twenty-four hours you'll ever have. You'll go through a mini-
labor, and you'll see a dead fetus. There will be no reward.
There will be nothing good about it."

"Except the rest of our lives," she said.

Abortion has been legal and permitted all over this country
since 1973. That's a whole lifetime for those who need it most—
for high school and college students—and most of their lives
for people under thirty. Maybe some thirty-five-year-olds have
a clear memory of prelegal days, as do women in their forties,
but even most women in that age group entered their childbearing years with a constitutional right to abortion, whether they
ever used it, or wanted to use it, or not. That's like all of us
knowing we have a right to trial by jury, although most of us
will never experience it or even ever think of it.

We don't like to have our rights taken away. And if ever a

right was in jeopardy, this is it. But as with anything we've grown up with, anything that has been an indelible part of our lives, it's difficult to imagine how things would be without it.

Like Social Security and not having to worry about old age, or having the right to vote, or drive a car, or own property, the right to abortion is ingrained in most people's understanding of what their basic rights are. If you've never seen the effects of a botched abortion, if you've never lost anyone to a back-alley abortionist, if you've never felt the panic that accompanies an unwanted pregnancy, it's hard to believe what it could be like. You have to go a long way back to find people who remember.

"Why am I working for abortion rights? It was more than forty years ago, but I remember my abortion. Illegal, of course. The worst thing about it? I was told to wait on a street corner at night. A man came up behind me and told me not to turn around. I was blindfolded and shoved onto the floor of a car. We drove around for a long time, turning corners so I wouldn't know where I was going. They never let me take the blindfold off. I never saw the person who did the abortion. Afterward they put me back in the car and left me at the same corner. It was degrading and horrible. But it was the only way then."

"My mother had a botched illegal abortion thirty years ago, when I was five. She died from it. I never missed having a brother or a sister—but I sure missed my mother."

"In the forties, one of my neighbors needed an abortion. Every woman in the building did something. They used my kitchen table. The doctor came in the afternoon. I stood guard at the door; another woman waited outside in case the woman's husband were to come home early. Someone else took her kids. She wasn't even someone I knew awfully well, but you had to stick together. You never knew when it might be you."

*   *   *

Circa 1912, a young woman named Sadie Sachs, the mother of three small children, lived with her truck-driver husband, Jake, on the top floor of a New York tenement, just barely making ends meet. The apartment had no running water, so every morning before he left for work, Jake carried up buckets of water for his family's use and carried the refuse down again at night. It was ghetto life in the city.

Like many people in the tenements, Sadie and Jake had little faith in hospitals—they'd seen too many people go in and never come out, except on a morgue slab. What health care they got, they got from public-health nurses. The nurse had warned Sadie not to get pregnant again. She was frail, and three children were enough.

Sadie had visited the local doctor and asked how to avoid pregnancy. His response? "Sleep on the roof." When she protested, he said, "Tell Jake to sleep on the roof. Take turns." She asked the nurse for help, but the nurse knew of nothing. The available contraceptive methods, like condoms, cervical caps called "the veil" and douches and pessaries—not very effective but better than nothing—were all so thoroughly suppressed that not even nurses had access to them.

A few months later, a frantic Jake Sachs pounded on the nurse's door. Sadie was delirious from septicemia. What had happened was evident. Pregnant again, she had gone to the local abortionist and paid him five dollars—the going rate. She died in nurse Margaret Sanger's arms.

Sanger went home, hung up her nursing cap and started a campaign to provide women with what she called "birth control." She was never able to forget Sadie Sachs, or the three children made orphans by Sadie's death. The idea of limiting reproduction as a way of making women independent wasn't original with Sanger, but as a tireless campaigner and a true believer, she made it work.

*   *   *

Essayist Philip Wylie once wrote, "This is a world of religion, not science. The people in it would rather guess than know, think than learn." But we can't let guessing run our lives. If we think that limiting abortion rights will somehow make us better people, aren't we missing the point? It will only make some of us parents against our will, and others it will make dead.

Although survey after survey shows that Americans want abortion to remain safe and legal, religious and political groups keep mounting well-funded crusades to prevent women from having safe, clean abortions, and their message appeals to many well-meaning people. Nobody's *for* abortion—how could anyone be? The medical community, though, remembers what it was like before *Roe* and *Doe*—the guys wth the coat hangers and the lye, out to make a buck. The AMA and ACOG are pro-choice, but so far they haven't mounted a successful counterattack to the movement that, in denying free access to abortion, will very likely reopen the door to the back alley.

I don't think there's anyone doing abortions who hasn't wished at some point that the situations creating the demand for them wouldn't just go away. That includes me. There have been plenty of times when I've wanted to say, "Enough! This is more human tragedy than I want to deal with." But that would require a different world—no poverty, no contraceptive failures, no rape or incest, no genetic defects, no maternal illness, better birth-control education, better support for women and children, better day care, better health care, no unprotected moments of passion, no human fallibility. We can start toward it, but we're a long way from home.

I close my eyes and I see a woman. She is too tired, too poor, too lacking in resources, too alone, too young to deal with a pregnancy. She wants a child, but not now, not without a husband, not on her meager take-home pay, not in the cramped little apartment that's all she can afford. Even with only herself to think about, she's barely making it. To go back to her hometown, to her family, with a baby that has no father—

unthinkable. Even if they'd take her in, they'd never let her forget it. She's in trouble.

If she had the money, she could go to another state, perhaps another country. But she doesn't. Her public hospital doesn't do abortions. Her public clinic isn't permitted to mention them. And time is running out.

So she gets a name. A doctor, an ex-pharmacist, a dentist, a nurse if she's lucky, but maybe only a woman who once successfully aborted herself. And she ends up in a hospital emergency room—bleeding, in shock, in coma, dead.

I can see it all too well.

But it doesn't have to be this way. If we can learn to see the abortion issue clearly—not religion but science, not ethics but rights, not sexism but equality for women—we can begin to work on the dilemma.

Index